Bandidos

Bandidos

THE VARIETIES OF LATIN AMERICAN BANDITRY

EDITED BY

Richard W. Slatta

Contributions in Criminology and Penology, Number 14

Greenwood Press
NEW YORK • WESTPORT, CONNECTICUT • LONDON

Library of Congress Cataloging-in-Publication Data

Bandidos : the varieties of Latin American banditry.

(Contributions in criminology and penology,
ISSN 0732–4464 ; no. 14)
  Bibliography: p.
  Includes index.
  1. Brigands and robbers—Latin America.
2. Outlaws—Latin America.   3. Latin America—Social
conditions.   I. Slatta, Richard W., 1947–   .
II. Series.
HV6453.L29B36   1987   364.1'552'098   86–12124
ISBN 0–313–25301–3 (lib. bdg. : alk. paper)

Library of Congress Catalog Card Number: 86–12124
ISBN: 0–313–25301–3
ISSN: 0732–4464

First published in 1987

Greenwood Press, Inc.
88 Post Road West, Westport, Connecticut 06881

Printed in the United States of America

The paper used in this book complies with the
Permanent Paper Standard issued by the National
Information Standards Organization (Z39.48–1984).

10 9 8 7 6 5 4 3 2 1

Copyright Acknowledgments

The author and the publisher gratefully acknowledge permission to reproduce from the following
copyright materials:

"The Oligarchical Limitations of Social Banditry in Brazil: The Case of the 'Good' Thief Antônio
Silvino," World Copyright: The Past and Present Society, Corpus Christi College, Oxford, England.
This article is reprinted with the permission of the Society and the author from *Past and Present:
a journal of historical studies*, no. 82 (Feb. 1979).

Five maps from *Maps On File*, © 1985 by Martin Greenwald Associates. Reprinted by permission
of Facts on File, Inc., New York.

" 'La Chambelona': Political Protest, Sugar, and Social Banditry in Cuba, 1914–1917," reprinted
from Inter-American Affairs, Spring 1978, with permission of Inter-American Affairs Press.

For Zoya Maxine, with love

Illustrations

Acknowledgments

A collection of essays, even more than a monographic work, requires joint effort and cooperation. I thank the contributors for providing the high-quality research and writing that went into this book.

Others who added constructive comments or editorial assistance include Peter Singlemann, Maxine P. Atkinson, Christa Howertown, and Gary Hill. Deborah Jakubs, of Duke University Library, extended helpful bibliographical assistance. Edna Gutiérrez de Moolick helped to translate two of the essays from Spanish into English. The efforts of those scholars whose works appear in the bibliography also merit our thanks and recognition.

Two of the contributions are reprinted from other publications. Thanks to the late T. H. Aston and to Paul Slack, of The Past and Present Society, for permission to reprint Linda Lewin's essay from *Past and Present*. And our gratitude goes to Simon G. Hanson, editor of *Inter-American Economic Affairs*, for permission to reprint the essay by Louis A. Pérez, Jr. Maps are reprinted by permission of Facts on File, Inc., New York. Mildred Vasan guided the project initially at Greenwood Press. The staff of the History Department at North Carolina State University, notably Amy Hosokawa, provided secretarial support for the project. Funds from the Faculty Research and Professional Development Program of North Carolina State University facilitated research on banditry in Argentina. Research in Venezuela was facilitated by a Tinker Foundation post-doctoral fellowship. And a final thank-you to Adam Osborne for putting microchips into an affordable, functional computer that helped to reduce the drudgery of rewriting.

Bandidos

1

Introduction to Banditry in Latin America

RICHARD W. SLATTA

Of the myriad actors on the historical stage, few have generated more excitement and intrigue than bandits. Most of the creative media—novels, poetry, plays, film, and painting—abound with dangerous, frightening, but captivating images of highwaymen and henchmen. And police and judicial records add substantive historical evidence of the seemingly omnipresent bandit. Owing to their great notoriety and popular fascination, bandits exist in a netherworld between fact and fiction.

Only recently have growing numbers of scholars attempted to untangle the twisted web of mythology, folklore, and official documentation that shrouds these figures. As with other elements of rural Latin American society, bandits defy conventional research methods because much of their lives escaped conventional documentation. Bandits can be defined legally as those convicted of property theft. But as will be seen in these essays, the term was also used as an epithet to characterize the rural lower classes or political opponents in many Latin American nations. We use the term bandit to mean persons (nearly always men) who worked in groups to steal property or rustle livestock.

The systematic study of banditry took a giant step forward in 1959, when Eric J. Hobsbawm published his provocative examination of *Primitive Rebels*, including social bandits. Ranging over the world and through time, the British social historian developed powerful, convincing images of pre-political or ''archaic forms of social movement,'' such as millenarianism, urban mobs, labor sects, and social banditry. A decade later he expanded his vignette of the bandit element, bolstered it with more evidence, and published his seminal portrait of *Bandits*, reissued in slightly revised form in 1981.[1]

Bandits touched off research on the topic around the globe, and revisions, refutations, and emendations began to appear in print. The more important contributions include those of Anton Blok in 1972, Peter Singelmann in 1975, Billy Jaynes Chandler in 1978, Linda Lewin and Pat O'Malley in 1979, Richard White in 1981, and Paul J. Vanderwood et al., in 1982. Despite these prodigious research efforts, Hobsbawm could still lament in 1981 that "comparative studies other than by the present author are scarce."[2] This collection of essays presents a major comparative testing of Hobsbawm's model of the social bandit.

Our works use nineteenth- and twentieth-century archival sources in Mexico, Brazil, Cuba, Venezuela, Colombia, Bolivia, and Argentina to detail the varieties of bandit activity in Latin America. We also analyze the significance of our evidence for current criminological theory. After presenting evidence from individual countries, we summarize our findings on the historical reality of Latin American banditry and offer revisions of Hobsbawm's concepts.

We conclude that the social bandit model fails to capture the significant historical variations of banditry in Latin America. Other models, including the political bandit and the guerrilla-bandit, are required. But we concur with Hobsbawm in stressing deep social divisions and conflicts as well as elite monopolization of economic opportunity as causal factors in Latin American criminality.

Hobsbawm described social banditry as "a universal and virtually unchanging phenomenon." These ubiquitous social bandits, according to Hobsbawm, were

peasant outlaws whom the lord and state regard as criminals, but who remain within peasant society, and are considered by their people as heroes, as champions, avengers, fighters for justice, perhaps even leaders of liberation, and in any case men to be admired, helped and supported. This relationship between peasant communities and the rebel, outlaw and robber is what gives the phenomenon of social banditry its political and social significance.[3]

Hobsbawm engendered his model with distinctive, universal characteristics. The figure appeared to be invulnerable to attack by police and the state—virtually superhuman—and could be defeated only by betrayal. The bandit came from rural, peasant stock and, like his peers, was young, single, and uneducated. A matter of honor or principle, accepted in peasant society but condemned by the state, often pushed a young man into a life of banditry. By attacking the class enemies of the poor and powerless, the bandit became a symbol of social protest, even though his actions stopped short of a revolutionary challenge to lord and state.[4]

Despite the social roots of bandit motivations, Hobsbawm concluded that "social banditry has next to no organization or ideology, and is totally inadaptable to modern social movements." Social bandits, like peasant society as a whole, were backward-looking. Their goal was to reestablish a traditional, vanishing social order that was being eroded rapidly around them. They lacked both the practical skills and the political vision to lead society toward a new, revolutionary order.[5]

If class acts of injustice motivate individual peasants to take up the bandit life, then what social conditions gave rise to wider outbreaks of banditry? Hobsbawm cites "pauperization and economic crises . . . , wars, conquests, or the breakdown of the administrative system" as circumstances likely to trigger a surge in criminal activity. At such conflictive and stressful times, the surplus rural male population, marginalized and unintegrated into modern society, might be forced into banditry.

Refusing to bow to class and social pressures, "stiffnecked and recalcitrant" men might take to the bandit life and, by their resistance to authority, "make themselves respected" within peasant society. A forceful, modernizing government, however, could eradicate banditry with improved public administration, communications, and economic development.[6]

Among the greatest difficulties in analyzing banditry historically is the problem of distinguishing myth from social reality. Hobsbawm acknowledged the conceptual and methodological difficulties inherent in the "rather tricky historical" sources that he used. Most societies harbor appealing popular legends based on the lives of famous bandits. The power and allure of these images come in part from a seeming need for even highly urbanized societies to retreat to a "sometimes heroic past." Myths allow modern man to savor nostalgically the lost virtue, the "freedom, heroism, and the dream of justice" that the social bandit gallantly fought to reassert.[7]

But Hobsbawm's use of popular and folk sources led him to conclusions different from those of other researchers working with documents from police and judicial archives. Anton Blok and others have suggested that many of the poems and ballads that inform Hobsbawm's studies may reflect idealized aspirations rather than social reality. Some of these literary sources project the values of urban middle-class writers who romanticized bandits rather than the oral traditions of a peasant folk culture.[8]

Some of the images and myths of social banditry in Latin America emanated from the pens of urban middle-class writers, not from folk sources per se. And in the case of the filmic images traced by Allen Woll, whatever folk roots that once existed disappeared amid Hollywood's flash and glitter. This does not negate the value of such materials as historical sources. On the contrary, Hobsbawm merits praise for his creative use of literary and folk materials. But such sources must be handled carefully and cross-checked against other types of data. In Hobsbawm's defense it is well to remember that he creatively used those sources available to him at the time. Much of the probing, archival research with Latin American police and judicial records has only been accomplished since the publication of the original edition of *Bandits* in 1969.

Paul J. Vanderwood ("Nineteenth-Century Mexico's Profiteering Bandits") finds strong economic motives behind banditry in Mexico from the late colonial era through the trauma of revolution in 1910. In Mexico "outsiders who wanted in" often turned to crime for personal advancement. Although the nature, scope, and intensity of banditry changed over time, bandits throughout the nineteenth century acted on the basis of self-interest and opportunism, not in defense of peasant class interests. Many willingly hired out as mercenaries to the highest bidder.

Peasants did not universally support Mexican bandits. Many instead hunted them to collect a reward. Men changed sides during the independence and civil wars and even perpetuated the fighting to reap further plunder. Many showed an equal willingness to rob or to chase robbers, depending on the relative rewards offered.

Vanderwood traces increased banditry directly to Mexico's succession of weak central governments that were unable to impose authority over much of the national territory. Bandit gangs created and effectively profited from widespread social disorder. When Porfirio Díaz consolidated his dictatorship over Mexico during the 1880s, the nature of banditry changed to resemble more closely social protest against his dictatorship. Vanderwood links the social roots of banditry to political conflict and tensions of modernization, but he finds little of Hobsbawm's noble robber in the profit-seeking outlaws of Mexico.

Miguel Izard and Richard W. Slatta ("Banditry and Social Conflict on the Venezuelan Llanos") detail the lives of a violent equestrian subculture of South America, the llaneros of Venezuela. Like the gauchos of the Río de la Plata, llaneros existed beyond the pale of urban-based "civilization." Despite efforts by bureaucrats at the capital in Caracas to subdue them, the social and legal conventions of a remote national government concerned the plainsmen little. Banditry, cattle rustling, and other evidence of conflict place the llanero within a subculture of frontier violence that also typified other plains regions of Latin America.

Despite some surface similarities between the persecuted existence of the llanero and the social bandit, Izard and Slatta conclude that the Venezuelan plainsman does not fit Hobsbawm's model. Social bandits enjoyed the succor and protection of peasant society, whereas llaneros existed autonomously and independently as a separate people. Although labeled bandits and criminals by national authorities, llaneros were independent frontiersmen, not social bandits.

"Civilization" seldom impinged on the llanero except when the ravages and demands of the independence and civil wars swept him into national conflict. Under these circumstances, llaneros willingly became what Christon I. Archer has termed "guerrilla-bandits."[9] As in the case of Mexican independence, guerrilla-bandits changed sides according to the perceived rewards of following the patriot banner of independence or that of the Spanish royalists.

Richard W. Slatta ("Images of Social Banditry on the Argentine Pampa") finds recognizable variations of Hobsbawm's social bandit among the images of banditry in nineteenth-century Argentina. The class conflict envisioned by Hobsbawm emerged in the social and legal relations between authorities who enforced the interests of powerful ranchers and the gaucho masses of the great Argentine plains or pampas. Single, illiterate, marginalized rural males made up the ranks of many bandit gangs.

Like the figure described by Hobsbawm, gauchos remained backward-looking and pre-political, not revolutionary, in their social vision and actions. Many turned to the outlaw life because of unjust or arbitrary treatment at the hands of military or civil authorities. Gauchos attempted to maintain a set of traditional behaviors and values that modernizing elites considered "barbarian" and antithetical to their own class interests. And gauchos as a social group came to symbolize (even to urban middle and elite groups) a nostalgic longing for bygone days of lost virtue and freedom.

But gaucho bandits differed significantly from Hobsbawm's noble robber figure. Living in a frontier culture of violence, gauchos engaged in gratuitous violence for sport, unlike the noble robber, who exercised his considerable strength only with just provocation. Owing to the great dispersion of population on the plains, gaucho outlaws operated on the far fringes of society. The putative ties between peasant and bandit seldom operated on the pampa.

Linda Lewin ("The Oligarchical Limitations of Social Banditry in Brazil") analyzes the career of one of the most famous Brazilian bandits, Antônio Silvino, active during the first decade and a half of the twentieth century. Drawing on a blend of official archives and folkloric sources, Lewin achieves a full portrait of the bandit as both historical figure and popular symbol.

Like Vanderwood for Mexico and Slatta for Argentina, Lewin finds clear elite-bandit cooperation in Brazil. She concludes that Silvino was much closer to the planter elite of the Brazilian Northeast than to the region's peasants. The images of Silvino recorded in regional popular literature (*literatura de cordel*) diverged markedly from the reality of the prominent bandit's existence.

Billy Jaynes Chandler ("Brazilian *Cangaceiros* as Social Bandits") lodges a far-reaching critique of Hobsbawm in his challenging portrait of another Brazilian outlaw who was active through the 1930s—the "bandit king" Lampião. He convincingly refutes Hobsbawm's depiction of Lampião as "the avenger." Oddly, the revised version of *Bandits* issued in 1981 fails to mention Chandler's book-length study of Lampião published in 1978.[10]

In searching for motivations among Brazilian bandits, Chandler finds more local, familial, and personal than broad social roots. Family feuds, endemic to the backlands, not class injustices, moved many to the outlaw life. Like Vanderwood, he sees personal desires for economic betterment as central. Banditry offered an easier, remunerative, adventurous life to the rural poor of the sertão. In social composition the gang headed by Lampião varied substantially from the social bandits envisioned by Hobsbawm.

Chandler also offers compelling evidence that a volatile culture of violence permeated the backlands. This confrontational milieu, coupled with "rugged individualism, an exaggerated sense of personal honor, and an extreme concept of manliness," interjected conflict and violence into interpersonal affairs. As social pressures of the twentieth century broke down the traditional authority exercised by the landed elite, criminal activities by Lampião and other outlaws increased.

On the other hand, the traditional social hierarchy and political order tightly constricted legitimate economic ventures. The capricious application of the law alienated the rural masses from the official organs of power. Anti-establishment ballads and tales gained great currency among the poor of the backlands. Chandler attributes Hobsbawm's faulty portrait of Lampião to Hobsbawm's overreliance on popular ballads and sensationalized stories developed by urban middle-class writers with little knowledge of or empathy for peasant culture or values.

Indian and mestizo communities of the Andean highlands provide yet another theater of Latin American bandit activity. Erick D. Langer ("Andean Banditry and Peasant Community Organization") examines the very different tactics adopted in two regions of the Bolivian highlands—Tomina and Tarabuco—in the face of late–nineteenth- and early–twentieth-century rural changes. He shows that Indian communities with a high degree of internal cohesiveness could use more politically sophisticated tactics, such as mass rebellion or litigation through the courts, to address their grievances.

Mestizo communities, lacking such internal cohesion, experienced higher levels of banditry in response to economic crises. Rather than representing a prepolitical form of protest, banditry in the Andes was an alternative political strategy used when mass mobilization was not feasible.

The next two essays examine the linkages between political violence and banditry in two contexts. The island of Cuba, Spain's last colony in the Western Hemisphere, suffered a violence-ridden history. Slave revolts and abortive independence movements during the nineteenth century threatened the hold of Spain and the landed elite on the island. After independence in 1898, partisan conflict marred the new nation's political growth. Outbreaks of banditry often accompanied these other forms of violence and political protest.

Louis A. Pérez, Jr., ("La Chambelona") details one episode of Cuban banditry and relates it to the broader political conflict occurring on the troubled island during World War I. As in Mexico, Venezuela, and other Latin American countries, political disruptions provided a fertile climate for banditry. Pérez shows how an elite-led political revolt by the Liberal party quickly degenerated into banditry as a form of rural social protest. Once again, the links between political turmoil and bandit activity emerge.

The most recent major episode of Latin American banditry came during the horrifying period of the *Violencia* in Colombia, which disfigured the nation from the late 1940s through the mid–1960s. Gonzalo G. Sánchez and Donny Meertens ("Political Banditry and the Colombian *Violencia*") also trace the rise of banditry to previous partisan conflict. The "political banditry" that they document exhibits some characteristics similar to social banditry. But the Colombian political bandit is subtly but substantially different from Hobsbawm's model because partisanship confounded class solidarity during the *Violencia*.

Some political bandits began their careers during the armed struggles of the 1950s as liberal or conservative guerrillas. The accord reached by political elites stripped guerrillas of their national political support and legitimacy. Realigning themselves with local elites and peasants, political bandits evolved extensive support networks and profit-making schemes, particularly in the rich coffee-growing regions.

But an inescapable dilemma haunted political bandits. These outlaws suffered from the lack of firm, consistent class or partisan bases of support in the countryside. Elites of their own political party branded them bandits and joined with the army in a war of extermination. Bandits also alienated peasants by turning to terror and revenge, rather than loyalty, as tactics to secure support. Failing to resolve this class-partisan dilemma, political bandits lost to the vigorous counter-insurgency campaign waged by the Colombian army.

If Hobsbawm created a striking and memorable image of the noble robber, the fertile minds of Hollywood generated a different image of the Latin American bandit. Allen Woll ("Hollywood Bandits") briefly traces the origins of the unflattering cinematic outlaw of Hollywood born in the violent years of the Mexican Revolution. Negative, racist stereotypes of "the greaser" emerged during those years of turmoil from 1910 to 1920—the antithesis of Hobsbawm's noble figure. Cold-blooded murder, even baby killing, no deed was too dastardly for the base "greaser." These vile images became mixed with documentary footage of Pancho Villa and others and resulted in films that showed the worst images of Mexico and Mexicans.

Latin American threats of economic boycotts prompted a revision of the cinematic bandit by the time that the silent era ended in the late 1920s. The 1930s witnessed more positive, even heroic and admirable figures in place of the "greaser." Films such as *The Robin Hood of El Dorado* (1936) presented a romanticized, sympathetic portrait of the outlaw. Based on the life and legend of the California bandit Joaquín Murieta, the film showed racism, exploitation, and injustice forcing a good man to the outlaw life.[11]

Bandits abruptly disappeared from movies about Latin America during the World War II push for hemispheric solidarity. But the 1960s witnessed the rise of the exploitative and gratuitous violence of productions by Sergio Leone and Sam Peckinpah. The villainous "greaser" returned to center stage. With gushing Technicolor and stomach-churning slow-motion photography, Hollywood resurrected the durable stock image born a half-century earlier. Protests by Hispanic-Americans notwithstanding, negative stereotypes of Latin Americans (bandits and others) continue to populate the Hollywood cinema.

The widespread phenomenon of banditry in Latin America provides ample evidence for the comparative testing of criminological theory. Dretha M. Phillips ("Latin American Banditry and Criminological Theory") draws on the evidence assembled in this book to critique prevailing theories of criminology that have been developed largely on the basis of experiences in the United States and Western Europe. Some theories with explanatory shortcomings in the United States, such as the conflict perspective, perform better in the Latin American context. But no extant theory is satisfactory in accounting for the variety of causes and patterns of Latin American banditry.

The critique of theory by Phillips offers compelling evidence of the need for more research in comparative criminology, especially in cross-cultural contexts. In particular, she suggests that a theory of subcultures may offer fruitful guidance for future research and theory testing.

Overall, the social reality of banditry in nineteenth- and twentieth-century Latin America exhibits far more divergence from than convergence with Hobsbawm's model. The rural masses clearly used banditry more for economic gain than for pre-political protest. When other tactics and avenues were available to them, peasants often chose options other than banditry. Much bandit activity occurred where peasant-bandit solidarity could not be established—in sparsely populated frontier regions, without settled peasant communities. Elite-bandit ties appeared much more frequently than the peasant-bandit union posited by Hobsbawm.

The historical reality of Latin American banditry differs from Hobsbawm's conceptualization. Nevertheless, the sociopolitical images of bandit legends in the region appear much as Hobsbawm describes them. Middle-class urban writers often generated these stirring bandit myths because of their great appeal to popular audiences. The variance between historical reality and political mythology did not stop people from believing in social bandits. As is often the case in history, the power and influence of myth and image far exceed that of social reality.

NOTES

1. The genesis of the social bandit concept appeared in Eric J. Hobsbawm, *Primitive Rebels: Studies in Archaic Forms of Social Movement in the Nineteenth and Twentieth Centuries* (Manchester: Manchester University Press, 1959), pp. 13–29. See the fuller treatment in *Bandits* (New York: Pantheon, 1969, rev. ed., 1981); and the summary in Henry A. Landsberger, ed., *Rural Protest: Peasant Movements and Social Change* (London: MacMillan, 1974), pp. 142–157.

2. Quotation from Hobsbawm, *Bandits*, p. 170. See the critiques by Anton Blok, "The Peasant and the Brigand: Social Banditry Reconsidered," *Comparative Studies in Society and History*, 14, 4 (Sept. 1972): 494–503; Peter Singelmann, "Political Structure and Social Banditry in Northeast Brazil," *Journal of Latin American Studies*, 7, 1 (May 1975): 59–83; Billy J. Chandler, *The Bandit King: Lampião of Brazil* (College Station: Texas A&M Press, 1978); Linda Lewin, "The Oligarchical Limitations of Social Banditry in Brazil: The Case of the 'Good' Thief Antônio Silvino," *Past and Present*, 82 (Feb. 1979): 116–146 (reprinted in this volume); Pat O'Malley, "Social Bandits, Modern Capitalism and the Traditional Peasantry: A Critique of Hobsbawm," *Journal of Peasant Studies*, 6, 4 (July 1979): 489–499; Richard White, "Outlaw Gangs of the Middle Border: American Social Bandits," *Western Historical Quarterly*, 12, 4 (Oct. 1981): 387–408; and Hobsbawm's responses in "Social Banditry: Reply," *Comparative Studies in Society and History*, 14, 4 (Sept. 1972): 503–505; and *Bandits*, pp. 11–15, 138–164; Paul J. Vanderwood, ed., "Social Banditry and Spanish American Independence," special issue of *Biblioteca Americana*, 1, 2 (Nov. 1982).

3. Hobsbawm, *Primitive Rebels*, p. 5; Hobsbawm, *Bandits*, pp. 17–18.

4. Hobsbawm, *Primitive Rebels*, pp. 14–17, 20, 22–25.

5. Quotation from Hobsbawm, *Primitive Rebels*, p. 5; see also Hobsbawm, *Bandits*, pp. 26, 98–101, 107–108.

6. Hobsbawm, *Bandits*, pp. 19, 22, 33, 35, 67.

7. Ibid., pp. 131–132.

8. Ibid., p. 10; James A. Inciardi, Alan A. Block, and Lyle A. Hallowell, *Historical Approaches to Crime: Research Strategies and Issues* (Beverly Hills, Calif.: Sage, 1977), pp. 32–33, 54. See also Linda Lewin, "Oral Tradition and Elite Myth: The Legend of Antônio Silvino in Brazilian Popular Culture," *Journal of Latin American Lore*, 2 (Winter 1979): 157–204.

9. Christon I. Archer, "Banditry and Revolution in New Spain, 1790–1821," *Biblioteca Americana*, 1, 2 (Nov. 1982): 88.

10. Hobsbawm, *Bandits*, pp. 59–60; Chandler, *Bandit King*, pp. 238–247; Lewin, "Oligarchical Limitations."

11. See Pedro Castillo and Albert Camarillo, eds., *Furia y muerte: Los bandidos chicanos* (Los Angeles: Aztlán, 1973), pp. 33–51; Frank F. Latta, *Joaquin Murieta and His Horse Gangs* (Santa Cruz, Calif.: Bear State Books, 1980).

2

Nineteenth-Century Mexico's Profiteering Bandits

PAUL J. VANDERWOOD

On their arduous journeys up and down the twisting trails and rutted roads of nineteenth-century Mexico, travelers fully expected to encounter bandits. They dressed down for the occasion and carried fewer valuables than normal. Some updated their wills before departure, but they were in the minority, for Mexico's brigands were as well known for their gentlemanly qualities as they were for their boldness. They might rob a bishop and then kiss his ring as an act of contrition. Bandits frequently asked the forgiveness of victims for what, they insisted, was the necessity to rob them of their property. At times they declined to take a person's last peso, noting that the money was needed for a meal.

Of course, bandits could be truculent, even vengeful, especially if their efforts netted little booty. Then they might strip their prey of everything, including clothing, down to undergarments. Some travelers were undoubtedly relieved by the sight of the blackened skull of a notorious brigand nailed to a tree by authorities who caught and executed him as a warning to others. But by and large, travelers appeared to be more fascinated by than fearful of bandoleros. In fact, they seemed disappointed if they finished their trip without at least one meeting with bandits. They wanted stories to tell on arrival, and the escapades of bandits were the talk of the day.[1]

Bandoleros permeated the past century of Mexican history, although their style, mode of operation, and measure of success changed as the nation modernized along capitalistic lines. Bandit activities always reflect their times, which is why they are invaluable sources for historical study. Throughout the nineteenth century, however, the motives of Mexico's brigands seem to have remained much the same. Bandits demanded a share of the profits from a society that offered them few legitimate chances for advancement.

Bandits were, in the main, ambitious outsiders who wanted in. Toward this

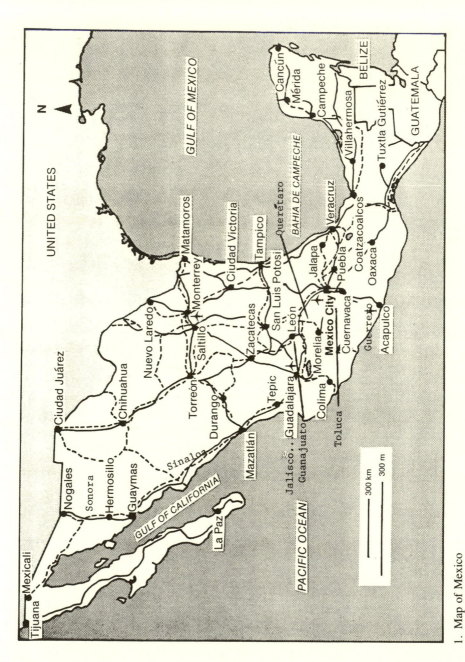

1. Map of Mexico

From: *Maps On File,* © 1985 by Martin Greenwald Associates.
Reprinted by permission of Facts On File, Inc., New York.

end they frequently treated with rural power brokers and vice versa. Elites normally preferred to exterminate brigands rather than to bargain with them, but at times they had no choice. Bandits often understood the local commerce as well as the merchants to whom they fenced stolen goods, and disgruntled bandits could be nasty business competitors. Under these circumstances, partnerships made good sense.[2]

Brigands held strong cards for much of Mexico's nineteenth century. In some regions they set the terms of trade. Just past mid-century they were powerful enough to force their demands on the national government itself. In effect, they said, "Incorporate us, or else." And the government acquiesced by employing known bandoleros as federal policemen—a wise move that had precedents in other places in earlier times. As policemen, bandits worked both sides of the law to their advantage.[3]

In the latter part of the century new and powerful capitalistic incentives lured away their well-placed traditional allies. It became more profitable for country strongmen to ally themselves to the central government rather than oppose it. Former business partners preferred to finance security forces to hunt them down, so Mexico's brigands experienced less fortune in their direct confrontations with authority. Yet bandits met the challenge, and in doing so they enhanced their image in the public mind; never mind that the image distorted reality.

For bandits are not only men; they are also myths. It does not seem to matter that a bandit's routine involved constant flight from the law, holing up for indeterminate stays in comfortless hideouts, and a persistent fear of betrayal. A brigand's lifestyle can hardly be described as a good life. Nor were many brigands lucky in love. Bandits were lonely people, and their few writings exude self-pity. Certainly more brigands died in a bloodbath than in bed, the victims of disillusioned, greedy, or desperate associates who salvaged their freedom by selling to police the secrets of the clan. Simply stated, the lives of bandits are tragic, frequently in reality and normally in myth, but it is this truly tragic aspect of their existence that nourishes their myth and earns them immortality.

How Mexicans loved their bandits: "Here comes Heraclio Bernal, the Thunderbolt of Sinaloa"; or Santanón's amphibious, phantomlike raids near Veracruz; or the clever, burlesquing antics of Chucho el Roto around Mexico City. Some thought that Chucho el Roto would be a fine federal deputy, better than most of the deputies already seated, because he so well understood the economy. Others sought his advice as a prison reformer.[4] Regardless of social position, people seemed to appreciate the brigands as representing independence, free will, even protest, in a social setting increasingly marked by personal frustration and outright oppression. Insofar as myth was concerned, bandits declined to trade their freedom for security. Many people still applaud such a stance, even when they will not chance it for themselves.

Colonial Mexico, or New Spain, certainly was not devoid of banditry, but the incidence of brigandage during most of the period seems to have been low. Travel accounts, even hostile ones such as that by Thomas Gage, do not relate encounters with bandoleros. And military historians have noted that muleteers did not particularly arm themselves for defense against bandits. Colin Mac-Lachlan, who studied criminality in the colony through the royal institution meant to control it, the *Acordada*, found few criminal prosecutions for banditry. He concluded that the *Acordada* served more as an instrument for centralized political control than as an instrument for law enforcement.[5]

Banditry, however, did become a serious problem in the last two decades of the colony. William Taylor notes an upsurge in Nueva Galicia, around Guadalajara, and ties it to, among other things, the rapid increase of economic activity in the district. In the 1790s, he says, banditry became a characteristic form of outlaw activity in western Mexico, as "more wealth and more trade meant movement on the highways and more opportunities for bandits to gain quick access to portable wealth and the material benefits offered by a cash economy."[6] Using trial records, Taylor sketched a profile of the typical bandit: "He was in his late twenties or early thirties, a day-laborer or poor artisan without regular work, illiterate, and likely to be classified racially as a Spaniard or an Indian."[7] And finally, as the Independence wars after 1810 approached, banditry in Nueva Galicia became widespread.

Some people took advantage of the unprecedented opportunities for self-advancement offered by the breakdown of royal authority during the turbulence of the Independence movement. New power bases were established and defended against competitors. Material wealth was redistributed by force. The followers of bandits nicknamed "The Crate," "The Castrator," and "Colonel of the Colonels," along with the Ortíz brothers and Pedro de Negro, became infamous for their crimes. Royalist generals looted along with the guerrilla nationalists, and all changed sides at will. The bandit García joined the Spaniards at Orizaba, but when overall Spanish resistance declined he returned to brigandage. Mexicans complained about his brutalities, and in response García began to bury his victims alive. He was eventually captured and exiled to California, where he resumed his robberies.[8]

Christon Archer has found that people on both sides—royalists and rebels—deliberately kept the war going because it offered so much easy plunder, all in the guise of patriotism. The line between Mexican guerrillas, supposedly patriots, and bandits became so blurred that Archer labeled them "guerrilla-bandits." Insecurity of the roads forced merchants to hire militarylike units to protect goods in transit. So domestic commerce depended on the will of the army and the bandits, who took advantage of the disorder to enrich themselves. Brigands sold plunder to merchants who then marketed the goods in cities like Guanajuato. Agustín Iturbide, who ruled as Mexico's monarch in the early 1820s, sold exit permits to Spaniards who feared death from the disturbances. His profiteering depended on continued disorder. Only the opportunity for much greater rewards persuaded Iturbide to betray his kind and participate in the negotiations that led to formal independence.[9]

After a brief flirtation with monarchy under Iturbide, a clique of Mexican leaders settled on a federal republic, to a large degree forced on the country by the realities of national disorder and confirmed in the Constitution of 1824. Armed debate among the power brokers followed. With no effective institutions to mediate differences, Mexicans suffered 800 revolts between 1821 and 1875.

Banditry, village uprisings, predatory armies, and caste wars all combined to keep Mexico in turmoil. No property was safe, no trade route secure. The two forces most responsible for sustaining the turbulence were the bandits and the army, who often worked together, selling stolen goods for their mutual profit. Bandits emerged from the Independence strife in small gangs with disparate backgrounds but united by a common desire to get ahead. They had pillaged as both monarchists and republicans during the war, and when it ended, they would not go back home. They meant to deal with the new power brokers. The brigands were reinforced by peons who had been handed weapons and told to fight. After victory these commoners refused to surrender their rifles, and when the national treasury could not afford to buy their continued services, they turned to banditry. So did others who were determined to protect from centralist encroachment the land they had occupied during the upheaval. All these people became rebels, determined to redistribute prestige and goods in their own favor, although not in accord with any ideology.[10]

These new brigands were not yet strong enough to regulate business by themselves; therefore, many became retainers for competing regional interests. No common cause existed in provincial Mexico, unless it was a mutual determination to keep central authority at bay. Caudillos, rural strongmen, were frequently at one another's throats—contesting economic advantage, political influence, and social prestige. The number of guns that a man could count on often determined the victor.

The relationship between outlaws and the people of power resembled a partnership more than an employer-employee arrangement. Wealthy ranchers normally would rather hang a brigand than treat with him, and they proved it later when backed by the dictatorship of Porfirio Díaz and his rural mounted police force, the *Rurales*. But given the uncertainties of post-Independence conditions, the propertied had to make deals with brigands for commercial service, protection, and retribution. Merchants also courted bandits out of fear and gain. Like the *hacendados* (ranchers), they would have welcomed effective policing, but none was available. So they sold to the robbers the goods needed to sustain their bandit activities. When they did so, authorities and the propertied looked the other way. If the outlaws could not fulfill their needs one way, they would do it another.[11]

Brigands also served in the armies raised by politicians in pursuit of power, even the presidency. Bandits who welcomed the chance to plunder within the bounds of a political cause were more reliable recruits than Indians, who might desert and return home to plant and harvest their corn. If their side won, so much the better for the bandits. If not, common practice pardoned the defeated and perhaps rewarded them in the hope of buying their allegiance. That was the kind of insurance that suited bandits; later national leaders gave them police work in the service of the state.[12]

Mexico experienced an epidemic of banditry after Independence, but it was not until the outbreak of civil war between Liberals and Conservatives in 1857 that brigands began to command regional control. Reformers, loosely grouped as Liberals, took control of national affairs in 1854, with plans to reorder society. They curtailed traditional privileges of the army, the Catholic Church, and the Indian communities in their determination to build a nation and a political constituency. At the same time, they overlaid the new structures with republicanism and capitalism meant to modernize Mexico along the lines of the United States and Western Europe. Such disruption of the former order naturally created new disorder. But even as the Liberals triumphed in civil war, foreign interlopers, sponsored by French imperialists and encouraged by Mexican dissidents, disrupted the country's leadership during the 1860s. Civil strife became entangled with national sovereignty. Nothing cultivates banditry like ineffective central government mired in a war for survival. Distinctions between soldier, brigand, patriot, and avenger simply disappeared.

By mid-century, bandits could be bought, but at their own price. They did not hesitate to change sides when promised better remuneration elsewhere or when fortunes shifted on the battlefield. Brigands did not scout, gather intelligence, or maintain communications between dispersed military units for pay in the usual sense. Rather, they were allowed to plunder as they went, and pillage sustained and rewarded them. However much that participants lamented the necessity of employing bandits as combatants, they did it just the same, especially the beleaguered Liberals.[13]

The Liberals were barely hanging on during the 1850s, but the bandits saw them through. Bandits raised so much havoc in the countryside that Conservatives in the capital could not finance their pacification. Banditry bled the Conservative treasury dry. When French imperialists threatened to end republican resistance to the imposition of a European monarch, bandit-guerrillas rampaged behind their front. They denied the foe victory until the end of Civil War in the United States and until the Prussian threat in Europe convinced Napoleon III to recall his troops and end the intervention in Mexico in 1867.[14]

How these plundering adversaries fought! Antonio Rojas and his *Galeanos* in Jalisco were hunted by the likes of the French army captain Berthelin and his French counterguerrillas. Rojas was a cutthroat of the worst order. He burned down entire towns that were not warmly hospitable to his band. He murdered Mexicans who declined to furnish comfortable lodgings and tasty meals. A necessary embarrassment to the Liberals, he maintained their cause in much of central-western Mexico in the critical year of 1864. Still, the republicans were somewhat relieved when French regulars shot down Rojas in January 1866, near Tocolotlán, Jalisco.[15]

Berthelin was, if possible, worse than Rojas. The Frenchman was a bloodthirsty racist, a tiger even in victory. Distinguished by effeminate attire, he adorned himself with jewelry, flamboyant rings, cosmetics, and perfume. Liberal forces killed him and took a large chunk of his scalp to Coalcomán so that the citizenry could sniff the greasy pomade in the hair.[16]

Mexico's decade of continuous turmoil, from 1857 to 1867, produced all kinds of banditry, from full-scale combatants like Rojas and Berthelin to small gangs and soloists like "La Carambada." Dressed in male clothing, she accosted travelers around Queretaro. After robbing one victim, she waved her pistol in one hand and bared a breast with the other. "Look who has looted you," she crowed, in a frontal assault on machismo.[17]

Supply trains during this period fell victim to brigands less often than did passenger stagecoaches because the convoys were well guarded, sometimes by hired bandits. Stagecoaches also had security guards, but they were notoriously undependable and often in league with brigands. Or the guards would charge the travelers a fee and then disappear.[18] A kind of toll system developed, but it was not as well organized as in Spain, where journeyers could buy travel insurance, called a *Viaje compuesto*, against being robbed. Or they could pay less for their ticket and take their chances, with a *Viaje sencillo*.[19]

In Mexico safe conduct could be purchased in Veracruz. It was also possible to purchase safe passage from the first robber encountered for the remainder of the trip. Otherwise, a voyager stood the possibility of suffering a succession of despoliations. There often was little left for the last robber in line, so he usually took all the personal clothing of the itinerants. More than a few arrived at their Mexico City hotels wrapped in newspapers, and their dash from the coach to the Hotel Iturbide raised quite a stir among onlookers.[20]

The best-known bandits of this period were the Plateados of Morelos, who, like most bandits, were both feared for their raw power and admired for their haughty dash. Above all, they were generally respected as a Mexican national type: the *charros*, best of all cowboys, possessed of a carefree, masculine arrogance, famed as horsemen and lovers. No bronc escaped their lasso nor any victim their shot. They dressed in high-crowned, wide-brimmed sombreros, suede bolero jackets, and tight-fitting trousers, all trimmed with silver sewn into swirling designs. The Plateados earned their title with ornate outfits, including silver spurs and saddles loaded with silver patterns. These men did not consider themselves mere outlaws. Like ostentatious Chinese bandits, the Plateados left their leggings open to expose an expensive inner lining to prove that they were no common robbers. The Plateados had class and they dressed the part. They were, however, neither gentlemen nor Robin Hoods. Their social cause was their own enrichment. They were crass competitors in a system that still lacked well-developed institutions for exchange and legitimate means to profit.[21]

The Plateados emerged because of the inability of ranking Liberal generals, like Jesús González Ortega, to reward volunteer troops with much more than thanks after they had taken Mexico City from the Conservatives in 1860. Compensation during the campaign had been in the form of plunder, but the capital had been declared out of bounds to looters. After sampling returns in the field, these veterans were in no mood to go home and subsist, so they kept their weapons and equipment and turned to brigandage.[22]

The Plateados were not just one huge gang, but a social phenomenon that occurred elsewhere in Mexico. Counterparts, also called Plateados, sprang up in Veracruz, Puebla, and Guerrero. These bands were large, up to 1,000 men, and they ran businesses in the areas where they worked. Their hideouts were well known: Monte de las Cruces on the Toluca road; Río Frío from the capital en route to Puebla; Cuesta China over toward Queretaro and Tlaltizapán in Morelos. Hacendados gave them horses, money, lodging, and even banquets, under the threat of losing much more, perhaps everything. The rich had to come to terms with the brigands. To whom could the propertied appeal for protection? No effective federal police force existed in the country, and to denounce a bandit invited revenge. When bandits kidnapped the manager of a hacienda, they reinforced their ransom demands with promises to destroy a recalcitrant hacendado's crops, cattle, and home. Deals had to be made, and hacendados furnished goods, arms, and safety to bandits. More than one traveler complained of being robbed in sight of a hacienda or of being refused a hacendado's help after being looted.[23]

These Plateados were not hired retainers, as were many bandits of earlier decades. They remained their own bosses. Bandoleros in this Golden Age of banditry did not often reciprocate a hacendado's favors. In fact, one of the more clever of the Plateados, Felipe "El Zarco" (Blue Eyes), is said to have worked his way into the highest social circles in Cuernavaca. After he won the confidence of the wealthy, he suggested outings in the countryside and promptly misguided his highly placed acquaintances into a nest of robbers.[24]

The Plateados, by late 1861, had paralyzed commerce in large areas of Morelos. Goods moved only at their will, and they demanded heavy duty for the right to roll the wagons. Authorities, some undoubtedly in league with the robbers, declined to prosecute them, and when they did, understanding judges, perhaps fearful of revenge, set the robbers free. Collusion based on fear and profit sustained the operation.[25]

Faced with the French Intervention, President Benito Juárez amnestied the Plateados and enlisted most, but not all, of them as republican guerrillas. Ever the pragmatists, many of the bandits sided with the French for higher pay and what they expected would be a more fruitful future. When the tide turned against the interventionists, the imperial bandits changed sides. In the wake of victory Juárez had to reward his brigand allies or face their return to banditry. But Juárez, like many other rulers faced with a similar reality, showed the good sense to mold the outlaws into his lawmen. In this way bandits became the core of Mexico's famed rural police force, the Rurales.[26]

Banditry persisted during the long dictatorship of Porfirio Díaz (1884–1911), but it took on an entirely different hue. Gone were the great bandit gangs of the past, such as the Plateados, and their power to control regions and enforce demands on the government. Instead, there appeared a number of loners with relatively small coteries of comrades, who loomed high in the public imagination but posed no serious threat to public order. They reflected a changing Mexico. As investment capital flowed into the country, it became more profitable for regional powerbrokers, who had formerly induced and supported banditry as a curtain of disorder against central control, to remove such barriers and join the dictatorship in mutual self-enrichment. So bandits lost their influential partners in the countryside, and those who had once encouraged and sustained them now financed security forces to hunt them down.[27]

This rupture in the former relationship between brigands and their accomplices did not mean that Mexicans-at-large shunned this new generation of bandits. However, the public attitude toward them changed. Mexicans had long celebrated their bandoleros because of their group power and haughty regional control. The Plateados were admired because they were stern rulers, not because they were troublesome subjects. But Porfirian bandits were lauded because they burlesqued the established order. With verve and wit, they challenged authority, but they were tragic figures doomed to defeat and early death. Bandits of the Porfiriato seemed to express an independence that many Mexicans sensed they had lost or had never enjoyed, and the popular culture of the time, specifically the folk ballads called *corridos*, clothed them in a legitimacy that augured danger for constituted government.

Chucho el Roto (Jesús Arriaga) was a low-income mestizo cabinetmaker in the capital who supplemented his income through banditry. Rumor held that frustrated love had driven him into brigandage. In a moment of passion he kidnapped and raped a young lady he loved but could never possess because she was of elite status.[28] A myth, quite likely, but one that underlined the real and uncrossable barrier between rich and poor.

His crime supposedly forced Chucho into full-time banditry, more as a gentleman Robin Hood than as a murderous desperado. Arriaga boasted that he never killed a victim, and the public believed him. The church provided a favorite target. He kidnapped priests and sued the bishop for ransom, or he simply picked the pockets of wealthy patrons attending mass. Chucho insisted that he was a Christian. When a local political boss in the state of Mexico offered 2,000 pesos for the bandit's life, Arriaga upped the ante: 3,000 pesos for the life of any available jefe and a bonus of 1,000 more for his particular adversary. Again, probably myth, the tale indicates where jefes stood with the populace. They were undoubtedly the *bêtes noires* of the regime.[29]

Mexico City's *El Correo de Lunes* in 1884 called Arriaga a "civilized bandit"—sociable, cultured, elegant, and well educated—and noted that Mexican high life was full of Chuchos, all of them after money, but none so frank or impudent as the bandit. The paper even nominated Chucho for Congress.[30]

Arriaga, a short, husky, bearded man with a kind face, was captured at age forty in Orizaba, where his cabinet shop was said to be a front for the intended robbery of a local cigar factory. Police found him in the company of three other bandits (one the well-known Francisco Valera) and in possession of a considerable cache of weapons. But prison could not long hold Chucho, and his escape in 1882 made people swear that he was more mirage than human. Three times he fled imprisonment, once outfoxing 200 soldiers guarding the jail. After each recapture, several of the capital's best lawyers handled his legal defense. Middle-class Mexicans cherished their relationship with the bandit and tried to shield him from prosecutions. *El Monitor Republicano* complained that authorities tried to saddle him with a number of unsolved crimes and demanded proof of his involvement.[31]

Jesús Arriaga was caught for good in 1884 in Queretaro, where he had lived with his woman for two years, making cabinets and picking the pockets of the populace, at times disguised as a woman. He had come to Queretaro dressed as a Turk and got started in business by selling rosaries to the city's residents, whom he described as "very Catholic." He also robbed loan houses but later asked a reporter: "Since when is it a crime to rob usurers?" How had he been discovered? "Damn it. My love of art." Chucho was apprehended in a theater. His picture had been circulating for some time, and he was recognized by a scar on his hand, the result of a carpentry slip. Some had surmised that he had fled to the comforts of Europe, that he was bathing in the sea off Biarritz, but Arriaga proclaimed his patriotism. He intended to die in Mexico, and he declined to elaborate on reports that he robbed mainly to finance a daughter's education in Brussels. If Chucho could not be bourgeois, he at least wanted such well-being for his daughter.[32]

The bandit assured newsmen that he soon would be free and shaking hands with old friends, but he died in 1885 in the darkness of Porfirio Díaz's prison at San Juan de Ulúa, the harbor fortress at Veracruz. Rumors that he had been beaten to death inflamed public sympathy and caused an official investigation into his death. The final verdict: dysentery. But Chucho el Roto outwitted his captors after all; he survives and cavorts on Mexican television today.[33]

The Thunderbolt of Sinaloa, Heraclio Bernal, toiled as a youth in Sinaloa's silver-mining district. While he knew the harshness of life as a miner, it was state politics that nudged him into banditry. Sinaloa, after the French Intervention of the 1860s, split politically between Juárez and his challenger, Díaz. Heraclio, like his father, supported Juárez. With Díaz's victory at Tuxtepec in 1876, Bernal's political opportunities evaporated, and he turned to banditry. The foreign-owned mines of Sinaloa and Durango offered easy targets and great rewards. Smugglers awaited stolen silver along the Pacific Coast. With local success, Bernal's regional reality ballooned into a national myth.[34]

Politics permeated Bernal's banditry. Teasing Sinaloa's Porfirian governor made great sport and attractive headlines for the brigand. When the governor sponsored a state dinner for a visiting official, Bernal organized in a rural village an even more sumptuous banquet for his followers. He once invited the governor to a dance that he had sponsored for friends. The governor, as expected, sent troops, but the Thunderbolt was long gone. Mexicans loved Bernal's pranks, even the imagined ones. No prank was intended, however, when he raised Sinaloan support for adversaries of Díaz in the 1880 presidential election. The movement produced heat but no fire, so he returned to brigandage. "Here comes Heraclio Bernal" became a popular national slogan that suggested terror, justice, jest, respect. Bernal played any role but that of loser.[35]

The Thunderbolt of Sinaloa in 1885 apparently bid to enter government service. He sent word to Díaz that, in return for his loyalty, he wanted to be named *jefe político* (political boss) of a Sinaloan municipality. He also demanded 30,000 pesos to finance himself and a security unit, and the release of gang members held by the government, including his brother. The president scoffed at such presumptuousness. Díaz did not have to bargain with robbers. Bernal might be pardoned if he surrendered, but there would be no promise of employment. The rebel rejected such adverse terms. He would undoubtedly have made a fine policeman, but instead he remained a successful bandit.[36]

With a band that may have reached 100 strong, Bernal dominated parts of Sinaloa and neighboring Durango. He forced loans from wealthy residents of the towns he raided, attacked armories, and sold contraband silver to finance his operation. He fined the administrator of one hacienda 25,000 pesos for daring to oppose him. When the administrator could not raise that amount, Bernal made him sign a promissory note. Then he took 9,000 pesos and a hostage to make sure that the note would be honored. Despite the governor's threat to punish those who aided Bernal, the brigand maintained substantial business ties. Local people in a sense had no choice. To denounce Bernal invited reprisal, which the state had no resources to prevent. Better to cooperate with him than to risk everything on his mood. Besides, even policemen and soldiers understand that there is profit in selling guns and ammunition to brigands.[37]

Throughout, Bernal's political ambitions never diminished. If Díaz would not let him weasel into his administration, Bernal would have to overthrow it. He joined revolts against Porfirian rule, with no success, and in 1887 produced his own political platform, which called for adherence to the Constitution of 1857, in particular the section prohibiting reelections. But a constituency, which at one time might have supported such a proposal, now favored the retention of Díaz. Bernal's challenge was too late. His days were numbered.[38]

The end of war against the Yaquis in Sonora permitted the federal army to concentrate on Bernal. To assist the military, anti-guerrilla forces were raised among those who knew his habits and territory. No peasant solidarity existed here. Ordinary Mexicans declined to follow Bernal's revolutionary instincts and joined the manhunt. The governors of Sinaloa and Durango put up a 10,000-peso reward for Bernal, and two of the bandit's gang members took the bait. They helped to set an ambush in which Bernal died on January 5, 1889. His gang split up, and several members joined the notorious brigand Ignacio Parra, who is said to have tutored Pancho Villa. The federals killed Bernal but not the Thunderbolt of Sinaloa. Newspapers printed an epitaph that he supposedly wrote for himself on the eve of his death. Incredibly, it lamented his failure to discover a place for himself in Mexican society. What irony! People admired Bernal for his stance outside social structures, when all the time he wanted to join the administration. But Bernal has finally acquired his niche inside the system. Nicolé Girón, who has recently studied Bernal, the man and myth, found him celebrated in thirteen songs, four poems, and four motion pictures, some adapted for television. Mexicans seem to yearn for his return.[39]

Santanón, another acclaimed bandit, earned his nationwide notoriety on the eve of the revolution. For more than a year he eluded the heralded Rurales, who, by reputation, always got their man but could not get Santanón (nor, in reality, many more like him). Narrow misses bloated the myths that people wanted to believe about the brigand. Durango's *La Evolución* concluded in 1910 that the Rurales must be shooting blanks instead of bullets at Santanón. It was the only explanation for the bandit's hairbreadth escapes. Or perhaps the Rurales did not shoot straight, but no one dared to say that, let alone believe it—even though it was true.[40]

Santana Rodríguez Palafox (Santanón) grew up an illiterate and unruly mestizo on a sugar plantation near his hometown of San Juan Evangelista in Veracruz. He hated his bosses, let them know it, ran off, was captured, and ended up literally shackled to his miserable work. His obstreperousness got him consigned to an army infantry battalion in Oaxaca, but he deserted in 1903 and returned home, where he found his mother in some way mistreated by authorities. One report had her beaten to death, a detail perhaps concocted to legitimate his depredations. Others said that he fell in with gunslingers as a restless young man, or that he lapsed into banditry out of grief at the death of his young wife. Some insisted that he left decent plantation labor to become a cattle thief, or that he was unjustly accused of stealing cows and then consigned to the military.[41]

Santanón's frustrations, whatever their source, drove him into banditry aimed mainly, but not exclusively, at foreign sugar planters and owners of sugar mills in southern Veracruz. He murdered the American manager of one mill and attacked several others with a band of only seven companions. Failure to apprehend him fed the public fancy. Santanón, they insisted, used no firearms, only a machete. He was a centaur protected by the shadows of night. No one had really seen him; no one knew him. Moreover, he was amphibious, which explained how he raided river-going cargo ships without detection. The facts of his adventures spread as rapidly as the fiction. Santanón did not shy from the murder of exploiters, but he also force-recruited supporters from Indian villages and put them up front as cannon fodder when he attacked a target. He also shot deserters. Vengeful natives, with good reason, joined the federal forces in hunting Santanón.[42]

Porfirio Díaz became seriously concerned about Santana Rodríguez when he learned that the brigand might be flirting with the ideas of radical Liberals, who, from exile in the United States, advocated overthrow of the dictatorship. The president hurried sizable reinforcements to Veracruz, consisting of Rurales, a battalion of soldiers, and field artillery, with orders to get Santanón.[43]

Liberals in Veracruz, with connections to the exiles, had indeed tried to recruit the bandit. They had even named him commander of a nonexistent Liberal army.

Whether Santanón had any ideological affinity for the cause is not known, but he should have welcomed support from any quarter. Later reports placed Liberal plans for insurrection in the brigand's possession, but that may have been a government plot to justify repression of radicals throughout the country.[44]

A federal deputy, Salvador Díaz Mirón, better known for his poetry than his legislation, was, in a moment of Porfirian caprice, given army units to track down the brigand. There you have it: poet versus bandit. Mexicans could scarcely contain themselves. Many rooted for Santanón. *La Evolución* called him an outlaw but praised his outrageous defiance of authority. It headlined the story about him: "Hero of the day."[45]

Rurales finally caught up with Rodríguez at Mecayopán in October 1910. Rural police scouts flushed him and twenty-six companions from a campsite and a fierce firefight ensued. Nearby army units, quickly on the scene, sent the brigands packing after a six-hour fight, but the bandits left behind eight dead, including Santanón. The Rurales received credit for the kill because their commanding officer, Lieutenant Francisco Cárdenas, galloped to the nearest telegraph post to report the triumph to his superiors in the capital. (Cárdenas in 1913 murdered President Francisco Madero. For his role in the Santanón affair he earned a promotion to captain.) Most probably it was a regular army soldier who shot the brigand, and it is doubtful that the Rurales could have weathered their encounter with the bandits without army support. Such claims were, however, part of the image-building process that sustained the rural police force far beyond its performance.[46]

The disorder fomented by Mexico's Revolution of 1910 was the nation's most divisive and deadly to date. With Díaz in exile, competitors for power were better defined and better organized than ever before, one of the proceeds of capitalistic development. Campesinos, proletarians, foreign investors, an emerging bourgeoisie, traditional elites, a multitude of marginals, not to underestimate competing foreign powers, all had a stake in the outcome, which promised great rewards to the victor. For almost six years the battle raged, laced by hasty alliances and broken promises, until in 1917 a faction won uneasy control with middle-class elements in charge. But it took another three decades to forge their interests in place.

Released by the violence of revolution from the inhibiting structures of Porfirian society, many Mexicans gilded outlawry with a tinge of patriotism and pillaged at will to their own advantage. With Díaz gone by mid–1911, the new president, Francisco Madero, sought to curb the disorder with proven solutions. He offered these aggressive opportunists positions in his bloated federal police force, but the ploy did not succeed because the compensation for police work did not nearly equal the gain available from wanton plunder. Because of Madero's inability to curb this disorder, but, more important, because the revolt had not run its course, he lost his regime to a usurper, Victoriano Huerta, in 1913. For somewhat more than a year, revolutionary rivals, led by the present pantheon of national heroes—Pancho Villa, Emiliano Zapata, and Venustiano Carranza—

sufficiently curbed their fundamental differences to oust Huerta; then they returned to dispute the real meaning of the Mexican Revolution. With the common cause that had lent some shape to the struggle gone, brigands chose sides in accordance with their potential for profit and then switched over to an adversary when it seemed more profitable to do so.[47]

Bandits, such as José Inés Chávez García, terrorized the Bajío like the bloody bandit-patriots of the French Intervention. Chávez García may have been the worst of the lot. He called himself a Villista, although Villa disowned him, and from the middle of 1915 to 1918 he ruled Michoacán and bordering districts of Guanajuato and Jalisco. He and his troops celebrated victories by raping virgins in the villages they pillaged. Rape became the gang's trademark. Lázaro Cárdenas, Benigno Serrano, and Anacleto López led columns against Chávez García. The bandit eluded them with clever guerrilla tactics, but the Spanish flu, which swept large portions of Mexico in 1918, finally caught and killed him.[48]

Pancho Villa himself remains an enigma to bandit studies. As a young man in Durango he was a cattle rustler, but what drove him to it is not clear. Some argue personal grievances, others say the profit incentive. But when the revolution erupted, he was drawing a salary as a track foreman on a railroad-building project in Chihuahua. Leaders of the rebellion convinced Villa to bring his section crew into the fight.[49]

Villa had good luck in the initial phase of the revolution; he ended up on the winning side. The victors established him in Chihuahua's first meat-packing business, and he shipped beef to the United States. Where he obtained the cattle is not so certain, but his negotiation indicates that Villa understood business potential, as did most bandits, and was moved by it.[50]

During the fight to oust Huerta and the internecine struggle that followed, Villa proved himself to be both a social reformer and a profiteer, although there is substantial controversy among historians as to the balance between the two. Villa raised enormous armies in the North, although little is understood about his recruitment tactics and incentives. Many individuals must have believed in the man or his promises. At the same time Villa force-recruited men into his ranks. In some cases the choice was simple: join Villa or get shot, although such demands may be more attributable to the leader's undisciplined lieutenants than to the Supreme Chief himself.[51]

As his fortunes declined in 1916 and 1917, inhabitants of villages in Villa's home territory of Chihuahua created security units called *defensas sociales* to protect themselves and their pueblos against what they considered to be the depredations of the Centaur of the North. His men raped and pillaged in Namiquipa, a town that had earlier furnished soldiers for the revolution, some of them undoubtedly for Villa himself.[52] Finally, in 1920, the beleaguered rebel accepted from the government a hacienda in Durango in exchange for his peaceful compliance. In doing so, some said that he betrayed the revolution. Even as Villa grows in national esteem and as he becomes more celebrated in official rhetoric, he remains controversial.[53]

2. José Ynez Chávez García, Mexican bandit

Of course, individuals and groups view bandits differently. An outlaw to one person may be a hero to another. One merchant keeps a weapon handy to fend off brigands; another forms a partnership with bandits for their mutual profit. One campesino hides a hunted felon from would-be captors; others help police to hunt him down. An entire community might defend a bandit because the brigand's activities are not considered to be outside the morality and standards of the community. But the same bandolero might not find succor in a nearby village with a different sense of acceptable behavior.[54] Over time, public attitudes toward a bandit may change: feared in one epoch, he may be lauded in the next. And these swirling sentiments surrounding bandits are both stimulated and confounded by the fact that bandits are not only real, but also symbolic.

As symbols, they stand as heroes in a determined, even noble, pose against the fetters of the modern world. With a carefree disposition and a straight back, they challenge authority. And the powerful have responded by molding the bandit-symbols to their liking and co-opting them to their cause. Bandits well serve a motion picture industry dominated by corporate capitalism. Pancho Villa is an official hero of Mexico's one-party government.

The names and deeds of these bandoleros continue to excite the popular imagination in Mexico. They persist in novels and comic books; they are glorified in cinema and television and are both praised and lamented in those wonderful purely Mexican corridos. Furthermore, the bandits already mentioned are among the country's best-known brigands; they have achieved and retained a truly national stature. Nevertheless, hundreds of other bandoleros, equally appreciated but obscured by their regionalism and localism, survive through an oral tradition in isolated pueblos, among campesinos who still claw a traditional subsistence living from their *milpas*, and in hinterland *cantinas*, still the centers of country life. In these places people continue to chat of bandit heroes, although the names of these brigands may be unknown to official documents, police blotters, and travel memoirs.[55]

The name of a nineteenth-century bandit is still occasionally seen sprayed in paint on an adobe wall—a call to the past for relief in the present—although more evident these days are the names of a new breed of bandits, genuine revolutionaries dedicated to overturning, rather than joining, the present society.[56] But the bandits of the past continue to have their pull. Mexicans yet admire those daring, often haughty, outlaws of earlier times, who in their relentless search for self-betterment shucked personal security and aggressively challenged a social system that was sharply tilted against them. Symbols of protest? Perhaps. Nonetheless, the government has co–opted most of them for its purposes. So Mexico's nineteenth-century bandits, cloaked in new myths, have finally ended up where in real life they had always wanted to be: respected members of the establishment, where they may fulfill daydreams but hardly incite change.

NOTES

1. Paul J. Vanderwood, *Disorder and Progress: Bandits, Police and Mexican Development* (Lincoln: University of Nebraska Press, 1981), pp. 3–15.

2. Alejandra Moreno Toscano and Enrique Florescano, "El sector externo y la organización espacial y regional de México (1521–1910)," in James W. Wilkie, Michael C. Meyer, and Edna Monzón de Wilkie, eds., *Contemporary Mexico: Papers of the IV International Congress of Mexican History* (Berkeley: University of California Press, 1976), p. 83; Eric R. Wolf and Edward C. Hansen, "Caudillo Politics: A Structural Analysis," *Comparative Studies in Society and History*, 9, 1 (Jan. 1967): 170–173; Richard N. Sinkin, "Modernization and Reform in Mexico, 1858–1876" (Ph.D. diss., University of Michigan, 1972), pp. 181–182, 187–188; Eric J. Hobsbawm, *Bandits* (New York: Delacorte Press, 1969), pp. 13, 32, 79–82; Margo Glantz, ed., *Viajes en México: Crónicas extranjeras* (Mexico: Secretaría de Obras Públicas, 1964), pp. 44–45, 237–239; Josefina Zoraida Vázquez, "Los primeros tropiezos" in *Historia general de México*, 4 vols. (Mexico: El Colegio de México, 1976), 3:48; Brantz Mayer, *Mexico; Aztec, Spanish and Republican: A Historical, Geographical, Statistical and Social Account of That Country . . .* , 2 vols. (Hartford, Conn.: S. Drake & Co., 1950), 2:149.

3. Vanderwood, *Disorder and Progress*, pp. 51–53.

4. Moisés González Navarro, *Historia moderna de México: El porfiriato: La vida social* (Mexico: Editorial Hermes, 1957), p. 433; *El Correo del Lunes* (Mexico City), 9 June 1884, pp. 2–3 *El Cable Transatlántico* (Mexico City), 23 August 1881, p. 3 *El Monitor Republicano* (Mexico City). 1 June 1884, p. 3; 31 October 1885, p. 3; *El Tiempo* (Mexico City), 3 June 1884, p. 4.

5. J. Eric S. Thompson, ed., *Thomas Gage's Travels in the New World* (Norman: University of Oklahoma Press, 1958); letter from Christon I. Archer, University of Calgary, to Vanderwood, 22 March 1978; Colin M. MacLachlan, *Criminal Justice in Eighteenth Century Mexico: A Study of the Tribunal of the Acordada* (Berkeley: University of California Press, 1974), p. 51.

6. William B. Taylor, "Bandit Gangs in Late Colonial Times: Rural Jalisco, Mexico, 1794–1821," in Paul J. Vanderwood, ed., "Social Banditry and Spanish American Independence," *Biblioteca Americana*, 1, 2 (Nov. 1982): 56.

7. Taylor, "Bandit Gangs," p. 37.

8. Captain G. F. Lyon, *Journal of a Residence and Tour in the Republic of Mexico in the Year 1826, with Some Account of the Mines in that Country*, 2 vols. (London: John Murray, 1828), 2: 171–172; Julio Guerrero, *La génesis del crimen en México, estudio de psiquiatriá social* (Mexico: Librería de la Vᵈᵃ de Ch. Bouret, 1901), p. 204; Josefina Zoraida Vázquez, "Los primeros tropiezos," pp. 12–15; Lieutenant R.W.H. Hardy, *Travels in the Interior of Mexico in 1825, 1826, 1827, and 1828* (London: Henry Colburn and Richard Bentley, 1829), pp. 164–165; H. G. Ward, *Mexico*, 2 vols. (London: Henry Colburn 1829), 1:231; Wolf and Hansen, "Caudillo Politics," pp. 170–172; Edward Thornton Tayloe, *Mexico, 1825–1827: The Journal and Correspondence of Edward Thorton Tayloe*, ed. C. Harvey Gardiner (Chapel Hill: University of North Carolina Press, 1959), p. 35; Luis Villoro, "La revolución de independencia," in *Historia general de México*, 4 vols. (Mexico: El Colegio de México, 1976), 2:348–349; Luis González y González, "The Revolution of Independence," in Daniel Cosío Villegas et al., *A Compact History of Mexico* (Mexico: El Colegio de México, 1973), p. 85.

9. Christon I. Archer, "Banditry and Revolution in New Spain, 1790–1821," in Paul J. Vanderwood, ed., "Social Banditry and Spanish American Independence," *Biblioteca Americana*, 1, 2 (Nov. 1982): 60, 66, 71, 85; personal letters of Archer to Vanderwood, 4 January and 22 March 1979.

10. Francisco López Cámara, *La estructura económica y social de México en la época de la Reforma* (Mexico: El Siglo XXI Editores, 1967), p. 233; Nevin O. Winter, *Mexico*

and Her People Today. An Account of the Customs, Characteristics, Amusements, History and Advancement of the Mexicans . . . (Boston: L. C. Page & Co., 1923), p. 330; Zoraida Vázquez, "Primeros tropiezos," 3: 60; Guerrero, *Génesis del crimen*, pp. 213–214; John H. Coatsworth, "The Mobility of Labor in Nineteenth Century Mexican Agriculture" (paper presented at meeting of the American Historical Association, San Francisco, December 1978), pp. 10–11.

11.   Moreno Toscano and Florescano, "El sector externo," p. 83; Wolf and Hansen, "Caudillo Politics," pp. 170–173; Sinkin, "Modernization and Reform," pp. 181–182; Hobsbawm, *Bandits*, pp. 13, 79–82; Glantz, ed., *Viajes en México*, pp. 44–45, 237–239; Zoraida Vázquez, "Primeros tropiezos," 3: 48; Mayer, *Mexico; Aztec, Spanish and Republican*, 2: 149.

12.   López Cámara, *Estructura económica*, pp. 235–236; Guerrero, *Génesis del crimen*, pp. 213–214; Tayloe, *Journal*, pp. 67–68; *Archivo Mexicano: Colección de leyes, decretos, circulares y otros documentos*, 6 vols. (Mexico: Imprenta de V. G. Torres, 1856–1862), 2: 677.

13.   Guerrero, *Génesis del crimen*, p. 213; Salvador Ortíz Vidales, *Los bandidos en la literatura Mexicana* (Mexico: [Porrua], 1949), p. 21; Lamberto Popoca y Palacios, *Historia de la bandalismo en el estado de Morelos, ¡ayer como ahora! 1860 (Plateados), 1911 (Zapatistas)* (Puebla: Tipografía Guadalupana, 1912), pp. 62, 65, 73; Moisés Ochoa Campos, *La revolución Mexicana*, 4 vols. (Mexico: Talleres Gráficos de la Nación, 1966), 2: 87; Felipe Buenrostro, *Historia del primero y segundo congresos constitucionales de la república Mexicana*, 9 vols. (Mexico: Tipografía de F. Mata, 1874), 4:373–375, 5:415–416; Nicolé Girón, *Heraclio Bernal, ¿bandolero, cacique o precursor de la revolución?* (Mexico: Instituto Nacional de Antropología e Historia, 1976), p. 35, quoting José Bravo Ugarte, *Historia sucinta de Michoacán*, 3 vols. (Mexico: Editorial Jus, 1964), 3: 242.

14.   Vanderwood, *Disorder and Progress*, pp. 6–7.

15.   Ireneo Paz, *Algunas campañas, 1863–1876* (Mexico: Ediciones de la Secretaría de Educación Pública, 1944), pp. 33–34, 41–42; José María Vigil, "La reforma," in Vicente Riva Palacio, ed., *México através de los siglos: Historia general y completa del desenvolvimiento social, político, religioso, militar, artístico, científico, y literario de México desde la antigüedad más remota hasta la época actual . . .*, 5 vols. (Barcelona: Espasa y Compañía, [1888–1889]), 5:678–681; Angelica Peregrina, "Documentos: Antonio Rojas, un bandido jalisciense," *Boletín del Archivo Histórico de Jalisco*, 2, 2 (May-Aug. 1978): 10–11.

16.   María Vigil, "La reforma," 5: 678–681; Paz, *Algunas campañas*, pp. 33–34, 41–42.

17.   Ochoa Campos, *Revolución Mexicana*, 2: 87; Ma. Guadalupe Flores and Angelica Peregrina, "Historiografía: Las gavillas en Jalisco de 1856 a 1863," *Boletín del Archivo Histórico de Jalisco*, 2, 2 (May-Aug., 1978): 2–8.

18.   S. S. Hill, *Travels in Peru and Mexico*, 2 vols. (London: Longman, Green, Longman and Roberts, 1860), pp. 223, 270–271; Albert S. Evans, *Our Sister Republic: A Gala Trip through Tropical Mexico in 1869–70* (Hartford: Columbian Book Co., 1970), p. 203; John Lewis Geiger, *A Peep at Mexico: Narrative of a Journey across the Republic from the Pacific to the Gulf in December 1873 and January 1874* (London: Trubner and Co., 1874), pp. 96–97; José López-Portillo y Rojas, *Elevación y caída de Porfirio Díaz* (Mexico: Librería Español, 1921), p. 77; Brantz Mayer, *Mexico As It Was and As It Is* (New York: J. Winchester, New World Press, 1844), p. 10.

19. Enrique Martínez Ruiz, "La crisis del orden público en España y la creación de la Guardia Civil," *Revista de estudios históricos de la guardia civil*, 5 (1970): 58; Constancio Bernaldo de Quirós, *El bandolerismo en España y México* (Mexico: Editorial Jurídica Mexicana, 1959), p. 231.

20. Glantz, *Viajes en México*, p. 44; C. A. Stephens, *The Knockabout Club in the Tropics: The Adventures of a Party of Young Men in New Mexico, Mexico, and Central America* (Boston: Estes and Lauriat, 1884), p. 181; Edward Dunbar, *The Mexican Papers* (New York: J. A. H. Hasbrouck and Co., 1860–1861), p. 114; Henry C. Becher, *A Trip to Mexico, Being Notes of a Journey from Lake Erie to Lake Tezcuco [sic] and Back . . .* (Toronto: Willing & Williamson, 1880), p. 137; Antonio García Cubas, *El libro de mis recuerdos* (Mexico: Editorial Patria, 1945), p. 201; López Cámara, *Estructura económica*, p. 234; Thomas W. Knox, *The Boy Travellers in Mexico: Adventures of Two Youths in a Journey to Northern and Central Mexico . . .* (New York: Harper & Brothers, 1902), p. 75.

21. Hobsbawm, *Bandits*, p. 29; López Cámara, *Estructura económica*, p. 233; Popoca y Palacios, *Bandalismo*, p. 13.

22. Popoca y Palacios, *Bandalismo*, pp. 5–7, 92; María Vigil, "La reforma," 5: 444; Bravo Ugarte, *Historia sucinta*, 3: 242; Girón, *Heraclio Bernal*, p. 35; Geiger, *Peep at Mexico*, pp. 308–309.

23. Anton Blok, "The Peasant and the Brigand: Social Banditry Reconsidered," *Comparative Studies in Society and History*, 14, 4 (Sept. 1972): 497; Hobsbawm, *Bandits*, p. 77; Dunbar, *Mexican Papers*, p. 113; University of Texas at Austin, Benson Latin American Collection, Rare Documents; Mariano Riva Palacio Papers (MRP), No. 3513, Lorenzo Calderón to Mariano Riva Palacio, 30 November 1849; MRP, No. 8172, José María Verdiguel y Fernández to Mariano Riva Palacio, 21 October 1869; MRP, No. 9104, Francisco Limón to Mariano Riva Palacio, 9 February 1871; Dennis E. Berge, trans. and ed., *Considerations on the Political and Social Situations of the Mexican Republic, 1847* (El Paso: Texas Western Press, 1975), pp. 19–20; Girón, *Heraclio Bernal*, p. 56; Popoca y Palacios, *Bandalismo*, pp. 36, 40–41, 76–77; García Cubas, *Mis recuerdos*, p. 200; Edith B. Couturier, "Hacienda de Hueyapan: The History of a Mexican Social Economic Institution" (Ph.D. diss., Columbia University, 1965), p. 114; Ochoa Campos, *Revolución Mexicana*, 2:87; Ortíz Vidales, *Los bandidos*, p. 18.

24. Popoca y Palacios, *Bandalismo*, pp. 33–35; Ortíz vidales, *Los bandidos*, pp. 15–19, 33–36.

25. México, Archivo General de la Nación, Ramo de Gobernación, Legajo 1384, Expediente, Plateados. (Hereafter AGN, Leg., Exp.)

26. Vanderwood, *Disorder and Progress*, pp. 49–50; AGN, Leg. 1384, Exp., Plateados; Guerrero, *Génesis del crimen*, p. 217; Paz, *Algunas campañas*, p. 61; MRP, No. 7445, (cuaderno) Miguel Cardena Asunción (unsigned), 2 February 1862 to 20 April 1863; MRP, No. 7533, Miguel Cardena Asunción to Mariano Riva Palacio, 11 March 1863; Paul J. Vanderwood, "Genesis of the Rurales: Mexico's Early Struggle for Public Security," *Hispanic American Historical Review*, 50, 2 (May 1970): 323–44.

27. Vanderwood, *Disorder and Progress*, p. 94.

28. Quirós, *Bandolerismo*, pp. 343–349.

29. Ibid., pp. 349–355; Ortíz Vidales, *Los bandidos*, p. 66; *El Siglo XIX* (Mexico City), 2 June 1884, p. 3.

30. *El Correo del Lunes* (Mexico City), 9 June 1884, pp. 2–3; *El Cable Transatlántico* (Mexico City), 23 August 1881, p. 3.

31. *El Monitor Republicano* (Mexico City), 1 June 1884, p. 3; 21 June 1884, p. 3; *El Tiempo* (Mexico City), 3 June 1884, p. 4.

32. *El Tiempo*, 3 June 1884, p. 4; *El Monitor Republicano*, 3 October 1885, p. 3; González Navarro, *Historia moderna de México*, p. 433.

33. *El Tiempo*, 5 November 1885, p. 1; 13 November 1885, p. 3; 8 November 1885, p. 3; *El Monitor Republicano*, 31 October 1885, p. 3; Luis González y González, "El liberalismo triunfante," in *Historia general de México*, 4 vols. (Mexico: El Colegio de México, 1976), 2: 203.

34. Quirós, *Bandolerismo*, p. 366; Owen W. Gillpatrick, *Wanderings in Mexico: The Spirited Chronicle of Adventure in Mexican Highways and By-ways by Wallace Gillpatrick* . . . (London: E. Nash, 1912), p. 329; Mario Gill, "Heraclio Bernal, caudillo frustrado," *Historia Mexicana*, July-September 1954, pp. 141–147; Girón, *Heraclio Bernal*, p. 29; Antonio Nakayama A., *Sinaloa: El drama y sus actores* (Mexico: Colección Cientifica, No. 20, Instituto Nacional de Antropología e Historia, 1975), p. 210.

35. Gill, "Caudillo frustrado," pp. 141–147; *La República*, 5 November 1885, p. 1.

36. Alfred O. Coffin, *Land Without Chimneys: or, the Byways of Mexico* (Cincinnati: Editor Publishing Co., 1898), pp. 199–200; David A. Wells, *A Study of Mexico* (New York: D. Appleton & Co., 1897), pp. 19–20.

37. Girón, *Heraclio Bernal*, pp. 50, 57–58, 61, 65; *El Tiempo*, 12 November 1885, p. 3.

38. Gill, "Caudillo frustrado," p. 147.

39. Girón, *Heraclio Bernal*, pp. 19–20; Gill, "Caudillo frustrado," p. 139; *El Monitor Republicano*, 1 February 1887, p. 2; González, "Liberalismo triunfante," 3:29; Quirós, *Bandolerismo*, pp. 368–369; J. Ascensión Reyes, *Heraclio Bernal (El Rayo de Sinaloa)* (San Antonio, Mexico: Casa Editorial Lozano, 1920), p. 245.

40. *La Evolución* (Durango), 1 July 1910, p. 1; my examination of Rural Police targets preserved in Mexico's National Archive proves them to have been mediocre marksmen.

41. Quirós, *Bandolerismo*, pp. 370–373; *Periódico Oficial* (Veracruz) 27 October 1910, pp. 2–3; *El Nacional* (Mexico City), 15 February 1959, pp. 3, 9; *El Imparcial* (Mexico City), 19 October 1910, pp. 1, 5; 20 October 1910, pp. 1, 5; *El País* (Mexico City), 17 October 1910, p. 2; *El Dictamen* (Veracruz), 26 June 1910, p. 4.

42. *Periódico Oficial*, 27 October 1910, p. 3; Quirós, *Bandolerismo*, pp. 273–274; *El País*, 18 October 1910, p. 1; *El Dictamen*, 14 June 1910, p. 1; 15 June 1910, p. 1; 16 June 1910, p. 1; 18 June 1910, p. 1; 25 June 1910, p. 4; 2 July 1910, p. 1; 14 July 1910, pp. 1–2; 27 July 1910, p. 1; 28 September 1910, p. 1; 3 November 1910, p. 1.

43. *El Dictamen*, 18 June 1910, p. 1; *El Nacional*, 15 February 1959, pp. 3, 9; Cholula, Mexico; Universidad de las Américas, Archivo de Porfirio Díaz, Legajo XIX, No. 004020, 18 October 1910 (hereafter APD, Leg., No., date); *El Tiempo*, 19 October 1910, p. 1; Gustavo Casasola, *Historia gráfica de la revolución Mexicana*, 5 vols. (Mexico: Editorial F. Trillas, 1960), 1: 215; *El Imparcial*, 22 January 9, p. 1; José C. Valadés, *Historia general de la revolución Mexicana*, 10 vols. (Mexico: M. Quesada Brandi, 1963), 1: 193; Mexico, Archivo de la Defensa Nacional, XI/481.5/310, folletos 1–3.

44. C. D. Padua, *Movimiento revolucionario—1906 en Veracruz* . . . (Cuernavaca: [n. p.], 1936), pp. 46–48, 65–67, 75, 81; U.S. National Archives, Department of State, Records of the Department of State Relating to the Internal Affairs of Mexico, 1910–1929, Record Group 59, National Archives Microfilm Publication (Microcopy No. 274), 1910–1914, File No. 812.00/450, Wilson to Knox, 15 December 1910; *El Nacional*, 15 February 1959, pp. 3, 9; *El Dictamen*, 22 June 1910, p. 1; James D. Cockcroft, *Intellectual Precursors of the Mexican Revolution, 1900–1913* (Austin: University of Texas Press, 1968), pp. 154–155, 180.

45. Quirós, *Bandolerismo*, pp. 374–376; Pauda, *Movimiento*, p. 64; *El Nacional*, 15 February 1959, pp. 3, 9; *La Evolución*, 1 July 1910, p. 1; *El Dictamen*, 22 June 1910, p. 1; 22 July 1910, p. 1.

46. *Mexican Herald* (Mexico City), 25 October 1910, 3; *El Dictamen*, 19 October 1910, pp. 1, 4; 20 October 1910, p. 1; 22 November 1910, p. 1; APD, Leg. LXIX, No. 004021, 18 October 1910; Leg. LXIX, No. 004025, 19 October 1910; *Periódico Oficial*, 27 October 1910, pp. 1–2; Sonora, General Archive, Vol. 54, Nos. 182–183; Padua, *Movimiento*, pp. 78–81; *El Imparcial*, 19 October 1910, pp. 1, 5; 20 October 1910, pp. 1, 5; 22 January 1911, p. 1; *El País*, 20 October 1910, p. 3; 22 October 1910, p. 2; 1 February 1911, p. 3.

47. Vanderwood, *Disorder and Progress*, pp. 164–178.

48. José Valdovinos Garza, *Tres capitalos de la política Michoacana* (Mexico: Ediciones "Casa de Michoacán," 1960), pp. 12–27; Ernest Otto Schuster, *Pancho Villa's Shadow: The True Story of Mexico's Robin Hood as Told by His Interpreter* (New York: Exposition Press, 1947), pp. 246, 264; Casasola, *Historia gráfica*, 2: 1297.

49. Arthur E. Stillwell and James R. Crowell, "I Had a Hunch," *Saturday Evening Post*, 200, 32 (4 Feb. 1929): 38; Dr. Ira J. Bush, *Gringo Doctor* (Caldwell, Idaho: Caxton Printers, 1939), pp. 226–231; William H. Beezley, *Insurgent Governor: Abraham González and the Mexican Revolution in Chihuahua* (Lincoln: University of Nebraska Press, 1973), pp. 36–37; Vanderwood, "The Counter-Guerrilla Strategy of Porfirio Díaz," *Hispanic American Historical Review*, 56, 4 (Nov. 1976): 560–561.

50. Beezley, *González*, pp. 93, 107.

51. Printed material on Villa is voluminous and growing. Most of it is polemical, or at least highly biased. More scholarly investigations of Villa include Friedrich Katz, *The Secret War in Mexico: Europe, the United States, and the Mexican Revolution* (Chicago: University of Chicago Press, 1981); and Katz, "Pancho Villa and the Attack on Columbus, New Mexico," *American Historical Review*, 83, 1 (Feb. 1978): 101–130.

52. Ximena Sepúlveda Otaiza, *La revolución en Bachíniva* (Mexico: Departamento de Etnología y Anthropología Social, Instituto Nacional de Anthropología e Historia, 1975), pp. 11–12; Martha Eva Rocha Islas, "Del Villismo y las Defensas Sociales en Chihuahua, 1915–1920" (thesis, Universidad Nacional Autonoma de México, 1979).

53. J.W.F. Dulles, *Yesterday in Mexico: A Chronicle of the Revolution, 1919–1936* (Austin: University of Texas Press, 1972), pp. 66–70, 178–180.

54. Julian A. Pitt-Rivers, *The People of the Sierra* (Chicago: University of Chicago Press, 1954), pp. 178–79.

55. For current popular examples, see Anónimo, *Chucho el Roto* (Mexico: Cuadernos Mexicanos, SEP, Año I, nu. 4 [1981?]); Carlos Isla, *Chucho el Roto* (Mexico: Ediciones ELA, 1980). An excellent book on the corrido is Vicente T. Mendoza, *El corrido Mexicano* (Mexico: El Fondo de Cultura Económica, 1954).

56. Two recent examples are Genaro Vásquez Rojas, a schoolteacher from the state of Guerrero, killed by troops in 1972, and Lucio Cabañas, also a teacher, who for seven years fended off federal pursuit until 1974, when he was killed in a car crash or by federal troops—the circumstances are not clear. In the summer of 1982 newspapers reported the outbreak of banditry, headed by Robin Hood-type characters, in the northern part of the state of Michoacán.

3

Banditry and Social Conflict on the Venezuelan Llanos

MIGUEL IZARD and RICHARD W. SLATTA

The llanos of Colombia and Venezuela is one of the vast plains frontiers of Latin America. In such regions criminal activity during both the colonial and national periods often stemmed from sociopolitical conflict between divergent groups. Urban elites in Caracas and Bogotá encountered virulent opposition as they tried to impose their will and law on frontiersmen of the Llano. Contraband livestock trade, a crime to political authorities but a way of life to llaneros, the horsemen of the tropical plains, provided a main focus of conflict. Plainsmen ignored the dictates of government and developed their own set of common law rules and traditions.

Other crimes against persons and property were committed, as in Mexico, by freebooters seeking to profit from general political disorder. Social anomie provided opportunities for those unscrupulous or desperate enough to take advantage of a chaotic situation. Such crimes persisted on the llanos until (a) central force could be applied effectively and (b) the llanos became an economic backwater with few opportunities for either legitimate or criminal gain. Although some social forces identified by Hobsbawm as contributing to social banditry existed on the Venezuelan plains, they gave rise to a range of criminal activity, not to social banditry per se.

SOCIAL FORMATION OF THE LLANERO

Conquering peoples have usually faced two very different responses from those they sought to subjugate. Sedentary, agricultural societies have often had no alternative but to yield to their conquerors, since dependence on crops tied them to the lands they inhabited. In contrast, nomadic tribes—hunters and gatherers—have been better able to avoid conquest because of their mobility. They

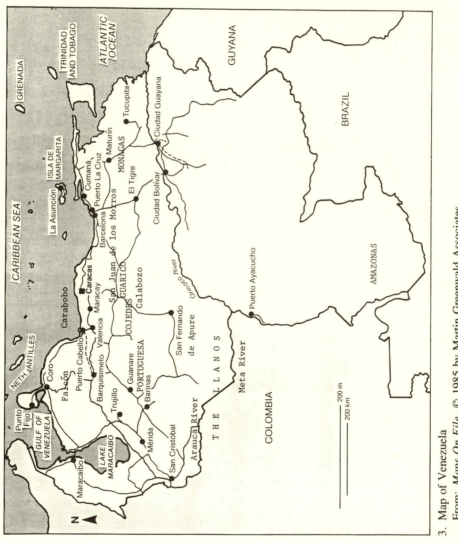

3. Map of Venezuela

From: *Maps On File,* © 1985 by Martin Greenwald Associates.
Reprinted by permission of Facts On File, Inc., New York.

have even taken the offensive and attacked invaders in order to weaken and deter them.

The expansion initiated by the Iberian crowns at the end of the fifteenth century represented a quantitative and qualitative change from similar activities that had taken place in the past. From the beginning of the sixteenth century, the Portuguese and the Castilians were protagonists in a massive overseas expansion. Their activities degenerated into the world's first colonialism on a continental scale in Latin America and disrupted the African continent with the search for black slaves to work in their new colonies.

In America the Iberian invaders subdued many agricultural peoples (often possessed of extraordinary, sophisticated cultures) and initiated bloody confrontations in frontier regions populated by nomadic groups. Some of the frontiersmen quickly became excellent riders and deadly mounted hunters, thanks to the livestock that arrived with the Europeans. Plains areas of South America, such as the pampas of the Río de la Plata and the llanos of Venezuela and Colombia, became formidable strongholds of opposition to colonial centralizing authority.

Plains regions present peculiar characteristics that set them apart from other geographical regions. Their borders are often fluid and vaguely defined, and their populations are also mobile and shifting. Given this dynamic frontier character, three distinct social groups developed on the llanos: (1) Displaced indigenous groups remained, with cultures largely intact, despite the conquering European presence.(2) Spanish and mestizo ranchers gradually asserted control over the wild livestock that roamed the plains and eventually gained title to the land itself. (3) Free but landless men, often of mixed blood, hunted the prolific wild livestock for sustenance and for hides and grease valued as exports. This latter group came to be known as llaneros, the wild cattle hunters of the plains. As on the Argentine pampa, conflict between independent-minded plainsmen and an acquisitive landed elite prompted the latter to use the law as a political weapon against the rural lower classes.[1]

During the eighteenth and nineteenth centuries the outlaw population of the llanos, like those of Mexico and Argentina, was also geographically and socially fluid. Some llaneros temporarily moved to more settled ranching areas and hired out as peons. Despite legal requirements for work contracts, labor-short ranchers and farmers seldom inquired about a peon's personal or employment history. The llanero population increased owing to flight from the more developed north-central coastal area, the valley of Caracas. Some of these fugitives would return to European-controlled regions, in hopes that their original crimes might have been forgotten. Others retreated still deeper into the frontier region, perhaps passing over the Orinoco River into the Amazonian jungles.[2]

The llanos early became an area of refuge for a wide variety of persons. Fugitives from authorities in the settled coastal areas found sanctuary in the vastness and anonymity of the llanos. Black slaves escaped to the plains from coastal sugar plantations. And Arawak Indians had already moved to the remote llanos after being driven out of the Caribbean in the early decades of the Spanish Conquest.

Another characteristic of plains regions is the longer time required to subjugate them to central authority. Confrontations between white elites and non-white masses began in early colonial Venezuela. But in the llanos the social conflict accelerated after the middle of the seventeenth century and more so toward the end of the eighteenth. Caribbean sugar production stimulated a heady demand for livestock. With pack animals, hides, and dried beef in demand, the ruling oligarchy in Caracas looked with greater interest to the potential wealth of the frontier. Llaneros violently resisted elite efforts to displace or subjugate them.

"CIVILIZATION" VERSUS "BARBARISM"

As in other parts of Latin America, urban authorities looked askance at frontiersmen. In the second half of the seventeenth century, Fray Ildefonso de Zaragoza marveled at the primitive life of the llanero. The plainsmen worshiped neither the true God nor false ones, recognized no authority, and rode about as wildly as the cattle they stalked.[3]

Socially, the llanos remained a region of outcasts and fugitives, despite the "civilizing" efforts of missionaries. In 1661 an official lamented the "many murders, robberies, and injuries committed by runaway slaves" living in the llanos.[4] In the early eighteenth century Fray Marcelino de San Vicente reported negatively on the mestizo population of the Llano. The inhabitants, charged the cleric, were "leading a scandalous life, more reprehensible than that of the heathen Indians, committing grave offenses without any of the exterior signs of the Catholic religion, for they live and die like barbarians in the hills."[5]

In the last quarter of the eighteenth century, missionaries in pursuit of Indians penetrated farther into the plains to the south. Between the Apure and Meta rivers they founded mission settlements, such as San Fernando de Apure. They suffered great difficulties, "not only because of the Indian's natural inconstancy and love of freedom, but also because of other people who failed to respect them." The priests required a military escort to protect them from the Indians and to destroy "a gang of zambos that turned the Indians into renegades."[6]

The marked prejudice against "barbarous" llaneros on the part of "civilized" Venezuelans persisted into the national period. The Caracas elite, with a distinctly North Atlantic viewpoint, could see little more than obstacles to progress in the inhabitants of the interior plains.[7] Far from the restraints of urban Caracas and the coastal plantations dominated by white Spanish masters, mixed-blood llaneros lived by their own rules.

CONTRABAND TRADE AND RUSTLING

Without question, cattle rustling was the most common crime of the colonial llanos. Like Argentine gauchos, llaneros held that free-roaming livestock could

4. Venezuelan Llaneros, 1862, from Ramón Páez, *Wild Scenes in South America, or Life in the Llanos of Venezuela*

be killed by anyone with the energy and skill to do so. This belief in use rights—the communal access to nature's bounty—was confirmed over time by colonial tradition and legislation.

As export markets for live animals, hides, grease, and dried beef expanded in the latter decades of the eighteenth century, urban elites sought to extend control over the profitable herds of the llanos. Economic self-interest reinforced the sociocultural prejudices of the elites against the plainsmen. Like Argentina's landed elite, Venezuelan ranchers used the law as a class weapon to control the livestock wealth of the llanos and subdue the unruly inhabitants. By regulating the killing of wild cattle and the branding of mavericks, officials declared much of the llanero population to be criminal.[8]

Contraband livestock trade became the economic mainstay of the region. A circular of October 18, 1777, decreed that *arrieros* (muleteers) carrying merchandise from Guanare, San Carlos, Carora, and Calabozo in the Llano to Coro on the coast (capital of today's state of Falcón) had to return with the same number of animals they brought. Muleteers were increasing their profits by selling contraband mules on the side.

Given the territorial vastness and the extensive fluvial network, government officials could do little to thwart illicit traffic down the Orinoco River to Caribbean island ports. And the occasional official who might pose a problem could be bribed into complicity. The complex, restrictive system of commercial prohibitions and high export and transit taxes further militated against legitimate livestock trade.[9]

Taxation and unfavorable conditions of internal trade stimulated the llanos to orient itself toward river ports, such as Ciudad Bolívar, and function economically apart from the valley of Caracas. In exchange for the hides and other contraband, produce came upriver from a variety of sources. A government report of 1692 complained that illegal goods "of all types" were being sold as far inland as "the llanos of San Sebastian."[10]

During the 1760s young mules could be purchased for ten pesos in the llanos, exported and sold illegally to foreigners for forty pesos. No such handsome profit could be gained in internal markets. During the 1770s illicit trade flourished between the llanos town of Barinas and ports downriver on the Orinoco.[11]

The economic expansion of Caribbean sugar islands in the late eighteenth century stimulated the livestock industry in the llanos. Island plantations required large numbers of draft animals as well as meat to feed their workers. Extensive contraband trade in hides with Jamaica, Curaçao, Trinidad, and other islands precipitated the wholesale slaughter of wild cattle. As on the pampas, meat was left to the vultures. The ranching elite of the llanos complained loudly of a rustling epidemic, but little was (or could be) done by way of enforcement. This boom in illegal hide exports drastically reduced the cattle population of the llanos and began a decline greatly accelerated by the depredations of the Independence wars yet to come.[12]

A PEOPLE BEYOND THE LAW

Because of the sociopolitical and economic antipathy between llaneros and urban elites, llaneros developed as a separate society, a people and nation unto themselves. In effect, virtually the entire llanero population was legally defined by the ruling class as criminal, much as gauchos in Argentina became, by definition, "vagrants and ne'er do wells." In Venezuela colonial officials declared llaneros to be "vagos y maleantes" (vagrants and corrupters) and forced them to labor at low wages.[13]

In the 1790s many llaneros charged with being of "bad life and customs" ended up in the Puerto Cabello prison on the coast, awaiting forced military service or labor on public works. Prison officials who received yet another fifty vagrants requested that police suspend further shipments because the prison was bursting at the seams.[14]

But the unique llanero way of life molded the plainsmen into formidable enemies of the state. Survival in the tropical plains required keen eyesight and hearing. By putting an ear to the ground, a llanero outlaw could sense approaching pursuers long before they might do him harm. He knew how to "bushwhack" cross-country and ford swollen rivers with safety. These frontier skills made fugitive llaneros elusive prey for soldiers or police.

Wily bandits, with extraordinary survival skills, became living legends. One example was "Guardajumo" (or "Guarda Humos"), an Indian who robbed ranches and traveling merchants between Barcelona on the coast and Calabozo (in today's state of Guarico) during the early 1780s. Among llaneros he was thought to be a witch who could turn himself into a smoke-covered tree trunk in order to escape the law (hence the nickname "Smokescreen"). The saying "worse than Guarda Humos" passed into folk wisdom to describe a dangerous character. The famous bandit met his end in May of 1802, when officials caught and hanged him in Calabozo.[15]

The lack of towns on the Llanos dictated that runaways and bandits had to live off the land. Superb hunters, llaneros could kill a variety of game for food, including deer, wild hogs, iguanas, and birds. They also fished in the many rivers. During the onset of the six-month dry season, fish became trapped in stagnant pools. Llaneros used their hammocks as nets to gather them up and then salted them down for later use. Beyond tobacco and coffee, the llanero had few needs not satisfied from the land.[16]

In short, llaneros were well suited to sustaining their protracted opposition to central control. They perfected sophisticated guerrilla operations, lived off the land, and used deadly irregular cavalry tactics. Ten-foot lances, used to down wild cattle, could just as easily be turned against opposing riders. Llaneros developed their own values and way of life. They pledged allegiance to no one save the *caudillo* (political strongman) who proved himself their better in terms they respected.

By the late colonial era llaneros had developed a life of subsistence and contraband trade that provided for their few necessities. For the most part the government tolerated *cuatreros*, or rustlers, probably because the activity was too extensive to police effectively. On the other hand, criminals who committed crimes against persons and real property were dealt with more harshly, if they could be caught. A decree of December 1772 ordered the death penalty for thieves (*ladrones abriegos*), but few were captured. In 1787 local officials expressed alarm at the "large number of thieves and malefactors" who had taken refuge in the hills between Araure (in today's state of Portuguesa) and San Carlos (in today's state of Cojedes).[17] But far removed from the repressive powers of the Caracas government, and often too formidable for local officials, bandits of the Llanos, like llaneros in general, made and lived by their own rules.

INDEPENDENCE WARS AND GUERRILLA BANDITRY

For skilled cavalrymen, such as the llaneros, warfare offered an attractive opportunity for employment. The plainsmen first rallied behind the fierce Spanish soldier José Tomás Boves. They did so because of their opposition to the repressive measures instituted against them by the creole patriot forces. In particular, llaneros objected to the strictures of the "Ordenanzas de los Llanos" (1811) that required them to register and limited their geographical mobility. Promises of booty and the charisma of José Antonio Paez led them to switch sides. Llaneros fought for the immediate material rewards of warfare rather than for abstract political goals. The *Gazeta de Caracas* of June 6, 1814, reported that "the booty was immense" after the first battle of Carabobo. Pillage sustained troops on both sides and became an accepted part of military conduct and a strong inducement to military service. The guerrilla-bandit was born out of the necessity for patriotic and Spanish forces to live off the land. The opportunity to profit from the disorder created by the Independence conflict blurred the distinction between brigand and soldier.[18]

Owing to their past reputation, llanero troops were blamed for most criminal incidents. Paez had no illusions about the moral character of his recruits. "In the lower Apure," he complained, "the only men to be found were execrable types; they formed bands to plunder the countryside, rob houses and commit crimes." The independence leader Simón Bolívar, in late 1813, ordered the formation of special units to combat bandits, who were taking advantage of the general disorder to rob towns, ranches, and travelers. Crime rose sharply in both city and country.[19] As in Mexico during the same period, disorder bred both illicit and licit opportunity. The rural poor would ride behind any leader who promised them the rewards of plunder.

Despite their association with theft and pillage, llaneros enjoyed some rehabilitation owing to their military prowess. Unencumbered by excess equipment, intimately acquainted with the terrain, the highly mobile llaneros harassed the Spanish expeditionary forces with lightning guerrilla raids. Paez forced the Spanish to retreat from the llanos without ever engaging him in formal battle. His irregular tactics impeded the Spanish search for supplies, especially food, and cut links between the main army and reserve units. The Spanish were reduced to feeding on their own horses and mules, which left them without mounts or pack animals for artillery and ammunition.[20]

REPUBLICAN BETRAYAL AND RENEWED BANDITRY

By the end of the Independence wars llaneros had achieved a military victory over the enemy armies, but nothing more. The hierarchical social structure remained intact, and the legislative machinery of Caracas continued to repress the llanero. Promises of compensation to llanero soldiers, made by a beleaguered Paez in the heat of battle, went unfulfilled. A law of 1823 assigned land to veterans, but the soldiers saw value only in cattle, not in real estate. Astute speculators and caudillos (including Paez) bought for a pittance the land certificates granted to ignorant soldiers. The end result was to increase the concentration of land ownership in the Llano and exacerbate rural social tensions.[21]

Warfare destroyed or dispersed most of the livestock on the llanos and created a huge class of landless, discontented veterans. The new republican elite extended its control over grazing lands, so that, by the mid–1820s, llaneros faced few legitimate prospects for economic survival. Not surprisingly, the energies of many landless, rootless ex-soldiers turned to rustling, pillage, banditry, or continued civil warfare behind regional caudillos. The conflict also retained the racial overtones of the colonial era, with mostly non-white llaneros increasingly at odds with the white elite. A description of Paez's troops held equally for llanero outlaws: "ferocious and valiant zambos, mulattos, and Blacks."[22]

New forces were added to those that had turned many llaneros to an outlaw existence during the colonial era. The *matuanos*, or criollo, ruling elite in Caracas, like the elite of Buenos Aires, constructed a legal labyrinth designed to corral the free-riding horsemen. Vagrancy and work laws proliferated during the early national period. Significantly, most labor regulations were administered through police and criminal codes—an indication of their coercive intent. Hesitant moves toward the abolition of slavery, finally completed by the mid-nineteenth century, further disrupted the labor supply and gave rise to more repressive legislation to force "free" persons to work.[23]

In the face of continued social disorder, legislation became increasingly harsh. The new leaders of Gran Colombia (which split into Colombia and Venezuela in 1831) decreed the death penalty for rustlers. The most notorious law passed was the infamous "Ley de Azotes" (Lash Law) of May 23, 1836. The law decreed death or imprisonment at hard labor for the theft of property and flogging for lesser crimes. This hated law inspired resentment and open revolt among the rural masses. Given the popular outcry, the use of flogging was repealed in 1845.[24]

Identification papers and internal passports (*libretas* and *papeletas*), like those imposed in Argentina, restricted the geographical mobility and the economic freedom of both agricultural and ranch workers. Planters, faced with even more labor shortages than ranchers, used tieing contracts, debt peonage, travel restrictions, vagrancy laws, and corrupt judges to repress workers. According to the police code of Carabobo in 1843, anyone caught gambling or without proper papers could be "condemned as a vagrant." Codes for other provinces provided similar penalties. The ordinance of 1847 for Barinas obligated ranch workers to complete any trail drive or other task begun, unless they became seriously ill.[25]

Simón Bolívar attempted to rebuild the nation's devastated livestock by restricting the export of animals. In 1819 he forbid the export of cows and vowed to "establish a severe policy against the killing of cattle." Seven years later he forbid the export of all livestock on pain of a 1,000-peso fine. The latter decree was reiterated in 1829.[26] The upshot was even more contraband trade.

High export duties, imposed by the impoverished new national government, also angered llaneros. In October of 1827 police captured a boat loaded with contraband cattle near Angostura. They recovered the cattle, but the perpetrator, José Natalio Mesa, escaped and fled to the area of Maturin (capital of today's state of Monagas). The labyrinthine Orinoco delta offered hundreds of avenues of access to the Caribbean. In general, the new, more vigorous republican efforts to eliminate this traditional, "normal" contraband were unsuccessful.[27]

But petty rustling and contraband trade did not employ all of the ex-pillagers of the Independence wars. Other forms of property theft also increased. In 1827 one audacious band attacked and plundered a village a mere five miles outside of Caracas. They bound the men, raped the women, and rode away with horses and cattle. "Los Guaiparos," a gang of about sixteen, murdered and stole from residents near Barcelona during the mid-1820s.[28]

An Indian bandit, Francisco Javier Perales, terrorized the area of Alto Apure and Casanare during the 1820s. Dionisio Cisneros worked the old province of Caracas for a full decade, beginning in 1821. Showing his caudillesque powers of persuasion, Paez talked him into retirement in 1831.[29]

Banditry, rustling, and political revolts all gave ample evidence of generalized social unrest on the republican Llano. The revolts of the plainsmen during the nineteenth century represented a continuation of resistance to oligarchic pressures on them. Many intellectuals and politicians scapegoated llaneros and their caudillo leaders as causes (rather than symptoms) of larger problems of national life. Like gauchos to the Argentine elite, llaneros were a wild fire that reddened the horizon—barbarous, destructive, and dangerously egalitarian.[30]

But the social conflict of the llanos can be interpreted in exactly the opposite manner. The prolonged struggles of llaneros were almost always defensive. The plainsmen did not seek to impose their will on anyone else. Rather, the llanero goal was to continue living according to old customs. They rallied behind regional caudillos in desperate and ultimately futile efforts to avoid encroachment and domination from the north. The frequent revolts in the llanos, climaxed by the bloody Federalist War of the 1850s, returned some llaneros to the life of rapine common during the strife of independence.

CIVILS WARS AND CRIME ON THE LLANOS

Outlaw gangs continued to operate with impunity, thanks to generalized sociopolitical disorder and the weakness of the central government. For some unscrupulous scavengers, politics became an excuse to deprive others of their property. Bandit gangs struck stores, travelers, and ranches and justified their thefts with a cry of "¡*Viva fulano de tal!*" (Long live whomever!).[31] As in Mexico, it became difficult to distinguish political rebels from common criminals.

Given the diminished number of livestock—victims of pillage and frequent epidemics—rustling became an even graver problem to ranchers. The old days of boundless herds of wild animals gave way to serious shortages of horses and cattle. In early 1844 the police chief of Pedraza, in Barinas province, requested reinforcements from the governor to combat gangs of rustlers. He had killed one gang leader, Eulogio Tapia, and arrested two "other men as perverse" as Tapia. The two confessed to a plot by a yet larger force of rustlers (*facinerosos*) to attack and burn villages in Barinas. Convinced of the imminent danger, Governor Pedro Arevalo dispatched five soldiers as reinforcements and solicited assistance from the secretary of state. Arevalo complained that his province was "highly indefensible because of its location—an immense range for malefactors."[32]

During the 1850s an area of Apure province once known as Setenta (renamed Independencia after 1821) became a center for banditry. According to one local official, the area had long been a "fortress for famous bandits, such as Moreno, Virguez, Vargas, Barsos, and another hundred." Brazen horse and cattle thieves, the gangs intimidated landowners to the point that the latter would not even visit their holdings. Dishonest merchants in the port town of Nutrias purchased the ill-gotten gains from bandits "who were used to marauding and boundless license."[33]

Such endemic banditry stemmed from two circumstances. First, most ranchers on the llanos tolerated or even colluded with rustlers. Second, the central government could seldom muster the force necessary to police effectively the vast plains. And government forces, always lacking adequate support, also had to live off the land. They sometimes became a plague more hated by residents than the bandits they pursued.

Merchants and officials, attracted by the handsome profits of contraband trade, formed part of a multiclass system of "contraband capitalism" on the llanos. Contrabandists gathered hides under cover of night at Nutrias, San Fernando, and other ports and shipped them downriver to Ciudad Bolívar, which became Venezuela's leading port for hides. Venal judges freed captured criminals in less time than it took to catch them. Late or non-payment of public salaries by the hard-pressed Caracas government increased the attractiveness of official corruption.[34]

As in other parts of Latin America, collusion between bandits and landowners also occurred on the llanos. Some ranchers brazenly hired known thieves to serve as ranch managers (*mayordomos*). Using a variety of wiles, unscrupulous employees would rustle livestock belonging to neighboring ranches. Some held premature summer roundups in order to seize the cattle of others before the usual fall rodeo. Some indebted ranchers even openly turned to banditry to retaliate against their creditors. The offices of creditors were attacked in San Fernando, Nutrias, and Guanare.[35]

Throughout the turbulent 1840s and 1850s the lines between bandit and rebel blurred. Defeated rebels often turned to banditry for maintenance. In 1858 a band of 200 stole horses in the name of political revolt and fled to the vastness of the plains. A loose federation of gangs known as "Los Indios Guaranitas" plundered villages in Barinas, Portuguesa, and Apure. Martín Espinosa's terrible band also pillaged Barinas. Banditry as a way of life became firmly established in the Llano.[36]

TRIUMPH OF THE CARACAS ELITE OVER THE PLAINS

For the remainder of the nineteenth century the llanos remained outside effective central control. Numerous bandit gangs preyed on travelers and townspeople in the llanos. During the 1870s highwaymen called "los Encarbonados" ("The Carbonized"), because they blackened their faces in disguise, operated from San Juan de los Morros south to Ortiz and Calabozo. Travelers journeyed in armed convoys for self-protection. Juan "Ovejón" Rodríguez robbed towns and ranches and, like "Guardajumo" before him, gained a mystical reputation. He repeatedly escaped from jail, used different names, and became an outlaw of mystery and renown. Captured in Cura in 1876, he was shot in cold blood by a guard who feared he would escape again.[37]

But the massive destruction of livestock herds during the Federalist War of the 1850s, coupled with the coffee boom of the north-central provinces, left the plains economically marginalized. After mid-century, livestock exports only accounted for a tiny fraction of total national exports.[38]

The centralizing efforts of Antonio Guzmán Blanco, in the 1870s and 1880s, aided by new elements of technology, also began circumscribing the life of the llanero and enforcing the law against remaining bandits. More modern firearms and telegraph service tipped the balance of force toward the government in Caracas. Guzmán Blanco attempted to impose peace and modernization on Venezuela, like his contemporary Porfirio Díaz was doing in Mexico. But the Venezuelan president was only partially successful.[39]

The modernizing dictatorship of Juan Vicente Gómez delivered the coup de grace to llaneros—bandits or otherwise—during the 1920s. Gómez organized the first well-equipped, motorized army. Growing oil revenues from Venezuela's rich Maracaibo Basin provided sufficient means to corrupt local officials and bring them into the national sphere of influence. His political tactics and centralizing vigor were reminiscent of the means used by Díaz in Mexico to subdue outlaws and subjugate local caudillos there. Shifting world and internal markets left the llanero with few means of livelihood—legitimate or otherwise. Migration drained the Llano of population as other oil-producing and urbanizing regions became more attractive.[40]

Gómez also established a livestock monopoly that excluded even other large ranchers. Thanks to his venality and mania for land, by 1920, 85 percent of Venezuela's cultivable land was held by 8 percent of the population. By the end of his rule, some fifteen years later, Gómez and his family controlled most of the usable land from San Fernando de Apure deep in the llanos to Caracas.[41] Caracas had finally triumphed over the plains. Centuries of effort to subjugate the llanero came to a successful close.

Despite the clear sociopolitical content of llanero crime, the llanero did not represent a social bandit type. Hobsbawm's social bandit operated with the aid and support of the peasantry. Like gauchos, llaneros evolved as a distinct social group that lived in frontier areas often beyond the reach of elite power. Llanero conflicts with central authorities might well be called international rather than civil wars because of the very different nature of the protagonists—virtually two different peoples, two different nations.

Llaneros represented a distinct society formed by outcast blacks, mestizos, mulattos, and a few whites over an aboriginal base. They functioned outside the dominant Venezuelan culture as a frontier society in constant flux, according to the growth or contraction of areas under oligarchic control. The frontier dividing the two was a social and geographical membrane penetrated by both sides in both directions.

Social conflict—the struggle of rural "barbarism" to avoid the imposition of urban "civilization"—clearly represented part of the fabric of llanos criminality. A few bandits, like "Guardajumo" and "Ovejón," achieved a magical reputation. Others, such as Zarate, a fictional character developed by Eduardo Blanco in an 1882 novel, achieved some literary fame. But it was the caudillos of the llanos, from Paez through latter-day rebels, such as Emilio Arevalo Cedeño, not bandits, who captured the imagination of the rural masses. True, the distinction between rebel and outlaw was not always apparent. Rural social conflict permeated the llanos from the first excursions of the Spanish in the sixteenth century through the early twentieth century. But, like on the Argentine pampa, the criminal types that emerged on the tropical plains of Venezuela provide little support for Hobsbawm's social bandit model.[42]

NOTES

1. Miguel Izard, "Tanto pelear para terminar conversando: El caudillismo en Venezuela," *Nova Americana*, 2 (1979): 41–43; John Lynch, "Bolívar and the Caudillos," *Hispanic American Historical Review*, 63, 1 (Feb. 1983): 5. For additional sources on the llanos, see Richard W. Slatta and Arturo Alvarez D'Armas, "El llanero y el hato venezolano," *South Eastern Latin Americanist*, 29, 2–3 (Sept. 1985): 33–41; Jane M. Rausch, *A Tropical Plains Frontier: The Llanos of Colombia, 1531–1831* (Albuquerque: University of New Mexico Press, 1984), pp. 294–304.

2. Miguel Izard, "Ni cuatreros ni montoneros, llaneros," *Boletín Americanista*, 31 (1981): 88–89.

3. Fray Baltasar de Lodares, *Los franciscanos capuchinos en Venezuela: Documentos referentes a las emisiones franciscanas en esta república*, 2 vols. (Caracas: Empresa Gutemberg, 1929–1931), 2: 70–76.

4. Carlos Siso, *La formación del pueblo venezolano: Estudios sociológicos*, 2 vols. (Madrid: García Enciso, 1953), 2: 284–285.

5. Ibid., pp. 168–169.

6. Ibid., pp. 290–304.

7. John V. Lombardi, *Venezuela: The Search for Order, the Dream of Progress* (New York: Oxford University Press, 1982), pp. 161, 170, 221, 259; Rausch, *Tropical Plains Frontier*, pp. 55–82.

8. Robert Gilmore, *Caudillism and Militarism in Venezuela, 1810–1910* (Athens: Ohio State University Press, 1964), p. 68; Lynch, "Bolívar," p. 5; see llanos laws and ordinances reprinted in Izard, "Ni cuatreros," pp. 53–83.

9. Miguel Izard, "Sin domicilio fijo, senda segura, ni destino conocido: Los llaneros de Apure a finales del periodo colonial," *Boletín Americanista*, 33 (1983): 19; Izard, *El miedo de la revolución: La lucha por la libertad en Venezuela, 1777–1830* (Madrid: Tecnos, 1979), p. 203.

10. "Diversos," 2: 102, Archivo General de la Nación, Caracas (hereinafter AGN).

11. Angel de Altolaguirre y Duvale, ed., *Relaciones geográficas de la Governación de Venezuela, 1767–68* (Caracas: Presidencia de la República, 1908, 1954), pp. 213–214; Izard, *El miedo*, p. 103.

12. Francisco Depons, *Viaje a la parte oriental de Terra Firme*, Paris, 1806, trans. Enrique Planchart (Caracas: Tip. Americana, 1930), pp. 317, 325–331; Robert P. Matthews, "Rural Violence and Social Unrest in Venezuela, 1840–1858: Origins of the Federalist War," (Ph.D. diss., New York University, 1974), pp. 90–91.

13. Izard, *El miedo*, pp. 85, 132. For further comparisons of gauchos and llaneros, see Richard W. Slatta, "Gauchos, llaneros y cowboys: Un aporte a la historia comparada," *Boletín Americanista*, 34 (1984): 193–208.

14. Izard, "Sin domicilio fijo," pp. 31–32.

15. Manuel Landaeta Rosales, *Gran recopilación geográfica, estadística e histórica de Venezuela*, 2 vols., 1889 (Caracas: Banco Central de Venezuela, 1963), 2: 235; Juan Uslar-Pietri, *Historia política de Venezuela*, 3rd ed. (Madrid and Caracas: Editorial Mediterraneo, 1980), pp. 18–19.

16. Izard, "Ni cuatreros," pp. 87–88.

17. Letter from Joseph Manuel Oropesa, 13 December 1772, "Correspondencia," 12: 302, Gobernación y Capitanía General, AGN; Izard, "Sin domicilio fijo," p. 35.

18. Lombardi, *Venezuela*, p. 132; Lynch, "Bolívar," pp. 6, 13; Germán Carrera Damas, *Boves: Aspectos socioeconómicas de la guerra de independencia*, 3rd ed. (Caracas: Universidad Central de Venezuela, 1964, 1972), pp. 32, 67, 69, 72, 74, 80; Rausch, *Tropical Plains Frontier*, p. 209.

19. Paez quoted in Rausch, *Tropical Plains Frontier*, p. 176; Carrera Damas, *Boves*, pp. 101, 164; Lombardi, *Venezuela*, p. 165.

20. Izard, "Ni cuatreros," pp. 121–122.

21. Uslar-Pietri, *Historia política*, pp. 101–102; Laureano Vallenilla Lanz, *Cesarismo democratico*, 3rd ed. (Caracas: Garrido, 1919, 1952), pp. 105–107; Lynch, "Bolívar," pp. 24–26; Rausch, *Tropical Plains Frontier*, p. 211.

22. Carrera Damas, *Boves*, p. 160; Vallenilla Lanz, *Cesarismo*, pp. 105–107; quotation from José Domingo Díaz, cited in Lynch, "Bolívar," p. 18; Matthews, "Rural Violence," pp. 94, 126; Rausch, *Tropical Plains Frontier*, pp. 195, 209.

23. Letter from Governor of Barinas, 4 March 1850, Interior y Justicia, 326: 55, 375–376, AGN; Fernando I. Parra Aranguren, *Antecedentes del derecho del trabajo en Venezuela, 1830–1928* (Maracaibo: Universidad de Zulia, 1965), pp. 56, 59; see police regulations and provincial ordinances in Facultad de Humanidades y Educación, Universidad Central de Venezuela, *Materiales para el estudio de la cuestión agraria en Venezuela, 1810–1865: Mano de obra, legislación y administración* (Caracas: Universidad Central de Venezuela, 1979), 1: 150–151, 201–202.

24. Matthews, "Rural Violence," pp. 132–133; Rausch, *Tropical Plains Frontier*, pp. 210, 212.

25. Facultad de Humanidades, UCV, *Materiales*, 1: 275–277, 379–381; Matthews, "Rural Violence," pp. 55–65, 73–74.

26. Facultad de Humanidades, UCV, *Materiales*, pp. 227, 486–487, 530.

27. Letter of 3 October 1827, Interior y Justicia, 2: 143–147, AGN; Rausch, *Tropical Plains Frontier*, p. 212.

28. Robert Ker Porter, *Sir Robert Ker Porter's Caracas Diary, 1825–1842: A British Diplomat in a Newborn Nation*, ed. Walter Dupuoy (Caracas: Walter Dupuoy, 1966), pp. 288–289; Landaeta Rosales, *Gran recopilación*, 2: 235.

29. Landaeta Rosales, *Gran recopilición*, 2: 235.

30. Izard, "Ni cuatreros," pp. 124–127.

31. Eleazar Cordova-Bello, *Aspectos históricos de la ganadería en el Oriente venezolano y Guayana* (Caracas: Ediciones Historia, 1952), pp. 39–40; Izard, *El miedo*, p. 52.

32. Letter from Police Chief Pablo Gonzales, 30 January 1844; letter from Governor Pedro Arevalo, 1 February 1844, Interior y Justicia, 294: 332–334, AGN.

33. Letter from Juan G. Illas, 15 February 1858, Interior y Justicia, 615: 103, 347–351.

34. Robert P. Matthews, "La turbulenta decada de los Monagas, 1847–1858," in *Política y economía en Venezuela* (Caracas: Fundación Boulton, 1976), p. 111.

35. Cordova-Bello, *Aspectos históricos*, pp. 41–42; Matthews, "Rural Violence," p. 279.

36. Matthews, "Rural Violence," pp. 138, 162, 276–279.

37. Landaeta Rosales, *Gran recopilación*, 2: 236.

38. See livestock export figures in Miguel Izard, ed., *Series estadísticas para la historia de Venezuela* (Merida: Universidad de Los Andes, 1970), pp. 184–185, 195–196; see also Izard, "Oligarcas temblad; viva la libertad: Los llanos del Apure y la Guerra Federal," *Boletín Americanista*, 32 (1982): 227–277.

39. Izard, *El miedo*, pp. 73–74; see also Mary B. Floyd, "Antonio Guzmán Blanco: The Evolution of Septenio Politics" (Ph.D. diss., University of Indiana, 1981).

40. Izard, *El miedo*, pp. 76–77.

41. William M. Sullivan, "Situación económica y política durante el periodo de Juan Vicente Gómez, 1908–1935," in *Política y economía* (Caracas: Fundación Boulton, 1976), pp. 265–266.

42. Izard, *El miedo*, p. 52; Èmilio Arevalo Cedeño, *Viva Arevalo Cedeño: El libro de mis luchas (autobiografía del General Emilio Arevalo Cedeño)* (Caracas: Seleven, 1936, 1979). The rebel leader claims that Gómez' livestock monopoly forced him into rebellion.

4

Images of Social Banditry on the Argentine Pampa

RICHARD W. SLATTA

Gauchos of the pampa shared some of the characteristics and experiences of the social bandits conceptualized by Hobsbawm. The two groups shared common motivations and life events that pushed them to a bandit existence: unjust treatment and persecution by corrupt or unscrupulous officials. They were single, uneducated males from the same social sector, the rural lower class. They were backward-looking and pre-political, not revolutionary precursors pointing the way to future sociopolitical change. And like Hobsbawm's bandits, the gaucho evoked an aura of nostalgia for lost virtue, justice, and freedom that gave rise to numerous mythical incarnations popular in literature and folklore. The gaucho, like the social bandit, lived according to long-established traditions and values at variance with state-imposed law that generally furthered the interests of the wealthy and landed.[1]

But gauchos also differed from the Hobsbawm model in significant ways. Unlike the "noble robber" or Robin Hood type, the gaucho outlaw did not always enjoy a reputation of invulnerability from police detection. One famous gaucho bandit, Juan Moreira, was renowned for his ferocity and ability to escape capture, but most of the bandits of the pampa lived on the run as fearful fugitives. Unlike Hobsbawm's bandits, who enjoyed a protective cocoon provided by peasant society, the gaucho outlaw usually fled to the sparsely populated frontier to face depredations by Indian raiders as well as the hot pursuit of police and soldiers. The gaucho bandit, like the noble robber, usually lived and worked alone, but the former did not have the reputation of giving to the poor what he stole from the rich. Whereas the noble robber killed only in self-defense or for justifiable revenge, the *matrero*, or gaucho killer, engaged in often fatal knife duels for sport and seemingly with little concern for human life.[2]

Overall, the reality and image of the gaucho outlaw placed him in an inter-

5. Map of South America
   From: *Maps On File*, © 1985 by Martin Greenwald Associates.
   Reprinted by permission of Facts On File, Inc., New York.

mediate position between the social and the anti-social bandit or common criminal. The experiences of gauchos, more social outcasts or marginals than social
bandits as defined by Hobsbawm, provide only partial support for his model.
The significant overlap lies in the social roots of forced criminality and margin-
ality, not in the precise portrait of the outlaw figures that emerged. The social
context of banditry—governmental repression and sharp social and cultural conflict—is far more striking a phenomenon than the characteristics of the bandit
population per se.

GAUCHOS AS BANDITS

The perception of gauchos as bandits extends well back into the history of
the Río de la Plata region to the very origins of the horsemen as a distinctive
social group. The staunchly independent riders, who slaughtered wild cattle and
horses (often illegally) for their hides, carried various names at different times,
but official opinion concerning them remained resolutely opprobrious. As ferocious cavalrymen fighting the Spanish in the cause of independence, gauchos
enjoyed a rise to somewhat greater, if limited, social acceptance in the early
nineteenth century. The image of gauchos as social bandits, rather than common
criminals, does not appear until the latter third of the nineteenth century and
then in formulations at variance with the Hobsbawm model.[3]

Although the term gaucho did not appear in print or documents until about
the mid-eighteenth century, several near synonyms were current that referred to
the wild cattle hunters who became identified as gauchos. Two Spanish scientists
exploring the Chilean coast first used the term gaucho in 1740 to mean country
people in general, a usage that became widespread by the mid-nineteenth century.
Juan Francisco Aguirre in 1783 observed that "gauchos or gauderios . . . are
people who . . . have, among other skills, that of slaughtering cattle for their
hides." He distinguished lawful ranch workers from *changadores*, who "are
gauderios who kill cattle without any government permit to do so."[4]

But government officials of the colonial era usually ignored such a distinction
and failed to identify good and bad gauchos—all were considered thieves. In
1790, Pedro de Lerena remonstrated against "vagabonds, otherwise known as
gauchos, who live by stealing cattle from the estancias and selling the hides at
less than their real value to the *pulperos*," owners of combination general stores
and taverns that dotted the pampa. Most officials condemned virtually all horsemen of the region as idlers, loafers, vagrants, and rustlers. Given the widespread
and endemic nature of contraband trade in the region, however, gauchos as a
social class were probably no more criminal than the merchants of Buenos Aires
and Montevideo or the corrupt Spanish officials who colluded in the illicit trade.[5]

Gauchos did not share the official vision of themselves as bandits. They held
a distinctive folk perspective on the nature of property—a vision rooted in the
venerable traditions and practices of the Río de la Plata. Juan de Garay, who
founded several Argentine cities and spread herds of cattle and horses along the

littoral, provided an initial underpinning for a communal definition of livestock wealth. In 1582, when he refounded the city of Buenos Aires, he declared all feral or wild horses to be community property and thus equally available to all residents. This belief in the communal ownership of livestock also extended to the *gando cimarrón*, or wild cattle, and the rich grasslands of the pampa. Ranching, cattle hunting, and land tenure policies were strongly influenced by these early communitarian values, and gauchos clung stubbornly to them.[6]

When colonial officials attempted to limit the traditional, communal rights of gauchos to avail themselves of the fruits of the pampa, they ran counter to well-entrenched cultural precedents that gauchos considered binding and valid. To the gaucho, the monopolistic royal official, attempting to change rules that had long governed the dispensation of natural wealth in the region, stood in violation of established rights and folk values. The new strictures had no validity to gauchos, but the determination of royal officials to limit access to wild livestock to the holders of licensed monopolies (*acciónes*) set them on a collision course with the gaucho population. In this sense, gauchos represented a backward-looking, traditionalist folk culture, like that of Hobsbawm's bandits. From the mid-eighteenth century through the 1860s colonial and national administrations persisted in attempts to circumscribe the geographical and economic freedom of the gaucho and impress him into the army and frontier militia to defend the interests of the landed elite.[7]

Provincial and national authorities in Argentina viewed gauchos as a dangerous, potentially revolutionary class. The progressive expansion and toughening of statutes restricting the rural population showed the government's growing determination to tame the wild gauchos of the pampa. Early restrictions, developed during the 1820s under Unitario governments, imposed relatively mild penalties for the common gaucho "crimes" of traveling without a passport, of lacking a work contract, or of failing to register with the military. In the following decades, under the dictatorship of Juan Manuel de Rosas, penalties and official zeal for enforcement increased. Rosas expanded the repressive legislation from its original intent of labor control to the broader motive of criminal and social control. Rosas, as well as the liberal elites after him, desired to contain the political-military potential of the gaucho and settle him into military service or sedentary ranch work. This process of legal circumscription came to a climax with the rural code of Buenos Aires province formulated in 1865. Other provinces quickly followed suit, and draconian vagrancy laws, passport requirements, and forced military service brought the long process of gaucho repression to a successful close.[8]

The extensive restrictions clearly indicate the gaucho's status in the official eye as a social and political threat. The intermittent rise of federalist caudillos of the interior provinces, who led frightening bands of *montoneros* (irregular cavalrymen) against the forces of centralism in Buenos Aires, realized the fears of many politicians. Mobilized and properly led, the gaucho masses could threaten the political power and economic interests of the landed elite of Buenos

Aires. Small wonder that the bulk of criminal legislation passed during the nineteenth century focused on rural social control.[9]

The continuities of criminal law, class, and power contrast sharply with the pervasive social and economic changes visited on the pampa during the latter half of the nineteenth century. Livestock production diversified to encompass sheep raising and modernized with fencing, refined pasturage, and improved breeds of imported animals. Ranchers employed immigrant tenant farmers to plant alfalfa for grazing in rotation with cash export crops such as wheat, corn, and flax. Like the landless gaucho, the immigrant farmer and farm worker seldom gained land ownership or appreciably improved their lot in life.[10]

The advent of modern ranching and the arrival of millions of Europeans in the littoral, combined with the continuing legal oppression, further marginalized gauchos in Argentine society. The sweeping changes even altered material culture and recreation on the pampa. Ostrich hunting, for example, had long been a form of entertainment and an important economic activity for the gaucho. Ostrich plumes found a ready market in European fashion circles. Barbed wire fencing and the assertion of property rights by *terratenientes* (large landowners) closed off this vestige of the gaucho's traditional lifestyle and livelihood. New clothing imported from Europe reflected ideological as well as socioeconomic change. In the eyes of the modern rancher and liberal politician, traditional gaucho dress represented the frontier "barbarism" of the past when plainsmen could subsist independently. By reducing economic options and eliminating old dress and activities, the elite successfully reduced the gaucho's status from self-sufficiency to dependent peonage.[11]

THE SOCIAL BANDIT IN POETRY: MARTÍN FIERRO

As the frontier and the gaucho vanished, literary and symbolic evocations of a romanticized past arose. Some commentators, drawing inspiration from Domingo F. Sarmiento's dichotomy of rural barbarism pitted against urban civilization, judged the demise of the gaucho to be desirable and necessary to the nation's progress. Others, echoing the social protest voiced on behalf of the gaucho by José Hernández, lamented his extinction. During this twilight era of the gaucho in the 1870s, images of the social bandit emerged from the writing of Hernández and other critics of the government's harsh treatment of the disappearing horsemen.[12]

Among the bandit images created by writers of *gauchesco* literature, none achieved greater cultural accolade and historical veracity than *Martín Fierro* by Hernández. The author brought to the poetic work not only consummate literary skills, but also a personal history of militant activism and intense opposition to the political forces that pushed the gaucho into an outlaw existence. In 1870 Hernández took up arms to fight against the political centralism of Bartolomé Mitre. The poet had firsthand knowledge of ranch life because he spent his youth on an estancia in Buenos Aires province. This experience served him well in

LA VUELTA

DE

MARTIN FIERRO

POR

JOSÉ HERNANDEZ

PRIMERA EDICION, ADORNADA CON DIEZ LAMINAS

SE VENDE EN TODAS LAS LIBRERIAS DE BUENOS AIRES

Depósito central: LIBRERIA DEL PLATA, Calle Tacuari, 17

1879

6. Cover of *The Return of Martín Fierro* by José Hernández, 1879

his evocation of the rhythms, values, and speech of gauchos. The poet also used stinging prose to trumpet federalist political values in the pages of his newspaper, *El Río de la Plata*, and in publications such as a biography of "El Chacho" (Angel Vicente Peñalosa, a caudillo of La Rioja Province). Better than anyone else writing about the gaucho, Hernández understood and expressed the social roots of the horseman's persecuted, outlaw existence.[13]

Hernández provided a valuable insight into the nature of pampean social relations by standing the civilization/barbarism dichotomy popularized by Sarmiento on its head. In *Facundo*, first published in Chile in 1845, Sarmiento charged that localistic, barbaric caudillos, such as Rosas and Facundo Quiroga, and the gaucho masses that supported them, impeded national progress. Hernández recognized the interplay between the city and the countryside and depicted the gaucho as a victim of oppression and injustices emanating from Buenos Aires. As he wrote in *El Río de la Plata* of August 19, 1869, "what more monstrous contradiction than that which converts the citizen of the countryside into the guardian of the interests of the capital more than his own?"

His epic gauchesco poem, however, not his prose or political service (he became a provincial legislator), brought the greatest diffusion of Hernández' thought. The characters of Martín Fierro, his sons, his friend Cruz, and Cruz's sons evoke the hardships and penuries visited on the gaucho because of unjust governmental persecution. Although Hernández evinced a change in political philosophy between the first part of the epic, published in 1872, and *The Return of Martín Fierro*, issued seven years later, images of the gaucho as a social bandit figure persist.

Like Hobsbawm's noble robber, Fierro's woes begin with his unjust treatment at the hands of legal authorities. Fierro opens his sad autobiography with the recognition of his status as a social outcast. He describes himself as a gaucho "in whose veins the blood of the Pampas runs, who married a wife and begat his sons, yet who nevertheless is held by some as a bandit grim and gory."[14] Impressed into military service on the distant, dangerous Indian frontier at the whim of a local commandant, Fierro explains the plight of the gaucho before legal authorities: "But now alas, he grows sour and grim, for the law and the police they harry him, and either the Army would rope him in, or the Sheriff have his hide . . . From the law's grim trap, not the Saints of heaven have ever saved a man."[15] In the classic sequence of the birth of a social bandit, Fierro is unjustly treated by an official, loses his family and scant personal possessions, and ends up a renegade and fugitive.

Hernández probed the condition of the gaucho beyond the surface exploitation by unscrupulous civil and military officials. He critiqued the Argentine national leadership for failing to educate and otherwise provide for the needs of the gaucho. Fierro apologizes to his listeners because "the only schooling I ever had, was a life of suffering: Don't be surprised if at the game, I've made mistakes;—that's not my shame—It's mighty little a man can know, if he's never learnt anything."[16] In the second part of the epic Hernández asserted that the government must provide the gaucho with "his rights as a citizen—a church, a school, and a home."[17]

Beyond criticizing governmental failure to aid the gaucho in adapting to the modernizing pampa, Hernández censured the gross inequities present in the Argentine legal system. The wealthy enjoyed immunity from prosecution while the poor, including the gaucho, suffered the brunt of legal oppression. "For the slightest slip that the gaucho makes, to the wilderness he's driven, to make his home with the ostriches, while others with more advantages, no matter what crimes they are guilty of, they'll always be forgiven."[18]

Hernández reemphasized the nexus between poverty and legal persecution at other points in the poem as well. "When the law bucks a gaucho over its ears, he doesn't fall on a daisy; unless he's got money the law is grim, there isn't a man will speak up for him."[19] "When the law gets down on a man that's poor, it's little they heed his pleadings."[20] In this criticism Hernández accurately reflected the gaucho's belief that he had been singled out for an extra measure of repression by Argentine authorities.

Regardless of political label or ideology, nineteenth-century politicians ably maintained the interests of the landed elite and labored strenuously to limit the options and movements of rural society's "dangerous classes"—the gauchos. Even when different social classes cooperated in illegal activities, such as the theft of cattle hides or wool that gauchos stole and pulperos fenced, the powerless of society were punished and the more influential often escaped and continued their illicit ventures with impunity.[21]

Although fictional, the characters created by Hernández accurately mirrored the sociopolitical realities of nineteenth-century pampean life. And his creations resonated deeply with the sentiments of the rural masses. The poem went through numerous printings and editions, both sanctioned and unsanctioned by the author. The first part of *Martín Fierro* ran through fifteen official editions, totalling some 60,000 copies, before the second part was published in 1879. The census of Argentina taken in 1869 gives a population of 495,107 for the city and province of Buenos Aires, the areas of greatest diffusion for the work. This meant that approximately one copy of the epic circulated for every eight men, women, and children in the province—a forceful indicator of the great popularity of the poem.[22] Hernández struck a sensitive chord not only among the literate, but also among the illiterate rural masses who gathered for readings of the poem at country pulperías that dotted the pampas. Fierro and Cruz, outcast rebels against constituted authority, became heroes to pampean society at the very time when oppression and modernization overwhelmed and doomed the gaucho.

THE SOCIAL BANDIT IN PROSE: JUAN MOREIRA

Other writers, who favored prose rather than poetic expression, vented social criticism similar to that found in *Martín Fierro*. Surprisingly, the gaucho figured only incidentally in Argentine fictional prose until Santiago Estrada published his picturesque depictions of rural life near Luján in *El hogar en la pampa* (1866). *Aventuras de un centauro de la América meridional* by José Joaquín de Vedia appeared two years later. Vedia presented the gaucho as a rebel against governmental oppression during the Unitario rule of the 1820s. He concurred with Hernández that the fugitive, non-conforming gaucho needed education to make him a productive citizen. An educated rural population would support able leaders rather than disruptive caudillos. The resulting good government would solve both the gaucho's and the nation's difficulties.[23] Vedia's work presented another variant of the pampean social bandit but never reached the mass audience claimed by the Hernández epic.

It remained for Eduardo Gutiérrez to exploit fully the potential of the gaucho novel as a genre and create the most famous image of the pampean social bandit after Martín Fierro. *Juan Moreira*, appearing as a serialized novel in 1879–1880 and later adapted to the stage, marks the beginning of a cycle of prose and dramatic depictions of the last oppressed days of the disappearing gaucho. Many of the social criticisms voiced by Hernández reappear in *Juan Moreira*: a lascivious, vengeful justice of the peace, a grasping, greedy foreign merchant, a *desgracia* (death of an opponent in a knife duel), and nomadic wanderings of a social bandit banished to the harsh frontier. Like Fierro and Cruz, Moreira is presented as a victim of circumstances and social injustices who would have been honorable and hardworking had society permitted it.[24]

Gutiérrez based his protagonist on the life of a real person named Juan Moreira. Little is known about the man's early life except that he was born about 1836 or 1838. Like others who walked the thin line between respectability and crime, he attached himself to a powerful political patron. By the late 1860s Moreira was serving as an enforcer and bodyguard for Adolfo Alsina of the Partido Autonomista Nacional. During the election of 1872 he killed the opposition strongman named Leguizamón at a polling place in the town of Navarro, Buenos Aires province. Some voters purportedly cast ballots for the Autonomist party because Moreira had shown the superiority of his cause in manly, gaucho fashion. The Latin American "cult of courage" shaped behavior in many areas, including the political arena, and a skillful knife fighter could be a valuable asset to a political movement. Moreira remained active with the Autonomist party through the presidential election held two years later.[25]

Violent, political activism, however, did not represent Moreira's sole source of notoriety. A police circular described him in unflattering terms in early 1874: "vagrant and ne'er-do-well," white male with pockmarked face, greenish eyes, thick nose, thin mustache, large mouth with gunshot wound in the lower lip, average to tall height, stocky, can neither play guitar nor sing.[26] In spite of his political connections (or perhaps partially because of them), Moreira was a wanted man.

A combined military and police force under the command of Captain Francisco Bosch located Moreira in April 1874, when he was hiding in the pampean village of Lobos, located southwest of Buenos Aires near the Río Salado. They first captured another outlaw in town named Julián Andrade, thinking that they had Moreira. After learning the truth the force converged on a house in which Moreira was reportedly hiding. As police and soldiers surrounded the building, the outlaw quickly flung open the door, stepped outside, and fired a blunderbuss from each hand. "I shit on the police of Buenos Aires," he yelled and then ducked quickly back into the house. A second time he boldly opened the door and fired, this time killing one and wounding another of the besieging party. A third time Moreira jerked open the door. He unexpectedly charged out into the patio and killed a second man as the panic-stricken soldiers fled in terror. As he was about to mount a horse and make good his escape, one soldier overcame his fright and leaped forward with rifle and bayonet poised. Sources disagree, but either Corporal Luis Lima or Sergeant Andrés Chirino stabbed Moreira through the back with a bayonet. According to one police report, he was then shot to death after he fell to the ground.[27] Moreira, bandit, vagrant, and bodyguard, was dead, but a mythical figure was to be born a short time later.

THE SOCIAL BANDIT IN THEATER

The rebirth of Moreira as a populist symbol emanated from the works of Eduardo Gutiérrez. It was a collaborative effort at drama, however, more than the novelized version, that reached the Argentine masses with the legend of Moreira the social bandit. In 1884 Gutiérrez combined his writing talents with the acting skill of José "Pepino el 88" Podestá, Argentina's leading circus clown, to produce a pantomime production of *Juan Moreira*. Podestá proved an effective dramatic actor, and the crude but evocative performance brought down the house time after time.[28]

In 1886 Gutiérrez added dialogue to the production, and the first spoken performance in the pampean town of Chivilcoy became an even greater success. The modern Argentine theater had been born in the sawdust and canvas of a humble circus ring. The play presented Moreira as a hero fighting against social injustices perpetrated by corrupt rural officials. A parallel theme, common in Argentine theater and literature, was the conflict between the gaucho and the gringo immigrant. This conflict comes to a head in the play when Moreira kills a cheating gringo pulpero named Sardetti. Although a badly conceived and poorly organized play, it was immensely popular, especially among lower-class patrons. Numerous imitative productions followed.[29]

The Gutiérrez/Podestá play depicts Moreira much like Hernández presented the fictional Martín Fierro. A once happy, innocent gaucho is beset by the nefarious forces of scheming merchants and evil officials. In both social bandit models the good gaucho is forced to a life of crime by unjust treatment. The pulpero Sardetti falsely accuses Moreira of lying about a debt that the merchant owes the gaucho (in an interesting reversal of usual debtor/creditor roles). Moreira avenges this deep insult to his honor and kills Sardetti in appropriate gaucho fashion, with his knife. The unscrupulous town mayor Don Francisco lusts after Moreira's wife. He engineers a confrontation to challenge the gaucho's honor and then has Moreira beaten by his henchmen. Finding himself betrayed by his wife, Moreira kills both the mayor and his unfaithful mate. In the dramatic version Moreira is cornered and killed in his own house.[30]

Like Fierro, Moreira bitterly criticizes the legal injustices of Argentina. In Act one, Scene two, he complains that "the law pursues me merely because it happens to wish to, and if tomorrow I should become a real criminal disgusted with this wretched existence, the law alone would be to blame. For it was the law that drove me to this road."[31] Elsewhere, Tata Vieja, a wise old gaucho, concurs: "Curse the law for treating gauchos of the Argentine so miserably!"[32] This social criticism of legal injustices, reinforced by palpable evidence from their own lives, found a receptive hearing among the rural masses of the late-nineteenth-century pampa who packed the circus tent for performances of the Moreira play.

Other gauchesco dramas also attracted mass audiences across the pampa. *The Return of Martín Fierro*, by Hernández, heralded the succession of the violent gaucho by an obedient peon. *Calandría*, a play written in 1896 by the traditionalist author Martiniano Leguizamón, also featured a good peon. The end of the old, wild outlaw gaucho made way for the modern, tractable creole peon who forswore violence and crime for a settled, responsible existence.[33] This revision and civilizing of the gaucho appeared in much traditionalist writing, but the persecuted, social bandit images also remained popular.

The porteño cultural elite scorned the gauchesco plays as they had the dialect poetry of Hernández. But some Argentines found plays such as *Juan Moreira* more than lowbrow and distasteful; they found them politically dangerous. Writing in the *Revista de policía* in mid-1900, a Pergamino policeman, Aquileo González Oliver, decried criollo dramas like *Juan Moreira*. He criticized the plays for denigrating the police and the criminal justice system and lionizing gaucho outlaws and murderers. González claimed that crime rates rose sharply after such plays were presented and urged censorship of the inflammatory writings. Beyond the danger of increased criminal activity, he warned that the "immoral, obscene" works might incite the masses to open rebellion against authority. To the policeman, the social bandit imagery invited regression to the barbaric customs of the past.[34]

Other evidence does not support the charges of social and political danger seen by González in the creole dramas, but he did recognize the potentially subversive nature of the glorification and sympathetic presentation of outlaws. Like bandit legends that developed in other cultures, the romanticized version of Moreira's life and death resonated strongly with the rural masses of the Argentine pampa. Whether they lived in the countryside or in one of the many villages and towns of the pampa, many had experienced or witnessed corruption, arbitrariness, abuse, and exploitation by public officials. The criticisms and complaints of official malfeasance made by writers manipulating the social bandit image also appear in contemporary newspaper accounts in Buenos Aires province.[35]

SANTOS VEGA

The third major figure of social banditry in gauchesco literature is that of Santos Vega, who, like Moreira, enjoyed several incarnations in various media. The distinguished poet of gauchesco themes, Hilario Ascasubi, introduced the character in his work of 1872, "Santos Vego or los mellizos de 'la flor.' " The poem developed a romanticized portrait of pampean life narrated by a skillful *payador*, or gaucho folksinger, named Santos Vega. The narrative traces the lives and fortunes of twin brothers: Jacinto, a good gaucho, and Luis, born under an evil sign. The latter early earned the nickname of "Tiger" and grew into a murderous outlaw. Like Martín Fierro, however, Luis renounces his past errancies and dies repentant in his old age.[36] In this initial appearance Vega narrates events rather than serving as a protagonist in his own right.

The prolific Eduardo Gutiérrez picked up the Vega theme for one of his thirty-one novels and published his *Santos Vega* in 1881. But it remained for the talented poet Rafael Obligado to raise Vega to the popular formulation of an oppressed gaucho that gained great favor with a mass audience. In his poetic rendering, published in 1887, Obligado depicts the gaucho as the beleaguered victim of the juggernaut of modernization and civilization. Encroaching science, technology, material progress, and European immigration are strangling the gaucho's traditional way of life on the pampa. These forces, symbolized by a mysterious payador named Juan Sin Ropa, defeat the gaucho. The stranger engages Vega in a singing duel, and the vanquished gaucho dies. Structurally, the poem consists of four parts that trace the rise and fall of the gaucho as he is pushed aside by "progress" in the late nineteenth century.[37] Although the gaucho of Obligado is not a true social bandit figure, he is ostracized and marginalized by the same forces that create social banditry.

The transition to the social bandit motif came in yet a third genre, the creole drama. A young Spaniard named Luis Bayón Herrera wrote a script for a dramatic production of *Santos Vega* that opened in Buenos Aires in June 1913. Like Fierro and Moreira before him, Vega bitterly complains of the legal injustices that have beset him. "And I fight the police because they come to take men before a thief they call a judge who tried to make slaves of free men and tents of their hides."[38] Thus the motif of the unjustly persecuted gaucho, forced to a life of crime by the repressive, inequitable policies of the state, persists in the gauchesco genre from the mid-nineteenth century through the twentieth.

The name and imagery of Santos Vega gained currency well beyond the drama authored by Bayón Herrera. Six months after the play opened in Buenos Aires, a traditionalist newspaper bearing the title *Santos Vega* was published. Other plays and poems drawing on the Vega motif also appeared. The story of the social bandit reached yet another medium in 1917, when Carlos de Paoli wrote a screenplay for a film version of the myth.[39] The gaucho bandit thus became transmitted by Argentina's young film industry to an even larger mass audience.

BANDIT MYTH AND REALITY

By the late nineteenth and early twentieth centuries the images of social banditry personified by Fierro, Moreira, and Vega had become well established among the Argentine masses. The transformation of the images from prose and poetry to drama and film, open to an illiterate public, maximized their diffusion and influence. The images, created by literary figures but drawing heavily on folk themes and values, touched the urban and rural masses. However, despite the fears of some police officials that social criticism and glorification of banditry would debase public morals and order, there is no evidence that social protest or crime increased as a result. In this sense the social bandit myths represented pre-political and traditionalist rather than political or revolutionary forces in Argentine society.

The only documented case in Buenos Aires province of gaucho masses banding together in an avenging act of violence was the massacre of about seventeen foreigners in the town of Tandil in 1872. Gauchos, inspired by representatives of a religious *curandero* (a folk healer) named Tata Dios, struck down the immigrants with xenophobic fury. But the isolated incident stemmed from millenarianism, not social banditry, although it was widely decried at the time as a harbinger of class warfare on the pampa.[40]

The widespread peasant support theorized by Hobsbawm for the social bandit did not prevail on the pampa. On the other hand, deserters, draft evaders, and rustlers could sometimes gain tacit and even open support because of the chronic labor shortage that plagued *estancieros* [ranchers] at roundup and branding times. Some ranchers hired known fugitives and sheltered them from the law because they needed any and all ranch workers that they could find.[41] But the complicitous network of peasant supporters who aided and abetted social bandits in their midst did not exist on the pampa. The high geographical mobility of the gaucho, the migratory and seasonal nature of ranch work, and the lack of access to land ownership may have prevented the formation of deep, localistic, peasantlike ties.

Notorious bandits, if not social bandits, were not hard to find on the pampa. In late 1853 the justice of the peace for Fortín de Areco, Domingo Olivera, warned that a prisoner named Eutaguio Galván [sic] was too "prejudicial" for the usual sentence of military service. He suggested that this "famous criminal" be temporarily imprisoned on Martín García Island in the Río de la Plata and thereafter transported to Patagonia for hard labor in a quarry. Not only was Galván a well-known bandit, but he had also fought for the "rebel" (presumably Rosista) army. On the recommendation of Justice Olivera, the criminal was supplied with necessities and shipped off to Patagonia, where he could not endanger life in Buenos Aires province.[42]

Alfredo Ebelot, a French engineer who worked on the pampas during the mid-1870s, reported the escapades of "El Gato Moro" in Corrientes province. This "gaucho bravo," whose name was Alberto Zarate, engaged in "open warfare" with provincial authorities. Ebelot emphasized the fierce criminal's skill with a knife but gave no indication of wider sociopolitical issues that might hint at social bandit status for "El Gato Moro."[43]

In marginal, sparsely populated lands some large bandit gangs appeared during the twilight years of the gaucho. But they existed largely in social isolation, preying on remote *estancias* [ranches] and then retreating to the vastness and solitude of the unsettled pampa. The Barrientos brothers, however, came closer to the social bandit model than did most frontier gangs. In 1881 their gang of five haunted the area of Tres Arroyos—lands only recently wrested from the Indians by Julio A. Roca in his "conquest of the desert." *La Prensa* of October 29, 1881, reported that the gang had engaged police in a two-hour battle of "blunderbuss fire." The Barrientos brothers escaped, and another police patrol under command of the *comisario* [police chief] of Tres Arroyos took up pursuit. A report by the minister of government complained that the "celebrated Barrientos brothers" had successfully evaded authorities and that local estancieros and merchants sometimes sheltered the outlaws. The report urged "honorable residents" to assist police in apprehending the gang as well as other groups of ostrich hunters and outlaws.[44] While operating in a frontier region the Barrientos brothers did apparently enjoy some popular support and assistance, like the social bandits of Hobsbawm.

In the same area threatened by the Barrientos brothers, gaucho *boleadores*, or ostrich hunters, roamed in gangs of up to seventy members. They hunted the pampean rheas for their feathers but occasionally felled a steer belonging to one of the frontier estancias. Fencing, increased police patrols, and the powerful political clout of the Sociedad Rural Argentina, representing the interests of the landed elite, closed off these last gestures of frontier indifference to the law by the late 1880s.[45]

Frontier bandits, like the Barrientos brothers and the ostrich hunters, represented the last gasp of gaucho rebellion against the closing of the open range and the strictures of the modern pampa. Rebellious gauchos opposed the constraints of modern export capitalism and asserted their traditional Iberian communal rights to livestock wealth—sometimes by rustling the cattle of terratenientes. The forces of modernization doomed the gaucho in a process not unlike that described by Hobsbawm in the decline of the social bandit. Like the social bandit, the gaucho acted in accord with traditional, folk values and remained an unreconstructed individualist fully determined to retain the ways of the old pampa.[46]

Hobsbawm recognized that non-conformist horsemen, whether the Mexican *vaquero*, the Venezuelan *llanero*, or the Argentine gaucho, did not necessarily represent social banditry. "Those 'who make themselves respected' do not automatically become bandits. . . . They are the exception which proves the rule."[47]

But on the Argentine pampa, where authorities automatically categorized gauchos as criminals, the individualistic, non-revolutionary social outcasts represented the rule, not the exception. In such a society of conflict one may find characteristics of social bandits and literary images of them, but they did not ride about the pampa amid popular support as posited by Hobsbawm. Gauchos were a marginal, oppressed class, not larger-than-life social bandits.

Nevertheless, the literary formulations of the pampean social bandit should not be dismissed. They form a functional piece of the folk culture of the region and show strong links with folk values and behaviors. The "folk-inspired literature," with its images of Fierro, Cruz, Moreira, Vega, and others, accurately and colorfully depicts the social realities of the Argentine pampa, even if the social bandit as such was a historical phenomenon.[48] Perhaps the widespread oppression and marginalization of gauchos as a social group rendered the social bandit mythology less central than in other cultures. Martín Fierro, for example, bore a resemblance to the social bandit but really represented the collective experiences of all gauchos.

The successful, long-term program of Unitario, Rosista, and liberal governments to domesticate the gaucho made the entire group an outcast subculture. Liberal leaders, who considered Rosas himself to be no better than his gaucho troops, were especially hostile to the gaucho and his way of life. Gauchos shared a collective vision and an experience of oppression visited on them by authorities, so perhaps the social bandit rising above all was unnecessary. On the pampa virtually every man, at least every gaucho, was viewed as a bandit by the ruling elite and the government. This historical reality, not social banditry imagery, dominated the lives of gauchos on the nineteenth-century pampa.

NOTES

1. Eric J. Hobsbawm, *Primitive Rebels: Studies in Archaic Forms of Social Movement in the 19th and 20th Centuries* (New York and London: W. W. Norton, 1959), pp. 15, 17, 23–24; Hobsbawm, *Bandits*, rev. ed. (New York: Pantheon, 1981), pp. 42, 131–132.

2. Hobsbawm, *Primitive Rebels*, pp. 14–15, 25; Hobsbawm, *Bandits*, pp. 17, 42–43.

3. See Richard W. Slatta, *Gauchos and the Vanishing Frontier* (Lincoln: University of Nebraska Press, 1983), and Slatta, "The Gaucho in Argentina's Quest for National Identity," *Canadian Review of Studies in Nationalism*, 12, 1 (1985): 99–122.

4. Madaline Wallis Nichols, "The Historic Gaucho," *Hispanic American Historical Review*, (hereafter HAHR) 21 (Aug. 1941): 419; Slatta, *Gauchos*, pp. 8–9.

5. Quotation from Nichols, "Historic Gaucho," p. 420; Richard W. Slatta, "Pulperías and Contraband Capitalism in Nineteenth-Century Buenos Aires Province," *The Americas*, 38 (Jan. 1982): 357–358.

6. Charles Gary Lobb, "The Historical Geography of the Cattle Regions Along Brazil's Southern Frontier" (Ph.D. diss., University of California at Berkeley, 1970), p. 11.

7. Richard W. Slatta, "Rural Criminality and Social Conflict in Nineteenth-Century Buenos Aires Province," *HAHR*, 60 (Aug. 1980): 452.

8. Ibid., pp. 455–461; Benito Díaz, *Rosas, Buenos Aires y la organización nacional* (Buenos Aires: El Coloquio, 1974), pp. 209–210.

9. Slatta, *Gauchos*, pp. 13, 76.

10. James R. Scobie, *Revolution on the Pampas: A Social History of Argentine Wheat, 1860–1910* (Austin: University of Texas Press, 1964), pp. 58–61.

11. Slatta, *Gauchos*, pp. 141–160.

12. Ibid., pp. 180–188; Slatta, "The Gaucho in Argentina's Quest," pp. 100–103.

13. Slatta, *Gauchos*, pp. 186–187; Walter Owen, "Introduction" to José Hernández, *The Gaucho Martín Fierro*, trans. Walter Owen (Buenos Aires: Editorial Pampa, 1963), pp. xxi-xxii.

14. Hernández, *The Gaucho*, p. 5.

15. Ibid., pp. 13–14.

16. Ibid., p. 294.

17. Ibid., p. 302.

18. Ibid., p. 86.

19. Ibid., p. 176.

20. Ibid., p. 175.

21. Slatta, "Pulperías," pp. 360–361; Slatta, "Rural Criminality," pp. 450, 468–469.

22. Hernández, *The Gaucho*, p. xxii; Argentine Republic, Superintendente del Censo, *Primer censo de la República Argentina, 1869* (Buenos Aires: Imprenta del Porvenir, 1872), p. 35.

23. Enrique Williams Alzaga, *La pampa en la novela argentina* (Buenos Aires: Estrada, 1955), pp. 135–137; Myron I. Lichtblau, *The Argentine Novel in the Nineteenth Century* (New York: Hispanic Institute in the United States, 1959), pp. 121–122, 126.

24. Lichtblau, *Argentine Novel*, pp. 127–130; Myron I. Lichtblau, "The Gaucho Novel in Argentina," *Hispania*, 41 (Sept. 1958): 297–298; Theodore Murguía, "The Evolution of the Gaucho in Literature" (Ph.D. diss., University of Washington, 1961), pp. 240–241.

25. Guillermo McLoughlin, "Juan Moreira: De la arena a la gloria," *Todo es Historia*, 2 (July 1968): 16–17; on the political ties of the social bandit, see Hobsbawm, *Bandits*, pp. 91–92.

26. *Filiación*, 18 April 1874, Navarro, quoted in McLoughlin, "Juan Moreira," p. 17.

27. Quotation from ibid., p. 18; see also p. 19.

28. Ibid., pp. 9–12.

29. Ibid., pp. 9–15; Amelia Sánchez Garrido, "Situación del teatro gauchesco en la historia del teatro argentino," *Revista de la Universidad*, 14 (May 1961): 23–27; Murguía, "Evolution of the Gaucho," pp. 240–241.

30. Murguía, "Evolution of the Gaucho," p. 242.

31. Edward Hale Bierstadt, ed., *Three Plays of the Argentine: Juan Moreira, Santos Vega, The Witches' Mountain*, trans. Jacob S. Fassett, Jr. (New York: Duffield, 1920), p. 7.

32. Ibid., p. 3.

33. Murguía, "Evolution of the Gaucho," pp. 245–247.

34. Aquileo González Oliver, "Los dramas criollos," *Revista de policía*, 1 (July 1900): 7–9.

35. *La Tribuna* (Buenos Aires), 15 February 1855; *Standard* (Buenos Aires), 18 January 1865; *Herald* (Buenos Aires), 25 October 1876.

36. Murguía, "Evolution of the Gaucho," pp. 170, 174–175.

37. Ibid., pp. 222–224.

38. Quotation from Bierstadt, *Three Plays*, p. 54; see also pp. xxxvi-xxxvii.

39. Madaline Wallis Nichols, *The Gaucho: Cattle Hunter, Cavalryman, Ideal of Romance* (New York: Gordian Press, 1968), pp. 123, 139.

40. See Hobsbawm, *Primitive Rebels*, pp. 57–58 on millenarianism. On the Tandil massacre, Hugo Nario, *Tata Dios: Mesías de la última montonera* (Buenos Aires: Plus Ultra, 1976).

41. Slatta, "Rural Criminality," p. 462.

42. Justice of the Peace Domingo Olivera to Minister of Government Ireneo Portela, 13 December 1853; Interim Captain of the Port Ramón Rodríguez to Minister of War Manuel de Escalada, 27 December 1853, Archivo General de la Nación, X 18–9–1 (Buenos Aires).

43. Alfredo Ebelot, *La pampa: Costumbres argentinas* (Buenos Aires: Ciordia and Rodríguez, 1961), pp. 37–48

44. Ricardo Rodríguez Molas, *Historia social del gaucho* (Buenos Aires: Editorial Marú, 1968), pp. 465–466.

45. Ibid., pp. 467–469.

46. Hobsbawm, *Bandits*, pp. 19, 24; Silvio R. Duncan Baretta and John Markoff, "Civilization and Barbarism," *Comparative Studies in Society and History*, 20 (Oct. 1978): 606.

47. Hobsbawm, *Bandits*, p. 36.

48. On evaluating literary and folk sources, see James A. Inciardi, Alan A. Block, and Lyle A. Hallowell, *Historical Approaches to Crime: Research Strategies and Issues* (Beverly Hills, Calif.: Sage, 1977), pp. 39–43.

5

The Oligarchical Limitations of Social Banditry in Brazil: The Case of the "Good" Thief Antônio Silvino

LINDA LEWIN

For many students of rural protest the Brazilian cangaceiro has been the "peasants' bandit," fighting on behalf of the people against an oppressive backlands establishment of landowners and merchants. Whether dramatically portrayed in the films and songs of the 1960s or ingenuously admired in the diminutive clay figurines adorning simple backlands homes, this heroic outlaw has readily assumed the character of a national metaphor of protest.[1] In her illuminating study of the phenomenon of banditry in Brazil, Maria Isaura Pereira de Queiroz expressed this symbolic value of the cangaceiro when she contrasted two conflicting views of her "bandit of honour" in the historiography: "For the foreigner and the rich," she remarked, "the cangaceiro is an outlaw who should be punished. For the true Brazilian, he is a man of justice, a liberator."[2]

More recently, in E. J. Hobsbawm's valuable studies of peasant protest, the cangaceiro has been analyzed as representing several distinct types of what that author has termed "social banditry." In Hobsbawm's work the "avenger," one type of social bandit, has been archetypically based in part on the twentieth-century career of the celebrated Brazilian cangaceiro Lampião (Virgulino Ferreira da Silva, fl. 1919–1938). The excessive and brutal cruelty of bandits like Lampião, according to Hobsbawm, gained them popular appeal as men who exerted power, demonstrating that even the poor and the weak could be terrifying.[3] As ambiguous heroes, however, such avengers were not considered "good" by the general populace, who nevertheless greatly admired them.

Hobsbawm also popularized and elaborated in greater detail a second, more common, idealized variant of the social bandit, the "noble robber" or "Robin Hood," who righted wrongs, stole from the rich to give to the poor, and killed

Reprinted from *Past & Present* 82 (February 1979): 116–46, with the permission of the editor.

LEANDRO GOMES DE BARROS

ANTÔNIO SILVINO O REI DOS CANGACEIROS

A' venda, Rua do Alecrim 38 E.

7. Woodcut of Antônio Silvino, king of the cangaceiros, from cover of chapbook by Leandro Gomes de Barros, 1896–1900

only in self-defense or for revenge.[4] Although Hobsbawm did not discuss specifically the case of Antônio Silvino (Manuel Batista de Morais, fl. 1897–1914), a number of Brazilian writers have interpreted this brigand as a classic "good" thief whose behavior closely corresponded to the archetypical noble robber developed in Hobsbawm's synthesis.[5] Finally, according to Hobsbawm, the social bandit could in certain historical contexts exemplify yet a third idealized type. By taking up arms as a primitive resistance fighter or guerrilla and cooperating in liberation movements, the social bandit might play a role as a limited, but nevertheless incipient revolutionary.[6]

Whether as an "avenger" or as a "good" thief the cangaceiro has, in the hands of his commentators, evolved from a figure originally condemned by nineteenth-century racist schools of criminal behavior for his "primitive atavism" to a stereotype who today embodies a heroic and unique national identity. In searching for their historical roots in the New World, Brazilian scholars have quite properly emphasized the significance of this colorful native popular hero.[7] The cangaceiro developed within a regional historical experience peculiar to the Brazilian Northeast. It is not surprising, however, that in the second half of the twentieth century he has been adopted as a national figure of protest against what an earlier "modernizing" generation defined as an economically backward and lawless past. Nor is it any wonder that recently he has been invoked as a symbol by the present generation to condemn the existing heritage of exploitation and inequality. Either as "primitive rebel" or as a metaphor of protest, therefore, the cangaceiro has transcended the limits of his own reality in Brazilian history. He has assumed the dual role of condemning the oppression of the powerful and promising a future of justice and equality.

Given the contemporary context in which the cangaceiro has been interpreted, the tendency in much of the scholarly literature has been to emphasize the socially positive side of this bandit by exaggerating his identity as a champion of the people. Unfortunately, the effect of this interpretation has been to obscure, even to deny, the cangaceiro's actual historical role as an instrument for maintaining the established order on behalf of local agrarian elites. The following discussion, therefore, suggests a number of ways in which an examination of the bandit career of Antônio Silvino revised or refined current popular notions about the behavior and role of such Robin Hood figures in the literature on Brazilian social banditry. In addition, this analysis offers an explanation for the failure of banditry to evolve into more revolutionary action directed toward transforming the traditional society. Deriving originally from the case study of politics and kinship in the northeastern state of Paraíba (Parahyba do Norte) during the Old Republic (1889–1930), the conclusions offered here are based on evidence drawn primarily from the private correspondence of the coronéis (local political bosses) with state and national politicians and from the local newspapers of Paraíba and neighboring Pernambuco during the same period.[8] These primary sources contain valuable new evidence from which to evaluate the cangaceiro's behavior, since all other interpretations of Silvino's career have relied heavily on secondary sources or ballads and memoirs that were written for popular consumption. The latter usually assumed as their purpose the articulation of a legendary Antônio Silvino at variance with much of the historical record.

Two aspects of what is commonly referred to as social banditry are analyzed from the perspective of the brigand whose career earned him his reputation as the "Brazilian Robin Hood." First, Antônio Silvino's nineteen years of bandit activity will be evaluated from a perspective that places him directly within the larger society in which he operated, a perspective that has not so far received sufficient attention. Accordingly, banditry is assessed within the context of the various structures of patronage that existed locally, but that were also directly linked to the state and national levels of the political system. This implies, of course, that the nature of local patronage relationships was a primary determinant of the extent to which such brigandage could be identified as social banditry. The Brazilian cangaceiro must not be seen as an abstract type, but as an individual directly related to specific but differing configurations of authority and dependency imposed by local structures of patronage. As a consequence of these relationships, banditry in Paraíba and in the adjoining territory of neighboring states was much more highly integrated with the *município* (county) or local political elites than has previously been acknowledged.

For this reason the crucial position of the *coronel-coiteiro*, the local boss who extended protection to bandits, deserves more attention. The conspiracy of silence surrounding this most elusive of actors in the scenario of banditry has rendered his role problematic, for he has received only oblique reference or been ignored altogether in the literature on brigandage. In view of the strong interdependence of the bandit and the *coiteiro*, the popular identification of the cangaceiro as a liberator demands critical re-evaluation.[9] Given this consideration, scholarly conceptualizations of the cangaceiro as an independent or "third force" whose behavior was directed toward championing the poor and punishing or checking the rapaciousness of the rich and powerful either neglect his dependence on the local establishment or fall short of confronting the central consequences of his behavior for the rural population. Therefore, the second respect in which this discussion seeks to re-examine banditry addresses the implications of such a brigand's behavior for the masses in rural society. If the cangaceiro happened to have been much less a social bandit than has previously been asserted, then such a revised interpretation raises the serious consideration that his presence was even an obstacle to more meaningful protest on a general level.

Complementing the analysis presented here, a brief biographical sketch of Antônio Silvino has been included in order to clarify both his professional evolution and the pattern of recruitment for his band. Much of Silvino's biography has been scattered; only fragmentary and often impressionistic accounts of his deeds have survived.[10] As the "Governor of the *Sertão* [the backlands]" Silvino operated for a span of almost two decades in a territory of approximately 100,000 square kilometers covering four states and populated by more than a million inhabitants. The most celebrated bandit in Brazilian history until the advent of the notorious Lampião ("King of the Cangaceiros"), Silvino remains the most adored and respected brigand in the Northeast's pantheon of heroic outlaws. Because he was disproportionately overshadowed by the more seductive, terrifying specter of Lampião, for whom he later became a virtuous foil in the hands of journalists, Antônio Silvino has never received the scholarly attention he deserves. In an era of brigandage in which regional historians elevated any bandit who survived for five years to historical immortality, Silvino's singular career offers some significant clues for the twentieth-century evolution of the *cangaço* (the phenomenon of banditry or its vocational role).

The cangaço's origins have generally been traced to the warfare that was endemic between powerful elite *parentelas* (extended families) even in the early period of the settlement of the sertão beginning in the late seventeenth century.[11] A number of more relevant factors, however, emerged in the latter half of the nineteenth century to contribute to the rise of the cangaço as a significant and unique political phenomenon, propelling it toward its historical apogee in the first quarter of this century. The emphasis that has been accorded the catastrophic droughts of 1877 and 1888, as well as subsequent periodic droughts of major and minor incidence, only superficially explains the increasing importance of the cangaceiro's role in regional life.[12] Extremely unfavorable climatic conditions, together with epidemics and the gradual abolition of African slavery before 1888, had undeniably contributed to the economic and social disorientation of the Brazilian Northeast by the close of Emperor Dom Pedro II's reign. With the collapse of his monarchy and the establishment of the republic in 1889, however, other factors fell more sharply into focus as important determinants in accelerating the historical trajectory of the cangaço's transformation into a major ingredient of backlands political life around the turn of this century. Economic growth owing to increased demand for export crops—cotton in the case of Paraíba— meant that the traditional family conflicts assumed larger, more lucrative, and more decisive proportions. In this respect the Paraíba sertão, which had still been an area of frontier settlement in the first half of the nineteenth century, witnessed increased strife with the disappearance of available good land for the more numerous offspring of the major parentelas. Consequently, traditional family antagonisms erupted in open warfare more frequently as the dominant kin coalitions rapidly disintegrated into fractious and less cohesive segmentary groupings.

Modification of the political structure considerably reinforced the tendency of economic change to increase family conflict. The constitution of 1891, for example, permitted more local political autonomy under a republic that was established with an emphatically federal distribution of power. In this context the coronel's role acquired an expanded dimension, that of a political "broker" between the local level and the state party machine. Despite the original decentralization of local control, the presence of the state was increasingly felt with each new decade of the twentieth century, by virtue of the patronage made available to family groupings that won local recognition by the state party machine. Certain writers have correctly emphasized increased taxation as a factor generating mass resentment in the Old Republic.[13] Given the booming export economy, at the local elite level taxation acquired a new relevance for the exacerbated rivalry of competing parentelas. More specifically, locally dominant families enjoyed both greater economic incentive and more immediate authority to enforce the collection of taxes. In a capital-scarce economy such as that which existed in Paraíba, município revenues were customarily appropriated by the members of the state oligarchy at the local level in order to finance their investment in the internal improvements necessary to make land more productive and markets more profitable in a growing export economy. Furthermore, the generally relaxed control effected by the presidential policy known after 1900 as the "politics of the governors" was reinforced by the extremely weak police powers of the respective state governments. The chronic insufficiency of law-enforcement contingents meant that small bands of brigands were often more than a match for either the state police or their newly created "flying columns (*volantes*)." When certain state governments successfully challenged local autonomy in the 1920s and 1930s, banditry entered a new defensive stage in its evolution.

Scholarly typologies notwithstanding, contemporary oral and written usage in the early decades of this century observed no rigid distinctions of vocabulary in bandit nomenclature. The terms cangaceiro and bandit (*bandido*) were used rather indiscriminately. In fact, individuals identified by those labels often exchanged roles themselves, alternately serving as hired retainers (*capangas*) or state police as well as operating as professional bandits who were popularly, but not consistently, identified as cangaceiros. Not surprisingly, these roles were interchangeable in a society where landlords, merchants, police officers, and bandit chiefs all recruited gunmen from a growing and fluid pool of the dispossessed and economically uprooted. Virtually all bandit leaders, and most bandits, "turned outlaw" to avenge a wrong done to them or their kinsmen because their family position in local politics made redress through the establishment's police and courts impossible. Yet another factor contributing to the emerging political role of the cangaço during the Old Republic derived from the less predictable and more frequent alternation of partisan control at the local level. The formerly Conservative or Liberal party family coalitions increased their persecution of each other and in so doing involved the cangaço more directly in município strife.

These political and economic changes that so abruptly altered the organization of backlands society at the end of the last century suggest why Antônio Silvino would represent a transitional type of bandit. He bridged the gap between the nineteenth century's traditional cangaço, established directly on parentela ties that limited it to a family-defined territory, and the twentieth century's professional cangaço, recruited broadly from the larger population with an area of operation embracing half a dozen states. In this respect Silvino's career is a useful historical watershed, dividing the formative stage of the cangaço, epitomized by his own Robin Hood kinsman Jesuíno Brilhante during the 1870s, from the fully matured and final phase of the cangaço in the 1920s and 1930s under Lampião.[14] Although it would be incorrect to characterize Silvino merely as a private retainer, his own rendering of "service" (servico), or, more properly, "favors," to many establishment figures outside the previously traditional family parameters observed by most of his predecessors suggested a basic change in the relationship of the cangaço to the political structure at large. In successfully expanding his operational territory and repertoire of exchange relationships with the rural establishment, Silvino presaged the full political potential of the cangaço so powerfully developed by Lampião after 1922.

Born Manuel Batista de Morais in 1875 in the remote Paraíba backlands município of Alagoa do Monteiro, Antônio Silvino grew up in nearby Afogados de Ingazeira, another notorious zone of endemic family conflict in neighboring Pernambuco.[15] Connected on both sides of his family to the major warring kindreds of that part of the sertão—the Batistas and their Dantas enemies who dominated the central plateau of Paraíba—Silvino counted several of the nineteenth century's most celebrated cangaceiros as his kinsmen. Ties of family affiliation over a large geographical region consequently linked him in dual lineage to the major zones of family warfare as well as to kinsmen who extended him their protection for the rest of his life. His parents were fairly prosperous, owning a dozen slaves and making a comfortable living planting cane and raising cattle. Pedro Batista Rufino de Almeida, Silvino's father, enjoyed political prestige in the 1880s as a law officer in Afogados, where he was also better known as "Big Batista" (*O Batistão*). He distinguished himself in local tradition as much by his "baptizing" powers with a gun as by his command of reading and writing, the latter perhaps the greater achievement among the largely illiterate backlands elite. Silvino "turned cangaceiro" in 1897 for the customary exaction of family justice after his father was murdered by an enemy cousin who could count on local political protection. He completed his apprenticeship as a brigand under the tutelage of his godfather and maternal uncle (or great-uncle), Silvino Aires de Cavalcanti e Albuquerque, the doyen of the preceding generation of cangaceiros who had incredibly eluded his pursuers for a quarter of a century.[16] Inheriting the leadership of his mentor's band after Silvino Aires's subsequent imprisonment, the young Manuel Batista began an independent career in 1899, adopting the *nom de guerre* "Antônio Silvino" in homage to his godfather, whom he swore to avenge.

Until he was finally betrayed and captured in Lagôa de Lages, Pernambuco, in late 1914, Silvino roamed the hostile back trails of the sertões of four states, selectively assaulting, robbing, or "liquidating" his enemies and destroying their property. During the twenty-three years he subsequently spent in the state penitentiary in Recife, he survived an initial attempt at suicide and reestablished old acquaintanceships with former bandit companions whom he joined in prison. Granting occasional interviews to a few interested local literati, Silvino converted to Protestantism and lived to be pardoned in 1937 by President Getúlio Vargas,

GENEALOGY OF ANTONIO SILVINO: KINSHIP RELATIONS WITH OTHER PROMINENT *CANGACEIROS*

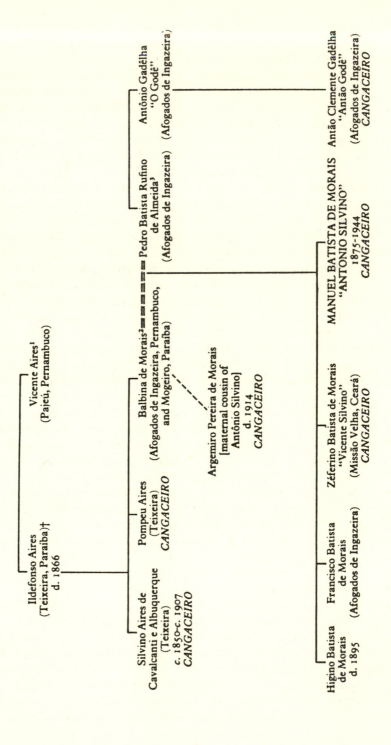

Notes

[1] Together with his kinsmen Antônio Gadêlha and Col. "Xico" Miguel da Silva, Lieut.-Col. Vicente Aires protected Silvino Aires. He is also remembered for having sent the Guabirabas, a notorious band of cangaceiros, to Paraíba in the 1860s.

[2] Balbina de Morais was related to the Morais of Paraíba, the Feitosas of the Inhamuns, Ceará, and the Brilhantes of Paraíba and Rio Grande do Norte.

[3] Pedro Rufino was a kinsman of Vicente Aires, on whose estate he resided. He was also a great-nephew of Andrelino Pereira (baron of Paieú), a cangaceiro pardoned by the Emperor Dom Pedro II. Antônio Silvino, therefore, was distantly related to Sebastião Pereira (Senhô Pereira) and his cousin Luiz Pereira ("Luiz Padre" or "Lulú-Padre"), two cangaceiros active between 1914 and 1920 and great-nephews of Andrelino Pereira.

‡ Locations in parentheses denote place(s) of residence.

* Sources: Trajano Pires da Nóbrega, *A família Nóbrega* (São Paulo, 1956), pp. 34-6; Carlos D. Fernandes, *Os cangaceiros: romance de costumes sertanejos* (Parahyba, 1914), pp. 100, 107, 113-15; Gustavo Barroso, *Heróes e bandidos: os cangaceiros do nordeste* (Rio de Janeiro, 1917), pp. 225-78; Gustavo Barroso, *Almas de lama e de aço* (São Paulo, 1930), pp. 75-89; José Américo de Almeida, *A Parahyba e seus problemas* (Parahyba, 1923), p. 497; Pedro Baptista das Chagas, *Cangaceiros do nordeste* (Parahyba, 1929), pp. 37-9, 49-84, 195-7; Maria Isaura Pereira de Queiroz, *Cangaceiros: les bandits d'honneur brésiliens* (Paris, 1965), p. 45; Mario Souto Maior, *Antônio Silvino, Capião de Trabuco* (Rio de Janeiro, 1971), pp. 29-34; *Jornal do Recife*, 30 Jan. 1897, 26 Nov. 1898; Abelardo Parreira, *Sertanejos e cangaceiros* (São Paulo, 1934), pp. 22-3.

8. Genealogy of Antônio Silvino

Key:

Direct descent |

Collateral descent

Collateral relationship not precisely specified

Marriage

who also gave him a minor government post. But he was unable to withstand the confines of his rehabilitated life as a petty bureaucrat in Rio de Janeiro and returned to his beloved Paraíba sertão for the last years of his life. He died impoverished in Campina Grande in 1944 with only a terse obituary to mark his passing.[17]

Antônio Silvino possessed a striking physical demeanor. A newspaper photograph revealed that his handsome features clearly belied the pejorative newspaper descriptions that Lambrosian journalists invariably ascribed to him.[18] Tall, well built, and strong in endurance, Silvino could cover sixty-five to eighty miles of trackless wasteland on foot in a twenty-four-hour period of relentless pursuit. A prize-winning marksman like his father and brothers, he used his legendary "golden rifle" to sever telegraph wires as well as to defend himself against his enemies. Besides exacting justice with his Winchester .44 and his "Brownie" (a Colt .45), he relied for protection on a silver-inlaid dagger and his inseparable *trabuco*, a type of scatter-gun that was standard equipment in the antiquated armories of backlands siege warfare. He rounded out this staggering portable arsenal with two large leather pouches of ball and powder and double belts of cartridges.

According to a frankly admiring witness, Silvino had only two personal weaknesses. The first was a fondness for diamonds. He usually wore them set in ostentatious gold rings on the fingers of both hands in the manner of his affluent establishment counterparts who advertised their social status with expensive jewelry. The other was his vain addiction to bathing his face in eau de cologne, followed by generous applications of brilliantine to his hair. He and his band reflected the cangaceiro's emulation of the establishment by adopting military dress. Depending on whether or not appropriate official garb had belonged to the state police or the national guard, Silvino respectively reserved for himself the dress and insignia of either a major or a lieutenant colonel. Both his men and the populace addressed him as "Captain Silvino" and colloquially referred to him as "Captain of the Trabuco." Something of a bandit bard, he has left as souvenirs of his intelligence and wit the punned rhymes he composed in honor of his enemies. Illiterate, he eventually learned to read the Bible in prison, where he also turned to raising birds and weaving birdcages to earn an income.

Before analyzing the historical evidence related to Silvino's career, it is worth reviewing the hallmarks of his legendary image as a "good" thief. Many of the events of his career described in the literatura de cordel also appear in the less flamboyant contemporary newspaper accounts. But many do not. Favorite legendary anecdotes describe how Silvino stole from the rich and distributed his booty among the poor, settled boundary disputes, arbitrated in domestic conflicts for backlands families, and, above all, respected "the honour of the family," that is, the wives and daughters of other men.[19] Legend chronicles Silvino's long-distance journeys to avenge wrongs and settle scores with an endless list of personal enemies. An oft-recounted saga describes his running war with the British-owned Great Western Railway Company in Pernambuco as its tracks and telegraph wires inexorably extended westward into the interior. Legend and ballad interpret his aggression toward these technological targets, including the mailbags he appropriated en route and destroyed, as motivated by his defense of his own "sovereign" territory, the sertão. His penchant for commandeering telegraph stations and pursuing his colorful "telegraph war" with Paraíba's governors from 1907 to 1912 enhanced his image as an anti-establishment figure and earned him his sobriquet, "Governor of the Sertão." Finally, legend further ascribed Silvino's phantomlike disappearances during gun battles and his inevitably sudden reappearances elsewhere to what every true cangaceiro possessed—a certain magical power that kept him out of danger. Significantly, the literatura de cordel singled out Silvino's own fighting prowess and shrewd cunning as the cardinal factors explaining his superhuman survival. Conscious of the value of his image as a "good" thief, Silvino himself constantly sought to promote it and was his own best propagandist. A Paraíba newspaper summed up his legendary reputation for close identification with the common people: "He protects the people, the anonymous masses with whom he divides his pillage and in whose bosom he has his best source of support. . . . He does not dishonour families and he has a mania for harming the public authorities, having become intransigent against those who pursue him."[20]

But was this the case? Legends are intended to immortalize individuals and their brave deeds, not to interpret their heroes' triumphs in terms of a broader context. Both the currently circulating stock of oral history about Silvino and the literatura de cordel fall under this rubric. On the one hand, they have ignored or underplayed the most important aspect of Silvino's long survival: his elaborately constructed web of collective security. On the other hand, they have omitted material from the historical record that would cast his deeds in an unfavorable light. Silvino's incredibly prolonged survival as a cangaceiro is explained by the fact that his most reliable protection derived consistently from his connections with the powerful rather than with the humble in rural society. And those connections defined him more as a landlord's bandit than as a people's bandit.

Turning to the specific ways in which structural considerations determined Silvino's local identity in rural society, patronage relationships on two political planes are crucial for an accurate interpretation of this brigand's behavior.[21] First, patronage connected individuals within the political establishment at the level of the local bosses in the município with those in the oligarchy at the level of the state party machine. Second, patronage on a lower level linked those bosses with the rural client population on their estates. Whether as the first set of establishment relationships within the state oligarchy or as the second set of relationships between the members of that oligarchy and the broad mass of the rural population, the patronage system was a means of offering security, albeit deteriorating security, to all its members.

The national political system rested on a base of local boss rule called coronelismo. This meant that coronéis delivered the votes of their clients in exchange for a free hand in local politics and a share of the spoils of officeholding. Powerful elite parentelas operated as units of political mobilization, and the dominant state oligarchy's partisan organization represented a coalition of the most powerful parentelas. Consequently, political conflict was organized according to vertical family divisions that locally reached downward into the mass of the rural client population. The police represented a form of patronage that extended from the state capital to local parentelas loyal to the state oligarchy who called for armed reinforcements against their immediate rivals. During Silvino's career the Paraíba State Police grew from under 400 to over 700 strong, although population increased by only 40 percent.[22] The police were nevertheless no match for Silvino and many other brigands because they were usually underprovisioned, outgunned, and, for that matter, even underpaid vis-à-vis their better remunerated and equipped bandit quarry. Finally, the much deserved reputation that police enjoyed for greater cruelty toward the rural population meant that cangaceiros were usually preferred as interlopers.

Silvino's behavior as a bandit fell within this structure of family domination and patronage, for coronelismo's organizational variations could influence his particular pattern of local accommodation. The extremely powerful coronel who controlled several municípios was limited in Paraíba to only several instances. Most frequently, political management by several tightly intermarried families of coronéis defined the predominant pattern of local rule. In other cases political control was contested in a município by two warring families in fierce and protracted, but evenly divided, conflicts. In addition to these local patterns of coronelismo the larger political structure also determined the types of relationships that Silvino established with members of the rural elite as well as the scope of his operational boundaries. Depending on the way in which local political influence could be exercised at the state and national levels of the oligarchy, his activities could be either openly tolerated, tacitly protected, or energetically discouraged. A few examples drawn from his own behavior illustrate the way in which bandits generally functioned as part of coronelista politics.

Silvino depended most consistently on an extensive network of protection in an area spanning the Paraíba-Pernambuco borderlands, bounded on the north by Campina Grande and Pilar and on the south by Bom Jardim and Timbaúba. Throughout his career he was sheltered and even entertained socially by landowners and merchants in this zone, although the range of his targets extended as far west as Crato and Milagres in Ceará and as far north as Acarí and Caicó in Rio Grande do Norte. This rugged territory spanning the Cariris Velhos, a mountainous area straddling the rich river valleys running parallel to the Paraíba-Pernambuco border, offered lucrative targets for his regular rounds of extortion and robbery. Owing to the common pattern of overlapping ownership of rural estates by various members of the same family, the kindreds who offered Silvino refuge were distributed on both sides of this border and included his own relatives and female consorts in a wide interstate area.[23] Because pursuing police were usually restricted to their own states, fleeing outlaws could with impunity cross and recross the borders to take advantage of these interlocking sanctuaries.

By 1900 Antônio Silvino had successfully made his reputation as a brigand in this border zone. His efforts to extort money had focused on many merchants in the Paraíba município of Umbuseiro, where he enjoyed protection and access to a chain of friendly properties defining his escape route in nearby Pernambuco. Citing the "manifest impotence of the state authorities" to repress the growing number of bandits in the interior, businessmen of the capital of Paraíba could only lament the serious interruption of their commerce with the interior. They protested Antônio Silvino's practice of entering backlands markets and collecting what he termed his personal *dizimo* (a state tax) under threat of death.[24]

Denunciations calling for the "cleansing of banditry from the backlands" became familiar front-page reading during the Old Republic but remained vain rhetoric until the 1920s. A small and still politically ineffectual force, the capital's merchants were by no means the only group to raise their voices against Silvino and other bandits who preyed on the interior. Silvino's choice of robbery victims, however, displayed no clear economic pattern beyond the fact that he struck at those who possessed the prized caches of money, jewels, guns, and merchandise. Landlords, merchants, tax collectors, and police were thereby equally favored, but merchants figured more prominently because of their readily available sums of cash.

Colonel Antônio Pessoa was the most prominent figure among those who have left private accounts of their situations as victims of Silvino's wrath. A prospering borderlands rancher from Umbuseiro (Paraíba) at the turn of this century, Colonel Antônio's experience illustrates the complexity of Silvino's relationship with a number of important figures in the rural gentry. Although he became governor of Paraíba in 1915, thanks to his younger brother, Epitácio da Silva Pessoa, himself a leading national politician and statesman of the Old Republic, Colonel Antônio Pessoa was in the political opposition locally in Umbuseiro during part of Antônio Silvino's career. For more than a decade his life was jeopardized by local enemies who extended protection to Silvino and used the bandit against the Pessoas and their clients.[25] In response to Silvino's numerous public vows to kill him, Colonel Antônio Pessoa intermittently pursued the bandit. But he never apprehended him—and for good reason.

Political power in Colonel Antônio's area of Paraíba was distributed in the most typical coronelista pattern of organization. A number of families collectively shared a precarious domination of the município; a less powerful agglomeration of allied families around Colonel Antônio Pessoa opposed them. Lacking effective political influence with the governor at state level, Colonel Antônio resorted instead to working through his powerful brother in Rio de Janeiro in order to compel the state oligarchy to deny Silvino support at the local level.[26] Epitácio's efforts to lobby on his brother's behalf in Rio de Janeiro with the leader of the Paraíba state oligarchy proved futile. The oligarchy was loath to intervene against

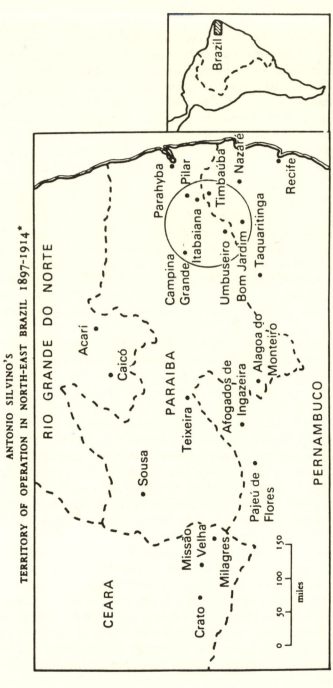

ANTONIO SILVINO'S

TERRITORY OF OPERATION IN NORTH-EAST BRAZIL 1897-1914*

* Source: Adapted from "Vias de comunicação", *Enciclopédia dos municípios brasileiros*, 36 vols. (Rio de Janeiro, 1957-63), iv, pp. 48 ff.

9. Antônio Silvino's Territory of Operation

the interest of its local partisans. An astute politician, Epitácio revealed in a letter to his brother the reason why the political structure would enable Silvino to coexist as an extralegal arm of Colonel Antônio's enemies:

You wrote informing me that you are pursuing Antônio Silvino, having put three men on his trail with strict orders. It seems to me that you should avoid these men going to the extreme. Consider that you, and above all I, have many enemies here [Rio de Janeiro] who would not hesitate to ensnare you with legal charges and by this means create trouble and difficulty in your life. I am unable in a mere letter to say everything to you in all candour. I can only advise you to be cautious and to avoid putting your hand in the trap.[27]

During the time Silvino identified himself openly in the family conflict against the Pessoas, Epitácio could only urge prudence on his brother. He recognized and feared that Silvino's capture might bring about the loss of the family estates to local adversaries whose influential position would assist them in the courts.[28]

Antônio Silvino rendered his "services" for his "friends" in exchange for protection and hospitality. However, he also maintained personal family claims on a number of coiteiros who construed their protection of him and their direct intervention with the governor on his behalf as personal loyalty to the memory of his murdered father, who had been their friend.[29] But Silvino's services were not always proffered merely as a gesture of personal loyalty or pragmatically dictated by mutually advantageous favors. Sometimes he received monetary remuneration. Silvino's custom of never receiving or paying money in the presence of his band and the obvious reticence of his protectors on the subject mean that his financial negotiations are exceedingly difficult to document. In 1904, however, it was well publicized and alleged that he had received payment for guaranteeing that the murderers of a prominent Pernambuco *senhor de engenho* (sugar estate owner) remained in jail to await trial.[30] His value to the rural elite before 1907 was melodramatically described in a letter to a major Recife daily paper:

Silvino *lived* in this district, in the most shocking partnership with the police authorities and . . . the political bosses served themselves with his *trabuco* in order to enhance their prestige and to get rid of their own political adversaries according to their criminal desires. . . . The local authorities fell all over themselves as the toadies of that bestial bandit, first as bearers of letters and messages [of extortion] and then undertaking [his] collection, bags in hand from door to door.[31]

The same author pointed out how such coiteiros protected their own families: "The authorities and the local bosses used to know beforehand the village which on the following day would be attacked by desperadoes and would order them to remember that their relatives resided there. And even though all the inhabitants were despoiled of their possessions [such] relatives were spared."[32]

Silvino's services appear to have extended to advancing his protectors' commercial interests. In one case he closed a local market and warned the towns-people that if they reopened it, he would exact revenge.[33] A number of independent sources definitely associated Silvino with regularly passing counterfeit money.[34] This practice linked him to the urban mercantile stratum, since only they were technically equipped to manufacture specious tender. Silvino's well-established and open relationships with the rich and the powerful were common knowledge to the general populace, which was regularly apprised of them in the daily press:

On 3rd March [1904] Antônio Silvino and his three companions . . . passed the day in the city of Timbaúba [Pernambuco] in the house of Sr. Juvino, record clerk of the jury in this *município*. They came after murdering Sr. Marroles [Marroces?]. This is not the first time they have been in Timbaúba because they have always at their disposal . . . the house of this businessman. Without a doubt Sipó Branco, Capibaribe and many *engenhos* are visited by them . . . because those places have often been refuges. Last week Antônio Silvino even went so far as to go deer-hunting in company with some *senhores de engenho* of the *município* of Nazaré.[35]

Elsewhere, when coronelista power was less collectively arranged and strongly divided between two warring family factions, Silvino adapted differently to the local patronage structure. His behavior in Campina Grande from around 1903 to 1908 is instructive in this respect. Campina Grande, the "gateway to the sertão," was the expanding entrepôt for most of the raw cotton exported from the Paraíba interior during the Old Republic. Merchant-landowners waged an internecine war for control of markets, warehouses, transport routes, and land. Bandits were an increasing reserve of reinforcements in their violent conflicts. The political opposition in Campina Grande was uncharacteristically strong, owing to special circumstances that had influenced the state oligarchy not to lend much assistance to the dominant local faction. Fairly evenly matched, the two family factions warred for several decades after 1889. Evidence suggests that Silvino allied with both sides, probably simultaneously at times.[36] By 1908, however, he appeared to have outlived his usefulness to either side, for he drew down on himself a fierce effort to capture or kill him after his alienation of powerful protectors in both factions.

By 1906 Silvino's aggressive depredations against the British-owned Great Western Railway Company in Pernambuco had antagonized it sufficiently for it to appeal for federal troops. The 27th Battalion was reinforced and the governor of Pernambuco was pressured to permit "hot pursuit" of Silvino across state lines. Furthermore, in 1908, the Pessoa faction in Paraíba gained an indispensable position in the oligarchy's majority in the state assembly and received new political consideration locally. Epitácio, therefore, successfully interceded at the federal level to ensure that his brother, Colonel Antônio, would have the protection of the Brazilian federal army locally.[37] Nevertheless, the soldiers clashed so often with both the state police and the civilian population, including the

Pessoas, that they had to be withdrawn. Even before that drastic step Silvino's protectors in Campina Grande had effectively neutralized the federal battalion's effectiveness, in all likelihood by suborning its commander. At least, Silvino bragged openly that he knew the routes of the army patrols before their officers received their marching orders; his success in eluding his pursuers confirmed that boast.[38]

Pressed harder in the field, Silvino made three unsuccessful attempts to secure a pardon from the governor.[39] His embitterment increased because of the large toll his enemies had taken of his original band of comrades-in-arms, all of whom were dead or imprisoned by 1908. These factors drove him to commit crueler acts, to seek new alliances, and to shift territory. In so doing he continued to adapt his behavior to the organizational patterns of coronelismo.

Extremely powerful coronéis who dominated their own and as many as a half dozen municípios were rare in Paraíba, but several local bosses attained relatively wide political domination in zones embracing two or three municípios. Despite their success as commercial landlords these coronéis were often contemptuously referred to as "feudal" bosses, for as powerful rural magnates they exercised the choice of either working with bandits or banishing them from their territories. After Silvino became alienated from his protectors in Campina Grande, he continued to rely on the sponsorship of several of these "feudal" coronéis because the police never dared to cross the boundaries of their estates and they offered the safest refuge. After 1908 Silvino could be more openly identified in local politics on behalf of these strong bosses, some of whom he endorsed electorally in public speeches.[40] In fact, where either one coronel was powerful or a group of them united, they could force Silvino to pay protection money to them. This concession was apparently not uncommonly extracted from him by those in a position to do so.[41]

When a full-scale backlands revolt erupted in Paraíba in 1912, led by Dr. Franklin Dantas and Dr. Augusto Santa Cruz, Antônio Silvino rode with them as they sacked a number of towns. On one occasion Silvino and his men collected "contributions" according to a list carried by Dr. Franklin and distributed election literature for the Dantas gubernatorial candidate.[42] An eyewitness left a rare and candid picture of his movements and protection:

The group of the famous Antônio Silvino outdoes itself. . . . His followers have been increased in number [to around thirty]; they go on horseback and now are no longer content with small booty. . . .

Lately he has cut the telegraph wires, ripped up mail-bags, and held up at gunpoint our wretched politicians in order to take his "modest tax," as he calls it. He has the most scandalous protection of many who are not only of the political opposition but also of the dominant party.

I know our police force is demoralized—to the point where the higher officers say they will not even give chase to Silvino because many of the local bosses in power and some very close to the government are the principal protectors of Silvino.[43]

Silvino continued to be active as a bandit in Paraíba until his capture in Pernambuco in late 1914, despite the fact that in 1912 Paraíba's new governor had effected the first interstate convention for cooperative pursuit of bandits. Although Paraíba's pact with its three neighbors marked a new offensive phase on the part of the state executive, the reality of banditry's coexistence with local politics subverted any legal initiatives intended to eradicate it. Paraíba's governor dismally summarized this situation in a confidential letter to state party boss Epitácio:

I agree with those who want to extinguish banditry. . . . We should [in this case] begin in our own house, with those party members and friends who live by banditry, with the estates which are filled with criminals having understandings with Antônio Silvino or with others they help. . . .

You know better than I the very true causes for which repression of banditry in the interior of the state was and will be ineffective. It is the local bosses who protect it . . . and politics originates from these bosses by virtue of their [control over] voters.[44]

The convention of 1912 was silent on the problem of coiteiros, leaving the structural underpinnings of banditry in local life unchallenged. Until his capture in 1914 Silvino continued to rely on his long-established network of protection in four states, and the press continued to observe that he always appeared to be promptly warned regarding his pursuers.[45] Depending on whether local family power was collectively shared, evenly divided between two warring factions, or extremely concentrated in one powerful coronel, Silvino accommodated himself accordingly. He therefore either served specific family political interests for reciprocal favors or remuneration, advantageously exploited two factions against each other, or wisely submitted himself to superior authority and bought his own protection.

Given his open identification or partnership with the establishment, Silvino's attacks on the rich and powerful deserve to be evaluated from that elite perspective. His reputation for "settling accounts" with many brutal backlands figures in the establishment quite naturally brought him heroic admiration from the rural poor, who in given situations logically identified him as a champion who delivered them from the excesses of such cruel individuals. In most cases, however, their deliverance was only fortuitous coincidence, for Silvino's motives were dictated by his own personal considerations of revenge and self-defense. He usually murdered someone because of his own personal grudge or one assumed on behalf of a friend.[46] His most typical victim was someone who had already sworn to kill him—a policeman, a retainer of a powerful local figure, or a relative of someone Silvino had murdered. He occasionally "evened the score" with an informer. By definition, his relationship with the political elite and his need for cash dictated that his victims would either be drawn from the establishment, owing to the political influence or booty they commanded, or be acting on behalf of the establishment as its agents. The cooperation of the poor, however, was frequently vital for Silvino's survival, if only momentarily, because they furnished intelligence and diverted pursuers. The poor, nevertheless, lacked the economic means to offer reliable security for long periods as well as the costly armaments needed to repel heavy police attacks. Although Silvino appears to have honestly sympathized with the oppressed rural population, especially when the oppressors were also his personal political enemies, its claims on his patronage were infinitely less important to his survival than the claims of the powerful.

Silvino gained much of his popular support from the rustic poor through his distribution of money and booty to them. In this respect analyses of his *noblesse oblige* generally overlook the fact that he himself required considerable amounts of money to continue to operate as a bandit. Suborning a policeman, for example, cost 200 to 600 *mil-réis* each time. Silvino's robberies or extortions were not undertaken for the principal purpose of redistributing rural income, but as a means of securing the personal income necessary for maintaining himself and his men as cangaceiros. It has been estimated that he and his band earned between six and ten *contos* per month, exclusive of more lucrative booty, which also suggests that they allocated only a small portion of their "collections" to the poor. For example, when Silvino "collected" 1 *conto* 800 *mil-réis* in the celebrated robbery in Pilar, he distributed only a modest tithe, approximately 200 *mil-réis*, to the poor.[47] His occasional distribution of money and his more frequent division of foodstuffs and merchandise among the indigent spectators of his robberies made good sense as well as bandit justice, for brigands who alienated the common people could be finished off by them. By the same token Silvino's assaults on the mails should not be construed as "primitive protest" against the state, but viewed as more pragmatically determined by his intelligent grasp of the tactics of his own survival. Mailbags carried messages of denunciation describing Silvino's efforts to bribe public officials and marching orders for his pursuers, which he wisely chose to intercept.[48] His attacks on the Great Western Railway might be construed similarly as anti-imperialistic attacks, but probably they were more related to his appreciation that the same company owned the telegraph wires carrying the latest news of his whereabouts and hampering his movements. In Antônio Silvino's eyes the company's English owners were attractive prey because they were rich before they were foreigners.[49]

Similarly, Silvino's respected code of personal conduct pragmatically furthered his advantageous relations with the landed gentry. Particularly in regard to his proverbial respect for the "honor of the family," his ethical code sealed his reputation as a "good" thief and assured him his privileged place at the tables of the first families of the sertão. Silvino's legendary scrupulous regard for the customary, prescribed restrictions on male behavior in the company of women is still the trait universally cited to recommend him as the "gentle cangaceiro." Practically speaking, however, he was aware that such "respect" toward women made even more good sense as respect toward the men of the political elite who exercised dominion over such women. Evidence suggests that Silvino's much-lauded respect for women was confined largely to those drawn from his own white, socially well-connected background. Even women of high social status, however, were occasionally subjected to public insult by him. A number of recorded incidents revealing his physical brutality and violent threats directed against socially inferior women contradict his unblemished legendary reputation on this score, although Silvino was probably no more excessive in this respect than many figures in the backlands establishment.[50] For him to have done otherwise than to "honor the family" would have been folly, for he would have provoked strong establishment resistance to his requests for refuge.

A second patronage relationship on a different level, that linking the backlands establishment and its rural client population, also circumscribed Silvino's activity as a bandit and stamped him as a typical patron figure. Silvino personified a patron both in the way he related to members of his own band and in the way the oligarchy locally forced him into direct confrontation with the rural client population, who consequently became included among his victims. His role as a patron in both of these contexts severely limited any potential his bandit behavior offered for either checking the excesses of the elite or championing their poor tenants.

From the mid-nineteenth century the leadership of the cangaço in Paraíba had been recruited from the losers in local elite conflicts over land, commerce, and the spoils of party patronage. With the arrival of the railroad after 1900, landowners quickly appreciated the greater opportunity to secure new markets. They increased their cotton production by seizing land. The first victims in land seizures were usually the weakest links in the chain of owners, often downwardly mobile and vulnerable freeholders or prospering *agregados*—the latter technically squatters but in reality often men of status with their own dependent clients. Judging from the family origins of bandit leaders like Silvino and his twentieth-century contemporaries, as well as those of their nineteenth-century predecessors, these two groups bore the brunt of intensified parentela conflict and constituted the predominantly white, socially well-connected leadership stratum of the cangaço.[51]

The rank and file of the cangaço were recruited from the less fortunate mass of the rural population. Poorer, undernourished, usually of darker complexion, and less likely to be political outlaws before entering the cangaço, such regular recruits more frequently assumed the life of a cangaceiro for reasons besides vengeance. For them, "turning cangaceiro" offered the additional incentive of better work at higher pay.[52] Bandit life offered more individual independence, and the camaraderie of the band was often more attractive than the isolation of the rural estate or the insecurity of membership in an agricultural labor force where customary tenantry rights were eroding. Above all, entering the cangaço as a deliberate and popular vocational decision reflected the positive attraction of a career of violence—the very antithesis of an agricultural tenant's passive existence. Nevertheless, the cangaço was still highly representative of the larger society from which it was drawn, for in choosing the life of a bandit a man exchanged one patron for another.

Antônio Silvino's band was organized hierarchically, according to degrees of loyalty reflecting either kinship to him or years of shared battle experience. Its members usually numbered six to eight men. Silvino's early lieutenant for at least six years, Cocada (Manuel Marinho), was a fellow *paraibano* (native of Paraíba) of obscure and indigent social origins but a bandit equally favored in intelligence, cunning, and fighting prowess. His personal and family ties in the borderlands area near Itabaiana (Paraíba) complemented Silvino's similar kin connections and contributed to their mutual security.[53] Silvino originally inherited his followers by virtue of his ties of kinship to Silvino Aires, but after maturing in experience he began to demonstrate different recruitment criteria. Around 1904 he divided his original band after an argument with Cocada, who apparently enjoyed sufficient stature to make his continued subordination to his chief problematic. Until Cocada's accidental death in 1907 the two leaders continued to coordinate their larger or more dangerous raids.[54] Silvino himself succinctly summed up his preference for excluding potential rivals in a terse comment offered in a prison interview: "Smart people did not enter my band; I only wanted more or less simple-minded types."[55] He typically recruited novices, personally teaching them to use a rifle, fight with a knife, and survive in the most desolate reaches of the backlands. In lending his personal sponsorship to their formation as bandits, he behaved as a patron, and he probably believed that such apprenticeships enhanced the loyalty he expected from those who fought with him.

By 1908, with the extinction of the band's original membership, there was an even more rapid turnover of recruits, owing to their distaste for an increasingly arduous bandit life. He occasionally even behaved as a responsible patron by assisting his men to reenter legitimate society, using his contacts within the rural establishment on their behalf. Booty was often converted to cash and meticulously divided in equal parts between Silvino and Cocada when they worked together, but the members of the bands were described as receiving a daily wage.[56] Silvino's superior position was also reflected in his income. He deposited considerable sums of money with his protectors and friends and also invested in cattle, apparently owning more than a thousand head.[57] Presumably he was looking forward to a day when he would be pardoned, or he was attempting to provide for the future of his offspring. Even his practical habits of survival set him apart from his men and reinforced his patron status. He negotiated his monetary transactions separately from his men, just as he customarily slept in a place unknown to them. He usually traveled alone, meeting his companions at a prearranged site. Although Silvino severely punished his men for infractions of discipline and occasionally even expelled individuals from his band, like any worthy patron he publicly praised their courage and considered it a personal obligation to avenge those who had been murdered.[58]

Silvino's role as a patron who was integrated within the rural establishment was further reinforced by the social and economic cleavages that existed on a number of levels in rural society. Both horizontal and vertical cleavages rendered the rural population responsive to the control of the patron stratum, which directly benefited as a political elite from the economic divisions among their dependent tenants. Horizontally, the agricultural client population was differentiated according to a hierarchy of privilege related to its conditions of land tenantry. Because dominant landlords controlled each group's access to credit, land, seeds, and water, as well as to price, sale, and ginning and baling, each type of tenant was isolated by differentiated privileges defined by the relations of production. Vertically, the population was further fragmented by the cleavages created by elite family affiliations, which reached downward to claim each tenant on behalf of his landlord's parentela. Because allegiance to a family head offered the only measure of safety, these prevailing patronage relationships between powerful landlords and their client populations dictated that inevitably Silvino would be brought into direct, violent confrontation with the lower orders of rural society.

Banditry directly impinged on the cleavage between landlord and peasant because the rural tenant's position in the patronage structure subjected him to the brunt of the attacks by his landlord's family enemies, whose agents could be either hired retainers, the police, or cangaceiros. Land wars and feuds over water rights were characteristically initiated by deliberately harassing a rival's tenants or stealing his livestock. The typical agricultural tenant could therefore expect to have his land seized, but more often his crops were burned, his livestock slaughtered, his fences destroyed, or his family assaulted. Furthermore, under the system of agricultural arrangements prevailing in the vast cotton zone of the interior, the tenant population contracted individually with estate owners not only for land and seeds, but also for the processing and marketing of their crops. Their productive surplus was therefore indistinguishable from that of their landlords. These economic arrangements marked rural tenants as logical targets for bandits striking at their landlords. Because the vertical family cleavages linked individuals of all social ranks on the same estate in mutual defense of the landlord's interest, peasants were jeopardized by their position in the patronage structure. Antônio Silvino was therefore drawn into situations where his victims included the humble as well as the great. As a locally protected bandit, he was expected to find his victims among his coiteiro's enemies, including their clients. In some instances those in the tenant population paid with their lives in defending their bosses' properties from Silvino's attacks. In other cases they were pressed into service under threat of death as his emissaries in extortion demands and then fell into the brutal hands of the police or enraged and defiant landlords. Particularly in Campina Grande, Silvino deliberately wreaked vengeance on the estates of his former coiteiros after he lost their valuable protection. He indiscriminately burned crops and slaughtered large numbers of livestock over a period of five years, taking his revenge on the entire population of selected estates.[59]

Survival in the cangaço implied varying degrees of accommodation to local structures of authority. Because even a bandit as formidable and shrewd as Antônio Silvino could not afford to place himself outside or above the basic patronage relationships that characterized political society, his behavior was circumscribed by the same oligarchical limits that also held peasants in check against collective rebellion. The existence of individual defiance among the lower orders of backlands society is only occasionally recorded in elliptical and terse references by rural bosses to the brutal deaths, rapes, and beatings the rural establishment meted out to anonymous individual rebels. In fact, the swift severity with which the establishment could retaliate with impunity against individual challenges to its prerogatives in local situations was effective in militating against more united and violent confrontations. More fundamentally, the economic reality of the rural masses' abject dependence on a landed elite, based on export agriculture and their local allegiance to a family head who still offered the best armed security, went further in explaining the absence of any meaningful movements of mass protest in Paraíba during the Old Republic.

Although the security offered by the rural establishment declined as economic change eroded much of the control traditionally exercised by the establishment, the growing numbers of marginal rural poor lacked both the economic means and the political influence necessary to transform the rural structure. Above all, leadership at the mass level failed to emerge because the historical conjuncture did not offer conditions favoring the merging of peasant grievances with those of other discontented urban sectors in the larger society. Banditry emerges, therefore, as an alluring but chimerical example of social protest precisely because the historical record of more meaningful mass dissent is such a barren one. Except for the Quebra-Quilos uprising in the 1870s, Paraíba experienced no *jacqueries* (bloody peasant uprisings) nor even indulged in militant millenarian revolts related to land or taxation, such as those of Canudos or the Contestado.[60] Religious fanaticism certainly existed as the popular analogue of banditry, but it similarly was sapped of its potential for transforming rural society by the political structure. Parish priests were extremely influential in public office in the state throughout the Old Republic and effectively militated against disruptive chiliastic alternatives by professionally mobilizing their own peasant clients. The padre-coronel was a familiar figure in backlands political life. During the Old Republic eight such clerical bosses sat in Paraíba's legislature, and one of them, Monsignor Valfredo Leal, shared the direction of the oligarchy in his capacity as either senator or governor from 1904 to 1912. As local political bosses, well over a dozen of these clerics assumed political leadership roles that were nearly identical with those of their lay counterparts.[61] They invested in land and commerce, delivered the local vote, distributed party patronage, and led their kinsmen and clients in local family wars and skirmishes. Their pulpits offered additional advantage as effective podia for electoral sermonizing, and even the threat of excommunication could be raised against the faithful who voted for the opposition, while their churches were customarily designated as polling centers. Such secularized priests had no intention of allowing their parishioners to succumb to messianic movements that might threaten their own political legitimacy and religious orthodoxy. Therefore, millenarianism, like banditry, was successfully blunted in its potential for generating clearly defined class dissent or outright rebellion because it, too, was circumscribed by strong oligarchical limitations. The established clergy, together with the political elite, remained an important obstacle to the rise of any movement that might have coalesced behind a popular thaumaturgic figure.

The further evolution of the cangaço after the termination of Antônio Silvino's career in 1914 is beyond the limited scope of this discussion. Yet the broad parameters within which the cangaço subsequently expanded its role in the region's political and social life in the 1920s and 1930s, only to vanish abruptly and pass into historical memory after 1940, can still be suggested. Banditry thrived because the local elites and the cangaço continued to be interdependent. Occasionally, where a local coronel was exceedingly strong and determined, banditry might be successfully combated within a narrow sphere. But as long as coronéis depended on cangaceiros as a necessary reserve force in their armed conflicts or found cooperation with the cangaço both economically and politically profitable, their working relationship remained a basic rule of coronelista politics. This fact was due to the absence of fundamental change in the political structure itself. Local family autonomy still defined a political system that was largely segmentary and in which power was often precariously held and violently contested. Local bosses were not encouraged or compelled to sever their reliance on the cangaço until the presence of the state was extended successfully to the backlands. Only a central state possessed the technical resources necessary to mount the geographically wide-ranging campaigns essential to discouraging bandits from manipulating their established networks of interstate protection and refuge. By the 1940s the central state had contributed to an effective and technically well-equipped military presence in the backlands, including an impressive system of access roads and the introduction of rapid communication tactics based on radio transmission and aerial surveillance, which meant that banditry finally faced its historical eclipse.

Nevertheless, the fundamental cause of banditry's demise was political. The commitment of greater resources to the eradication of banditry was both a reflection of the growing centralization of public power after the establishment of Getúlio Vargas's authoritarian *Estado Nôvo* (New State) in 1937 as well as the larger claim that urban and mercantile interests exerted on the use of state power. In certain limited cases, even in the 1920s, state governments had been effective in assuming the offensive against banditry. Lampião, for example, was virtually banished from Pernambuco after 1928 and sought more vulnerable operational territory in the state of Bahia.[62] Backlands coronéis in Bahia were not as yet subordinated to the ineffectual control of the state capital in Salvador. Generally, however, local backlands autonomy was not seriously challenged by either state or federal authorities until the 1940s, and even then many local political prerogatives that appropriated public authority for private ends were left intact.

Banditry ultimately disappeared as local elites realized that they had more to gain in cooperating with state and federal governments in the eradication of brigandage—thanks to new federal patronage opportunities as well as to punitive measures against those who abetted it—than they did by coexisting with it. Concurrently, the formerly grand scale of family warfare rapidly contracted. Never again did a backlands revolt challenge the authority of the state. The cangaceiro became part of the nostalgic folklore of the elite "great families" whose traditions of martial glory could only be maintained in oral narrative and personal memoir.

In seeking the cangaço, members of the rural poor had turned to an individual solution to their plight as a class that, as Anton Blok has suggested in the case of western Sicily, undercut potential for more meaningful change through mass action and revolt.[63] At best, as bandits they achieved upward mobility and relative personal independence from a landlord. They usually gained a better patron, a higher income, a more generous diet, and perhaps even some brief fame but often at the price of a shortened life span. The admiration that their fighting prowess and terrible punishments attracted from the rural poor, however, seemed to be due more to their unremitting war with the state police than to their individual acts of vengeance against particular establishment figures. Banditry in this context did not so much check the excesses of the powerful as it facilitated the settlement of old personal elite scores by broadening the arena of traditional family conflicts to incorporate larger numbers of police and cangaceiros. Superficially, the cangaço appears to be a genuine example of protest. Yet, in developing within an oligarchical structure that limited change precisely by diffusing the potential for meaningful mass dissent within its own patronage relationships, the cangaço exemplified the way protest in general in Brazil was traditionally circumscribed by a political system that was still patrimonial.

In conclusion, those who have idealized the bandit have neglected many of the implications of his behavior for the rural masses he supposedly defended. In this respect the historiography of Brazilian banditry has been heavily influenced by writers of a previous generation, often literati with family connections in the political elite, whose viewpoints were strongly colored by a wistful nostalgia. Others of a more recent generation have romanticized the cangaceiro in their eagerness to interpret him—with justifiable motives—as a contemporary political symbol of national protest. The historical reality was nevertheless quite different. Backlands life was harsh and brutal for those consigned to society's lower orders. Caught between the warring sides of cangaceiros and police, despoiled and threatened by both, the *matuto*, or humble rustic, had few, if any, champions in his world. He eked out a precarious existence in the presence of a "social bandit" who indeed was not even a reliable agent of social justice, much less a liberator. Nevertheless, as a vicarious executor of the unarticulated rage of most of the rural poor, the cangaceiro had popular appeal as an agent of superior violence. The cangaceiro's violence was an admired gesture of psychic affirmation in the absence of either justice or positive change. It is precisely in his vocation of violence that one should explain the popular attraction of the cangaceiro. This is the historical legacy of the cangaceiro, a legacy that continues to be appealing today.

NOTES

I gratefully acknowledge the assistance of a National Defense and Foreign Language (NDFL) Fellowship from Columbia University and a Woodrow Wilson Dissertation Fellowship from 1970 to 1971. Special thanks are due to Dr. Horácio de Almeida and Dr. Maurilio de Almeida for graciously putting their private libraries at my disposal. The Instituto Histórico e Georgráfico Brasileiro, Rio de Janeiro, and the Instituto Histórico e Geográfico Paraibano, João Pessoa, Paraíba, generously allowed me to consult their archives. Billy Jaynes Chandler, Robert M. Levine, Emília Viotti da Costa, and Joseph L. Love offered valuable comments on earlier drafts.

1. A discussion of the cangaceiro in Brazilian cinema and a filmography appear in Alberto Silva, "O cangaceiro, herói do Terceiro Mundo," *Cultura*, 4, 16 (1975): 13–19.

2. Maria Isaura Pereira de Queiroz, *Cangaceiros: Les bandits d'honneur brésiliens* (Paris, 1965), p. 196.

3. Eric J. Hobsbawm, *Bandits* (New York, 1972), pp. 50–53.

4. Ibid., pp. 34–36; Eric J. Hobsbawm, *Primitive Rebels: Studies in Archaic Forms of Social Movement in the 19th and 20th Centuries* (Manchester: Manchester University Press, 1959), ch. 2.

5. Silvino's earliest popularization as a "good" thief was in the literatura de cordel (chap-books "strung up" for display for sale) or popular ballads that circulated widely during his bandit career: Ronald Daus, *Der epische Zyklus der Cangaceiros in der Volkspoesie nordostbrasiliens* (Berlin, 1969), pp. 37–94; Mark J. Curran, *Literatura de cordel* (Recife, 1973), pp. 9–40. Carlos D. Fernandes (pseud. Jaime Aroldo) was the first to depict Silvino as a fictional, romantic hero: Carlos D. Fernandes, *Os cangaceiros: Romance de costumes sertanejos* (Parahyba, 1914), partly serialized earlier in *A União* (Parahyba), 1910, 1913. Other popular biographical accounts appeared in Gustavo Barroso, *Heróes e bandidos: Os cangaceiros do nordeste* (Rio de Janeiro, 1917), pp. 225–278; Gustavo Barroso, *Almas de lama e de aço* (São Paulo, 1930), pp. 75–89; José Lins do Rêgo, *Fogo morto* (Rio de Janeiro, 1943); (Cícero) Rodrigues de Carvalho, *Serrote Preto: Lampião e seus sequazes* (Rio de Janeiro, 1961), pp. 340–377.

6. Hobsbawm, *Primitive Rebels*, pp. 27–29; Hobsbawm, *Bandits*, pp. 84–93.

7. See Maria Isaura Pereira de Queiroz, "Notas sociólogicas sôbre o cangaço," *Ciéncia e Cultura*, 77 (1975): 495–516.

8. The private papers of the Paraíba politicians consulted are deposited in the Arquivo Epitácio Pessoa (hereafter AEP) at the Instituto Histórico e Geográfico Brasileiro, Rio de Janeiro, and the Arquivo Coronel Antônio Pessoa (hereafter ACAP) at the Instituto Histórico e Geográfico Paraibano, João Pessoa (formerly Parahyba), Paraíba.

9. A police officer who pursued Lampião offered the following insight into the reticence of writers to discuss the role of the coiteiro: "Respecting . . . the memory of those who no longer exist . . . I found it agreeable to remain silent regarding their [that

is the coiteiros's] connections and guilt in this matter": Optato Gueiros, *Memórias de um oficial ex-comandante de forças volantes*, 2nd ed. (São Paulo, 1953), p. 151.

10. Today Silvino's reputation in Paraíba is largely maintained through oral tradition, which displays a remarkably close familiarity with the literatura de cordel. See "Memórias de um cangaceiro," *Gente* (Brasília), May, 1975, for the reminiscence of one of Silvino's band.

11. Queiroz, *Cangaceiros*, pp. 35–36; Queiroz, "Notas sociológicas sôbre o cangaço," pp. 496–498.

12. José Américo de Almeida established that almost every prominent bandit operating during the great droughts of 1877–1879 and 1888–1889 was already active at an earlier date: José Américo de Almeida, *A Parahyba e seus problemas* (Parahyba, 1923), pp. 136–170.

13. Rui Facó, *Cangaceiros e fanaticos: Gênese e lutas*, 2nd ed. (Rio de Janeiro, 1965), pp. 87–88.

14. Jesuíno Brilhante (Jesuíno Alves de Melo Calado, fl. 1871–1879) was the subject of an early novel of the cangaceiro genre: Rodolfo Theophilo, *Os Brilhantes: Psychologia de um criminoso: Romance*, 2 vols. (Ceará, 1895). See also Raimundo Nonato, *Jesuíno Brilhante, o cangaceiro romântico, 1844–1879* (Rio de Janeiro, 1970).

15. *Jornal do Recife*, 29 November 1914. Biographical material was drawn from the following sources: Fernandes, *Os cangaceiros*, pp. 100, 107, 113–115; Barroso, *Heróes e bandidos*, pp. 225–278; Barroso, *Almas de lama*, pp. 75–89; Almeida, *A Parahyba*, p. 497; Pedro Baptista, *Cangaceiros do nordeste* (Parahyba, 1929), pp. 37–39, 49–84, 195–197; Queiroz, *Cangaceiros*, p. 45; Mario Souto Maior, *Antônio Silvino, Capitão de Trabuco* (Rio de Janeiro, 1971), pp. 29–34; *Jornal do Recife*, 30 January 1897, 26 November 1898; Abelardo Parreira, *Sertanejos e cangaceiros* (São Paulo, 1934), pp. 22–23. Sources conflict over the ancestry of Silvino's parents because probably they were cousins.

16. *Jornal do Recife*, 26 November 1898. Silvino Aires was the son of Paraíba Provincial Deputy, Col. Ildefonso Aires, an ally of the Dantas who served also as local political boss and police officer in Teixeira, Paraíba, in the 1860s.

17. *A União*, 1 August 1944. Silvino was captured on 28 November 1914 near Santa Maria, Taquaritinga: *Diario de Pernambuco* (Recife), 1 December 1914; *A União*, 4 December 1914; *Correio de Campina* (Campina Grande, Paraíba), 6 December 1944, Supplement; *Diario de Pernambuco*, 1 and 7 December 1914, 16 March 1915; Souto Maior, *op. cit.*, pp. 73–79, 121; Queiroz, *Cangaceiros*, pp. 72–73; Rodrigues de Carvalho, *Serrote Preto*, pp. 369, 377.

18. *A União*, 4 December 1914. Descriptive material is adapted from "João do Norte" (pseud. G. Barroso), *A União*, 5 May 1912. See Estácio de Lima, *O mundo estranho dos cangaceiros* (Salvador, Bahia, 1965), pp. 38–52, for a recent version of the biologically deterministic school of Brazilian banditry, deriving from nineteenth-century European writers like Gustav Le Bon and Cesare Lambroso whose racist explanations of criminal behavior gained wide intellectual acceptance in Brazil.

19. The itinerant balladeers Leandro Gomes de Barros (1868–1918) and Francisco das Chagas Baptista (1882–1930) were the first to popularize Silvino's deeds during his own career, beginning with the latter's *A vida de Antônio Silvino* (Recife, 1904), subsequently revised and augmented in final form as *A história completa do celebre cangaceiro Antônio Silvino* (Rio de Janeiro, 1919). Silvino was reported to have once paid Leandro de Barros a handsome two contos for his remaining stock of ballads: *O Estado de São Paulo*, 2

December 1914. Original chap-books are reprinted in the Casa de Rui Barbosa's series, *Literatura popular em verso: antologia*, 2 (Leandro Gomes de Barros) (Rio de Janeiro, 1976); 3, *Leandro Gomes de Barros* (Rio de Janeiro, 1977); 4, *Francisco das Chagas Baptista* (Rio de Janeiro, 1977). See also Daus's stimulating interpretation of the development of Silvino's career in popular poetry in his *Der Epische Zyklus der Cangaceiros*.

20. *A União*, 7 April 1910.

21. See Linda Lewin, "Politics and *Parentela* in Paraíba: A Case Study of Oligarchy in Brazil's Old Republic, 1889–1930" (Ph.D. diss., Columbia University, 1975); Linda Lewin, "Some Historical Implications of Kinship Organization for Family-Based Politics in the Brazilian Northeast," *Comparative Studies in Society and History*, 21 (1979): 262–292; Billy Jaynes Chandler, *The Feitosas and the Sertão dos Inhamuns* (Gainesville: University of Florida Press, 1972).

22. Estado da Parahyba do Norte, *Collecção dos actos da Parahyba para o anno de 1906* (and *1907, 1908, 1910, 1915–16*), 5 vols. (Parahyba, 1911–1917); Estado da Parahyba do Norte, *Almanach do Estado da Parahyba para o anno de 1900* (Parahyba, 1900). On police brutality, see Almeida, *A Parahyba*, pp. 143–145.

23. *Diario de Pernambuco*, 25 August 1906, 21 December 1914; *A União*, 2 April 1913, 6 December 1914.

24. *O Commercio* (Parahyba), 4, 5, 15, and 23 August 1900; *A Provincia* (Recife), 20 October 1900.

25. Epitácio Pessoa to Colonel Antônio Pessoa, Rio de Janeiro, 25 December 1904, 5 March 1906, 8 February 1907: ACAP/1; affidavit of Rio Preto, *Diario de Pernambuco*, 29 March 1906; anon. denunciation to Colonel Antônio Pessoa, 5 November 1906: ACAP/2.

26. Epitácio Pessoa to Colonel Antônio Pessoa, Rio de Janeiro, 8 February and 9 March 1903: ACAP/1. Epitácio served as Minister of Justice and Education, 1898–1902; as Attorney General and Supreme Court Justice, 1902–1905; as Chief Justice, 1905–1911; as senator from Paraíba, 1912–1919. From 1919 to 1922 he was president of Brazil.

27. Epitácio Pessoa to Colonel Antônio Pessoa, Rio de Janeiro, 11 February 1903: ACAP/1. See also Epitácio Pessoa to Colonel Antônio Pessoa, 6 January 1905, 4 December 1909; ACAP/1; Epitácio Pessoa to João Pessoa Cavalcanti e Albuquerque, Petrópolis, 13 March 1909, in Epitácio Pessoa, *Obras completas*, 28 vols. (Rio de Janeiro, 1955–1965), 20, *Miscellânea*, pp. 5–7.

28. Epitácio Pessoa to Colonel Antônio Pessoa, Rio de Janeiro, 1 August 1904, 16 January 1905: ACAP/1.

29. Letter of Mariano Rodrigues Laureano to the editor of *A Provincia*, 6 April 1906: repr. in *A União*, 12 April 1906.

30. Anon. to *A Provincia*, 7 and 11 February 1904; *Allegações apresentadas pelo Belarmino Antônio Vicente de Andrade, Advogado de Dona Maria Correia de Queiroz no processo criminal instaurado contra os assassinos de seu marido Capitão Porfirio Alysio Pereira de Queiroz* (Nazaré, Pernambuco, 1904).

31. Letter of Mariano Rodrigues Laureano to the editor of *A Provincia*, 6 April 1906: repr. in *A União*, 12 April 1906 (italics in the original).

32. Ibid.

33. *Diario de Pernambuco*, 26 November 1905.

34. *O Município* (Itabaiana, Paraíba), 3 March 1904; Barroso, *Heróes e bandidos*, p. 278. At his capture Silvino was carrying a large amount of counterfeit money: *Diario de Pernambuco*, 3 December 1914.

35. Anon. letter of denunciation, *A Provincia*, 3 March 1904; *O Município*, 2 February 1908; Barroso, *Heróes e bandidos*, p. 237; intelligence reports of Silvino's movements near Umbuseiro: ACAP/1, 2.

36. Anon. denunciation to Colonel Antônio Pessoa, (1906?): ACAP/2/201; Ildefonso Guedes to Amigo Antônio Pessoa, Rio de Janeiro, 16 March 1907: ACAP/2/104; *A Rasão* (Campina Grande, Paraíba), March 1908: ACAP/2/205; public statement of Antônio Silvino at the house of Augusto Rezende, *O Município*, 28 June 1908; *Diario de Pernambuco*, 9 June 1908; Barroso, *Heróes e bandidos*, p. 253; Queiroz, *Cangaceiros*, p. 69.

37. Epitácio Pessoa to Colonel Antônio Pessoa, Rio de Janeiro, 5 and 22 July 1907: ACAP/1. Epitácio personally intervened with Marshal Hermes da Fonseca, Minister of War and an old family friend, to send more troops: Epitácio Pessoa to Colonel Antônio Pessoa, Rio de Janeiro, 14 June 1907: ACAP/1. Gubernatorial message of Valfredo Leal, 22 November 1908: *Almanach do Estado da Parahyba do ano de 1909* (Parahyba, 1909), p. 218; Antonio Xavier de Oliveira, *O exército e o sertão* (Rio de Janeiro, 1932), p. 122.

38. *Diario de Pernambuco*, 31 December 1908; José Fabio de Costa Lira to Antônio Pessoa, Umbuseiro, 24 February 1907: ACAP/2/88.

39. *Diario de Pernambuco*, 1 March 1907; Rodrigues de Carvalho, *Serrote Preto*, pp. 376–377; Souto Maior, *Antônio Silvino, Capitão de Trabuco*, pp. 65–66.

40. Barroso, *Almas de lama*, p. 250; Rodrigues de Carvalho, *Serrote Preto*, pp. 360–367.

41. Dr. Antônio da Silva Mariz to Epitácio Pessoa, Sousa, Paraíba, 20 June 1912: AEP/10/186. Former Federal Deputy Mariz identified four municípios in Paraíba and Rio Grande do Norte where Silvino bought protection.

42. Anon. to Colonel Antônio Pessoa (1912): ACAP/2.

43. Dr. Antônio da Silva Mariz to Epitácio Pessoa, Sousa, Paraíba, 20 June 1912: AEP/10/186.

44. João Castro Pinto to Epitácio Pessoa, Parahyba, 28 July 1912: AEP/10/198.

45. *A União*, 30 April 1913.

46. The *literatura de cordel* identifies many of Silvino's victims.

47. Barroso, *Heróes e bandidos*, p. 24; *A União*, 5 May 1912; *Diario de Pernambuco*, 2 and 5 March 1907; Francisco das Chagas Baptista, *A história de Antônio Silvino* (Recife, 1907), pp. 34, 36. Agricultural wages in Paraíba for 1912 averaged around twenty-five *mil-réis* per month. (One *conto* equalled 1,000 *mil-réis* and the equivalent 1910 value of one *mil-réis* was thirty-two U.S. cents.)

48. Almeida, *A Parahyba*, p. 175; anon. to Colonel Antônio Pessoa, Umbuseiro (?), 1906: ACAP/2/202; Barroso, *Heróes e bandidos*, p. 239; affidavit of Ana Maria da Conceição (*amásia* of Rio Preto), *Diario de Pernambuco*, 6 and 10 April 1906; affidavit of Rio Preto, *Diario de Pernambuco*, 29 March 1906.

49. While burning mailbags before an assembled crowd Silvino declared: "I do this because I need money to confront the campaign the government makes against me" (*Diario de Pernambuco*, 17 February 1906). After robbing a Great Western Railway station he stated: "See the money that the English have here? The English don't need money!" (ibid., 29 February 1908). Others ascribed Silvino's feud with the Great Western to the company's failure to grant compensation to his family for access rights across its properties in the interior of Paraíba: Chagas Baptista, *A história de Antônio Silvino*, pp. 27–28.

50. *Jornal do Recife*, 1 April 1898; *O Commercio*, 8 February 1901; *Diario de Pernambuco*, 15 May 1906, 12 December 1914; *O Município*, 28 June 1908; Chagas Baptista, *A história de Antônio Silvino*, p. 8; Barroso, *Heróes e bandidos*, p. 232.

51. These generalizations about bandit leaders are based on information collected about nearly a dozen major brigands operating in Paraíba from the 1860s to 1930. A similar prosopography was constructed for the rank and file of Silvino's band.

52. See Amaury de Souza, "The *Cangaço*," in Ronald Chilcote, ed., *Protest and Resistance in Angola and Brazil: Comparative Studies* (Berkeley: University of California Press, 1972), pp. 109–132.

53. Silvino first operated as a bandit under his own name, "Né" Batista, and was part of the group briefly led by Luiz Mansidão of Geritacó, Pernambuco in 1898: Ulysses Lins de Albuquerque, *Moxotó brabo* (Rio de Janeiro, 1960), pp. 94–96. Leadership of Mansidão's band, originally led by Silvino Aires, passed to Antônio Silvino early in 1899 and included his cousins Antão Godé (Antão Clemente Gadêlha) and Pilão Deitado (name unknown), his brother Zéferino Batista de Morais (known as Vicente Silvino in Missão Velha, Ceará, where he lived), and probably Cocada and Relâmpago (name unknown): *A União*, 1 December 1914; Rodrigues de Carvalho, *Serrote Preto*, p. 354; Xavier de Oliveira, *O exército e o sertão*, p. 127; Fernandes, *Os cangaceiros*, pp. 100, 107.

54. Affidavit of Rio Preto, *Diaro de Pernambuco*, 29 March 1906.

55. *Diario de Pernambuco*, 7 January 1915.

56. Silvino interceded with Colonel Belém of Crato, Ceará, in order to assist three of his band in rejoining legitimate society as members of the Ceará State Police: *A União*, 17 April 1910; see also *Diario de Pernambuco*, 7 January 1915.

57. José Lins do Rêgo, *Meus verdes anos* (Rio de Janeiro, 1956), p. 275; anon. informant to the author, July 1975. Two of Silvino's daughters were educated in a good school in Recife while he was active as a bandit: Parreira, *Sertanejos e cangaceiros*, p. 23.

58. Luis da Camara Cascudo, in Souto Maior, *Antônio Silvino, Capitão de Trabuco*, p. 13; *O Município*, 28 June 1908; *Diario de Pernambuco*, 18 December 1914.

59. Dr. Antônio da Silva Mariz to Epitácio Pessoa, Sousa, Paraíba, 20 June 1912: AEP/10/186; Queiroz, *Os cangaceiros*, p. 69; Barroso, *Heróes e bandidos*, pp. 242, 248–249, 253; *Diario de Pernambuco*, 18 January and 24 February 1907.

60. On peasant revolts, see Roderick J. Barman, "The Brazilian Peasantry Re-Examined: The Implications of the Quebra-Quilo Revolt, 1874–1875," *Hispanic American Historical Review*, 57 (1977): 401–424; Euclides da Cunha, *Rebellion in the Backlands*, trans. Samuel Putnam (Chicago, 1944); Duglas Teixeira Monteiro, *Os errantes do novo século* (São Paulo, 1974).

61. See Eul-Soo Pang, "The Changing Roles of Priests in the Backlands of Northeast Brazil, 1889–1964," *The Americas*, 30 (1974): 341–372; Ralph Della Cava, *Miracle at Joaseiro* (New York: Columbia University Press, 1970).

62. I am grateful to Billy Jaynes Chandler for this observation on Pernambuco; see his *The Bandit King: Lampião of Brazil* (College Station: Texas A&M Press, 1978); Eul-Soo Pang, "The Revolt of the Bahian *Coronéis* and the Federal Intervention of 1920," *Luso-Brazilian Review*, 8, (1971): 3–25.

63. Anton Blok, "The Peasant and the Brigand: Social Banditry Reconsidered," *Comparative Studies in Society and History*, 14, 4 (Sept. 1972): 494–503; Anton Blok, *The Mafia of a Sicilian Village, 1860–1960: A Study of Violent Peasant Entrepreneurs* (Oxford, 1974), pp. 94–102.

6

Brazilian *Cangaceiros* as Social Bandits: A Critical Appraisal

BILLY JAYNES CHANDLER

SOCIAL BANDITS

The *cangaço* (banditry in the Brazilian backlands) has fascinated not only Brazilian scholars, but some foreign ones as well. Most prominent among the latter is British Marxist social historian Eric Hobsbawm, who has used the *cangaceiros* to help illustrate his concept of a special form of banditry that he calls "social banditry." In this essay I shall scrutinize Hobsbawm's model of the social bandit, point to weaknesses in the concept, and suggest an alternative view. I shall emphasize the time of Lampião (Virgolino Ferreira da Silva), 1922–1938, the period about which the most is known.

THE *CANGACEIROS*

Among nations of the Western world, Brazil occupies a noteworthy place in the history of traditional rural banditry. This reputation rests mostly on a seventy-year period from 1870 to 1940, the time when cangaceiros attained their greatest notoriety. The cangaceiros were bandits in the northeastern backlands, the *sertão*, who lived from robbery and looting, abductions for ransom, and extortion. Although most of them have long since been forgotten, a few were turned into legendary figures of regional and even national significance, a development made possible by improvements in communications that in the twentieth century linked the backlands to the outside world. By the third and fourth decades of this century, Rio de Janeiro newspapers were sending reporters to the far corners of the region to interview bandit leaders and cover police campaigns to eliminate them.

The reporters found much of interest, for many of the bandit chieftains were colorful characters, as were some of their followers. A number of the cangaceiro leaders, to be sure, came along too early to gain wide attention, and they performed their heroic and often fascinatingly bloody deeds in relative obscurity. Men such as Jesuino Brilhante of the 1870s, turn-of-the-century bandit Antônio Silvino, and Sebastião Pereira of the late 'teens played mostly on a local and regional stage.[1] But such could not be said of the last and most notorious of the northeastern desperados, "Lampião" (The Lamp), who became a legend of national prominence in his own time.[2]

That Lampião should have achieved fame is not surprising, since his story, with no need for embellishment, fits the traditional bandit legend so well.[3] Born in 1898 to respectable folk in the backlands state of Pernambuco, he became a bandit, he affirmed, because the police murdered his father. His first infamous deed was a raid in 1922 on the home of the aged widow of a nobleman of imperial days because, he said, of ties between her family and the authorities. In the mid-twenties the already well-known bandit almost made the leap to respectability when he was temporarily commissioned a captain by federal authorities seeking to combat the "Tenentes," the marauding rebel army led by Luis Carlos Prestes.

Denied the rewards and legitimacy that he had hoped for, Lampião quickly grew disillusioned by the experience and reverted to form. He organized a bandit army of his own that sometimes numbered as many as 100 men and met state mobile contingents sent to combat him on more than equal terms. Then his fortunes declined as Pernambuco officials strengthened their resolve to fight him. Down and almost out, he slipped across the São Francisco River into Bahia in 1928. He rebuilt a bandit empire, again defeating numerically superior but inept state forces who, like many other unsophisticated backlanders, came to see his uncanny cunning as superhuman.

For that matter, some important people fell under his influence too. Lampião, during the 1930s, dealt with political bosses as peers and even became friendly with a federal army officer then serving as governor of the state of Sergipe. And during the same decade he enhanced his image by taking a woman, the vivacious "Maria Bonita" (Pretty Mary), who deserted her village cobbler husband for the noted bandolero. She died by Lampião's side, machine-gunned down, as was he, in a remote mountain creek at Angicos in July of 1938. Appropriately, their deaths came as the result of betrayal by a trusted protector. True to the bandit myth, a man as cunning as Lampião could only be subdued through treachery. Newspapers splashed stories of their passing on front pages all over Brazil, although many backlanders, believing the infamous bandit leader to be perversely invincible, refused to accept them. From afar, even the staid *New York Times* noticed Lampião's death.[4]

But the cangaceiros were not just creations of the press. The cangaço (way of life of the cangaceiros) was a phenomenon in its own right. The term cangaceiro had apparently been used for a long time, denoting a gunman for hire or on his own, but became commonly used only during the late nineteenth century. By then it meant a member of a group of bandits who operated on their own, although occasionally they might hire out or do favors for someone else.[5]

The cangaço had a kind of internal unity in that, as time passed, its members increasingly identified themselves, not as common bandits, but as cangaceiros. Cangaceiros differed from ordinary bandits in that they dressed distinctively and allegedly shared similar reasons for falling outside the law. In their own minds cangaceiros stood apart from and above petty thieves and common criminals.

A properly dressed cangaceiro required at least two things. He wore an ammunition belt over his shoulder and crossing his chest. Two were preferred, not just for the additional firepower they afforded, but also for the striking appearance created by their intersection. But the main trademark of the cangaceiro was his hat, a modified, enlarged version of the traditional leather head covering of the northeastern cowboy, or *vaqueiro*. The wide brim was usually turned up in front and often decorated with elaborate stitching and insets of precious stones, gold and silver coins, and whatever else struck the bandit's fancy. Brilliantine on the hair, generous dousings of perfume, and numerous rings on the fingers rounded off the requirements. (These affectations were also the trademark of the ruthless French army captain Berthelin, part of the occupying force in Mexico during the 1860s.) They made quite a fancy picture—cangaceiros almost universally loved to be photographed—and it is no wonder that young village toughs throughout the northeast began to affect their styles. Drawn by these dashing figures, Maria Bonita and other young women forsook ranch and village life to join the cangaceiros as consorts.

Cangaceiros also increasingly adopted the argument that they were victims of injustice, that they had been mistreated by the authorities or oppressed by the powerful. Authorities did brutalize many persons. But for those who became cangaceiros, the claim of unjust treatment served mainly as a pretext to justify their criminal careers. In any case, their claims struck responsive chords in popular fancy, especially among those who knew the bandits only from the romanticized version of storytellers and big-city reporters. Few of those who knew the bandits firsthand shared those views.

In Hobsbawm's thesis, set forth in *Primitive Rebels* and *Bandits*,[6] a social bandit is a peasant who shares the moral values of the peasant community. He becomes an outlaw in defense of those values; he is a victim of injustice. He does not prey on other peasants. Rather, he maintains their trust and support, and their enemies are his enemies. Moreover, the true noble robber—the epitome of the social bandit—rights wrongs, redistributes wealth, and never kills unjustly. Social banditry is, in sum, social protest, although usually of an unconscious, pre-political nature.

Immediately a question arises. Is Hobsbawm talking about bandits in the flesh or the legends about them? He and many of his defenders argue that facts are less significant here than legends, but a reading of his works suggests that he is not making a case primarily for legend; rather, he really believes in his social bandits.[7] He does recognize, however, that his data in support of them are "rather tricky.''[8] The main problem is that he fails to find noble robbers in significant numbers and, in compensation, sprinkles his work liberally with ignoble robbers of all kinds. In his defense, Hobsbawm adds numerous qualifications to his thesis, and the second edition of *Bandits* refines the ideas still more.[9] Ultimately, however, the concept of the social bandit is valid or invalid. Social bandits either exist in history in sufficient quantities to constitute a significant pattern in human behavior, or they are so few as to be only colorful, interesting aberrations.

It need not be argued that Hobsbawm is totally wrong. His work is provocative, and the force of many of his ideas has an almost irresistible appeal. Bandits, especially when they lived long ago and, more crucially, far away, strike our fancy. His thesis has some validity, no doubt, even if peripherally. But it does not correctly interpret the Brazilian cangaço.

Hobsbawm does make a distinction between "noble robbers"—the genuine social bandits—and the class in which he placed the cangaceiros. These latter, he says, were "avengers" whose violence was so excessive that they were almost indistinguishable from common criminals. In general, he seems to think that while the cangaceiros were more the second than the first, they had characteristics of both. Nevertheless, he argues that they were social bandits and that their careers represented protests against social injustice.[10]

Hobsbawm does not probe deeply into cangaceiro history, nor does he probe deeply into any of the episodes of banditry that he uses as illustrations. Consequently, his ideas on banditry cannot be judged adequately by the data offered. The best way to evaluate the thesis is to test his model against specific episodes of banditry, such as those of the cangaço.

First, on peasant origins. No major cangaceiro chieftain was a peasant. Brilhante, Silvino, and Pereira were all "gentlemen" who came from quite substantial families, landed and prestigious. Lampião was of humbler origins but not a peasant. His father owned land and cattle, although not in abundance, and a mule team with which he transported goods over a large interstate area of the backlands. The Ferreiras identified with landed families, not peasants.

Second, on the origins of the fall of the cangaceiro chieftains into banditry. All of them were involved in bloody feuds between families or clans. Brilhante sought to avenge the death of his nephew, a *delegado* (county police chief), killed while rounding up recruits for the Paraguayan War. The delegado died calling for revenge, and Brilhante soon sent word to the rival family judged responsible for his nephew's death that he was going to exact revenge. In this way the feud started. Silvino became a cangaceiro futilely seeking to avenge the death of his father, a valiant man who had been much feared by his enemies. Pereira turned cangaceiro in 1916, after an older brother had been killed by the rival Carvalho family, this just one act in a lengthy chain of retaliatory acts involving both sides. Reportedly, it was Pereira's mother who urged him to avenge his brother's death. Lampião's case is similar to the others. A dispute with a neighboring rancher led to feuding, and finally, Lampião's family, the Ferreiras, was persuaded by local officials to move to the neighboring state of

Alagoas in an attempt to defuse the escalating conflict. But once there, the Ferreira boys would not let well enough alone and returned to raid their enemies. Thus before the police attack that resulted in the death of his father in 1922—the alleged reason for entering the cangaço—Lampião was already a cangaceiro.[11]

Assigning responsibility in these cases is not easy. Support for Hobsbawm's claim that social bandits are motivated by acts of injustice is not readily apparent. In Lampião's case, blame accumulated on both sides as valiant or foolhardly members of each side went out of their way to wreak havoc on the other. If the Ferreira brothers had been more prudent and less foolhardy, the tragedy of their father's death and their seemingly irrevocable leap into outlawry might not have occurred. Backlands family feuding, not class conflict, seems much more in evidence as motivation.

If cangacciro chieftains were not Hobsbawm's social bandits, what about their followers? Less is known of most of them, but enough is known to state that they became bandits for a variety of reasons, some of which fit Hobsbawm's characterization while others do not. Some shared the problems of the chiefs in that they tried to escape enemies or persecute them, in turn. Others joined gangs because of vigorous police persecution of those suspected of cooperating with outlaws. It is not clear, however, that these oft-cited reasons produced the majority of cangaceiros. A good many—petty criminals and army deserters, for instance—had the law after them already or had become estranged from their families because of their own reprehensible conduct. One of Lampião's men had seduced his own sister and was afraid his father would kill him. Another feared for his safety because he was a rival for the affections of his father's girlfriend. Many joined the cangaço because it offered a life free from ordinary toil, or money in abundance, or adventure, or even the excitement of danger. For others, an opportunity having presented itself, and having no particular fondness for the life they already had, they just went along.[12] In the latter case the dearth of economic opportunity in the sertão, not oppression per se, served as the stimulus.

It may also have been that the cangaço became virtually self-sustaining because in time, its notoriety attracted enough recruits to keep it alive. Many men may have enlisted mainly because they saw others living from crime and getting away with it and decided to try it for themselves. That they should have done so is not surprising, for there is ample reason to believe that a sizable group of potential outlaws may be found in virtually any society. It is equally obvious that when social controls are relaxed—as they were in the Brazil of the cangaço—the likelihood that potential outlaws would turn to crime is increased.

Hobsbawm asserts that social bandits did not prey on other peasants and sometimes even shared their loot with them. This assertion stems from Hobsbawm's penchant for establishing the confrontation of peasants united against the state and the landed elite. It is true that cangaceiros did not normally rob peasants. But then peasants had little of value to be taken. As to killing, cangaceiros killed in the main to terrorize people into submission, and whether their victims were peasants or landlords was incidental.[13]

Some of the cangaceiros gave somebody something now and then—they seldom lacked money. Lampião sometimes distributed goods plundered from merchants, even forcing unwilling people to accept them. He also threw coins in
the street for boys to scramble after.[14] But class identity with peasants? He never
identified with them; indeed, much of his rage lay in believing that he had been
denied the chance to become a prosperous rancher.[15]

To this point we have been dealing with individual bandits. It is true, nevertheless, that social phenomena may be collectively significant in a way that
individual parts are not. Hobsbawm has addressed this matter by arguing that
his social bandits were "primitive rebels," that their actions constituted unconscious, pre-political protest, forerunners, he says, of peasant leagues and socialist
movements.[16] Bandits, in this depiction, pass beyond the perverse and com-
monplace to central positions in the play of social forces. They do not arise
primarily from inherent human failings nor merely because social controls fail.
Instead, they are embodiments of social protest.

If this contention is to be sustained, one is burdened to offer some proof of
more or less direct links between bandits and social protest. There is little
evidence in the history of the cangaço that points to such links. Under other
circumstances such links could have existed, for just as there is no special affinity
between banditry and social protest, neither are there insurmountable barriers.
Pancho Villa, of revolutionary Mexico, to mention but one, bridged the gap. In
Lampião's case the possibility of his joining the forces of social protest was
broached on one occasion. Luis Carlos Prestes' insurgent column passed through
the Northeast early in 1926 on its long trek through the Brazilian backlands, and
it was suggested to Prestes that he invite the cangaceiro chieftain to join. The
future communist boss rejected the idea, and Lampião lost his closest chance of
becoming a revolutionary. His story would have been immensely more valuable
to Hobsbawm had the union taken place. Instead, the bandit king was briefly
enrolled by frantic government agents in the fight against Prestes. The main
point is that bandits are not automatically prohibited from playing significant
roles in society during those times when issues are decided by force. When
traditional controls crumble, bandits may exercise dominance merely because
they may be courageous men who have force at their command. What they then
become—revolutionaries, ordinary *caudillos*, power and property usurpers in
their own right, or whatever—depends on the circumstances of the moment.[17]

Hobsbawm, of course, does not in the main portray his social bandits as
conscious revolutionaries. To the contrary, he recognizes that few fit into that
category. He argues that most social bandits just tried to hold society to the
traditional rules of justice.[18] The defense of bandits as revolutionaries rests,
instead, on what he believes to have been their unconscious motivation. This
notion could perhaps be strengthened if it could be shown that a given outbreak
of banditry was of sufficient scope and intensity to qualify as a general rebellion
against the established order. This is the usual view of the cangaço, but it is
only partly true.[19]

The cangaço was made up of episodes, and those that lasted for significant lengths of time were led by one or another uncommonly capable bandit leader and were generally confined to limited areas. Brilhante, during his short career of the 1870s, operated in the Rio Grande do Norte-Paraíba border area. Silvino's years of brigandage, from 1897 to 1914, stretched over four states, but his base was a portion of the Paraíba-Pernambuco border region. Pereira's outlaw career, 1916 to 1922, was centered in a small area of Pernambuco and Paraíba. Lampião pillaged, robbed, killed, kidnapped, and worked the protection racket in six or seven states for seventeen years, but only limited areas ever suffered much at his hands. Of course, these four cangaceiro chieftains were not the only ones plying the trade in those years. But even in the worst of times, vast regions went untouched by unusual bandit activity, and many of the areas that suffered did so only because of invasions from the outside. Everywhere that it existed, banditry can most accurately be characterized as the actions of a few individuals. Nowhere was it a broad-based criminal subculture that had the participation and support of entire communities.[20] As in the Argentine case, banditry flourished in more sparsely populated frontier regions, not in areas of heavy peasant population.

Just how important the cangaço is to northeastern Brazilian history is an arguable point. It was surely not without social significance. But most of the shortcomings in Hobsbawm's analysis are related to his aims in writing about bandits. He was not, it appears, much interested in the field for its own sake, in the actual lives of bandits, in the complexities that plague historians and frequently render broad generalizations problematic. His purpose, it seems, was to help establish a history of revolutionary activity. Leftist intellectuals in the mid-twentieth century, losing faith in Marx's industrial workers as vehicles of revolution, began searching for a broader tradition. Hobsbawm contributed bandits, but they did not fit well. They did not realize that they were social rebels; they sought no basic changes in the structures of their societies. Hobsbawm recognized this, but since they practiced violence against property and lives, they were, in his view, making a political, or rather a "pre-political," statement. This conclusion did not proceed so much from a sound factual base as from fitting skimpy and often questionable data into a preconceived framework. Whatever merits the social bandit concept may have—and there may be some bandit episodes to which it is applicable—it does not contribute much to an understanding of Brazilian cangaceiros. On the contrary, its application to them appears to obscure considerably more than it enlightens.

THE LEGENDS

Before turning to the cangaço, as revealed in archival sources, it should be noted again that Hobsbawm built his case for the social significance of banditry not only on what he knew about bandits themselves, but also on his belief that peasants admire them and revel in heroic tales told about them. Central to this is the contention that peasants conceive of bandits as symbols of opposition to oppressive social, political, and economic domination. There may be some validity here, at least in the case of a true peasant bandit. Peasants may take satisfaction in seeing him rob, terrorize, and kill wealthy and powerful persons whom they dislike and envy, provided, of course, that he does not treat them similarly. But it should not be assumed that this rare, if classic, bandit is of much relevance to the cangaço.

In actuality, humble people of the backlands, such as *moradores* (tenants) and landless villagers, related to Lampião and his men in various ways. Some of them served him out of fear or because he paid well. Others ran afoul of him and were tortured and killed. Many were awed by him. His presence was commanding, and the stories told about him were compelling. Some few came to know him well and like him. He was not, after all, totally brutalized or even normally an unpleasant person. A man who as a young teenager visited his camp several times remembers fondly that the famed desperado called him "son" and often shared his food with him at mealtime. A poor woman fleeing from a drought, to whose sons the bandit had given coins, informed the press that "Mr. Lampião is not as bad as people say."[21] But even so, there is scant reason to believe that humble people identified with him. He was not one of them. His main relations, like those of powerful Mexican bandits, were not with them, but with ranchers, merchants, and political bosses.

The significance of Lampião and other bandits as legendary figures of popular interest is not easily dissected and explained. Storytelling, before the media explosion of recent decades, was a popular pastime, and inventors of stories sought the ingredients for them beyond the mundane happenings of ordinary life. Tales of lurid crimes, of the kind that seems to fascinate many people, were obvious choices. As such stories passed on for a generation or two or three, the commonly sordid figures of criminals sometimes turned into noble and heroic ones. Maybe, as Hobsbawm has contended, class elements were involved in these transformations. Common themes of popular stories do tell of how the unschooled outsmart the schooled, the "fool" makes a fool of the wise, the weak overcome the powerful, and so on. The much-told tale of the tortoise and the hare that still enchants children follows these themes, and such stories are basically entertaining. They also are more satisfying if the underdog is a lovable figure or at least has some admirable qualities. It may thus have been the desire to weave an appealing tale that caused popular storytellers to redraw the figure of the bandit.

It is also true that people historically have disliked authority. Such a point of view becomes even more understandable in societies where legal power is wielded in grossly capricious ways. Thus the popularity of stories of humble men twisting the tails of authority is not surprising. There are also within us bits of envy of the more powerful, the wealthier, or the more fortunate. And we enjoy stories of how the less favored among us profit at the expense of those more favored.

While recognizing that class elements may play a role in the popularity of bandit tales, I prefer to interpret the matter more broadly. There is little reason to believe that the stories are more appealing to peasants than to villagers, town tradesmen, landowners, or even city dwellers. Indeed, their appeal appears to be almost universal. The appeal is, after all, on a basic level, as is evinced by the fact that the essential ingredients in classic bandit tales are strikingly similar to those encountered in children's literature; yet children often have a remarkable lack of class consciousness. Maybe one of the main appeals lies in the classic bandit's representation of the "superman" that virtually every male at one time or another in his life yearns to become.[22] Such a conjecture, in any case, makes about as much sense as any other. In short, the roots of such stories are many, varied, and too widely diffused and illusive to be narrowly tied to one economic class. A special, exclusive relationship between bandit legends and peasant opposition to excessive oppression is not a self-evident proposition.

Nor is there much reason to believe that bandit tales are mainly, or even significantly, of peasant origin. Many come from more affluent people: middle-class writers, for example, who recognize the broad appeal and salability of such stories. Facile with pen and sometimes with a knack for verse, Brazilians have produced hundreds of thousands of words on Lampião and disseminated them throughout the nation by newspapers, magazines, booklets, and books.[23] Even today, not only does an average of a book or two appear on him each year, but also cheap little booklets, written in verse, that celebrate his exploits are still sold by peddlers on market day, just as they have been since the early years of his career.[24]

Understandably, the image of Lampião that comes through much of this popular literature is one that history would scarcely recognize. Many of the bandit's evil deeds are there, to be sure, for they, too, have their appeal. One also finds extravagant examples of his uprightness, generosity, and religious faith, including the view that he and the popular saint Padre Cícero were virtually blood brothers. There are also gross exaggerations, where none are needed, of his ability to outwit the police. The point is that the public image of Lampião has been created more from what has been written about him than from what he actually did. The transformation of criminals into heroes, thus, may not be as fraught with meaning as we might believe. Much of it reflects only the eagerness of storytellers to feed the popular hunger for vicarious thrills.

THE REAL WORLD OF THE CANGACEIROS

If the social bandit concept does not correctly interpret the cangaço, what, then, can be said about the significance of cangaceiros? Problems always accompany historical interpretation, and there are plenty of them here. Even the basic assumption, made by most historians and social scientists, that we can adequately explain human events by elaborating the particular societal conditions of their setting, is only partially valid. There seem to be some constants in human social behavior, and banditry and other similar forms of criminality have been so common as to appear to be among them. History is also full of apparent accidents and irrational acts; much of human action is simply mindlessly imitative. We might keep these things in mind before we explain historical events according to elaborately contrived and sometimes romantically based theories or before we regroup data to fit ideological commitments. The traditional wisdom, often the perceptions of those who worked within the limitations and exigencies of the moment, should be given a hearing before we leap to judgment.

One problem that we should seek to understand is why so few men become outlaws while others, in overwhelming numbers, subjected to the same or similar pressures, react in ways that are within the rules of civilized society. One thing is clear about the cangaceiros: they took roads at critical junctions in their lives that led to criminal careers, while others, undergoing similar difficulties, did not. Any theory that emphasizes general conditions to the exclusion of personal responsibility is, at the least, incomplete. This points to the need for studies of bandits that do more than skim the surface. Whatever answers are to be found lie at the point where individual temperaments interact with specific historical situations and events. We may understand at least as much about bandits by studying them carefully at close range as by concentrating on the general conditions of their societies, although neither approach excludes the other.

With these caveats, what, then, can be said about the cangaço's broader social significance? What produced the cangaço, sustained it, and brought it to an end?

On the first point—what produced it?—the answers are not readily found, but most writers on the subject point to a combination of crises in the backlands.[25] The drought of 1877–1879, as well as subsequent ones, produced such severe dislocations that the region did not settle down for many years, it is often argued.[26] Concurrent with this rootlessness, and perhaps feeding on it, were two more outbreaks of religious fanaticism: Antonio Counselheiro's Canudos and Padre Cícero's Juazeiro.[27] The first was short lived, but the latter played a major role in the rise of the Cariri region of Ceará. The area became the backlands' most populous, with people newly arrived and little subject to the controls that formerly had held them in check. The Cariri was, in any event, fertile soil for the recruitment of cangaceiros.[28]

Bad economic conditions also are said to have produced the cangaço. But while the economy of the Northeast was chronically depressed, it had its ups and downs. Cotton production was increasing in Paraíba. Commercial activity was on the increase at times in most parts of the backlands. The penetration of railroads into the interior of Ceará, for example, valorized agricultural products by making it possible to get them to markets. Sugar production rose and fell in Pernambuco, and so on.[29] In their totality these developments helped some people and hurt others. Yet what effects any of the foregoing had in the making of cangaceiros is hard to determine, for it is difficult to link directly their stories with economic change or even temporary disasters.[30]

It has been suggested that more commercial activity stimulated banditry by making more money and goods available to plunder, and such would appear to be a reasonable assumption.[31] The problem is that the histories of bandit chiefs like Brilhante, Silvino, Lampião, and others—those noted figures on whose backs the cangaço rested and whose reputations pulled so many others into it—do not support the contention. Their fall into outlawry had other roots.

On a broader scale Hobsbawm, as well as some of his followers, have attempted to link the cangaceiros to crises occasioned by the early stages of an aggressive and expanding capitalism that adversely affected the peasantry.[32] One noted Brazilian social historian has followed a similar thread in suggesting ties between Lampião's career and the problems of the Amazon basin rubber industry.[33] In fact, there is nothing in Lampião's story as recorded that suggests a tenable connection between his becoming a bandit and the misfortunes of the rubber industry or, for that matter, any other industry.

Did economic conditions have no part in the formation of cangaceiros? The answer would seem to be a qualified one. It is likely that had other attractive job opportunities been available to the region's adventuresome young men of that era, fewer would have become bandits. In that sense economic, as well as social and political, conditions helped to shape the particular forms that criminality took and influenced the incidence of it. It is not instructive to argue, however, that in a different situation, the cangaço would not have occurred; not, that is, if events are to be explained within their own historical context. If this is the case, it becomes apparent that allegedly worsening economic conditions were not the critical element.

Can one connect the origins of the cangaceiros to anything more than human perversity or random happenings involving individuals? Traditional wisdom suggests two possibilities. The first is the persistence of private vengeance because of the weakness of the public institutions of justice and the frequent use of force to serve private aims.[34] Close family ties also fostered violence, since loyalty to one's own meant more than subservience to the public good. Moreover, it seems that a complex of factors—including rugged individualism, an exaggerated sense of personal honor, and an extreme concept of manliness—dictated that a man did not leave justice to the state, but rather enforced it on his own. Clearly, these sociocultural conditions and the origins of the criminal careers of men like Lampião are closely intertwined.

The longstanding tradition of private vengeance, nonetheless, does not by itself explain the cangaço. Combined with another factor, however, a more plausible general explanation may be suggested. This was the general weakening of the traditional order on such a scale that it became more difficult to hold the passions engendered by the above within reasonable bounds.

Backlands society was seldom orderly—witness the many interparentela wars, for example—but a measure of order had been maintained by the landed potentates, each in his own dominion.[35] But this traditional order was eroding rapidly by the late nineteenth century, and the continuing division of holdings on the deaths of the owners made such change inevitable.[36] Maybe, too, the rotation of power during the Empire between the two major parties encouraged the fracturing of local private authority.[37] The political order of the First Republic, including intervention in state and local affairs (as in Ceará in 1914), may have carried the process further.[38] At any rate, it is clear that by the twentieth century private power in the backlands had seriously decayed, at the same time that institutions of public power were still fragile and often corrupt.[39] Under these circumstances little security was to be found in the traditional ways, for few of the landed were powerful enough to offer much protection.[40] Men sought justice and vengeance in whichever ways they could. Small quarrels, with little to restrain them other than fear or prudence, grew into big ones. Slights, affronts, and injustices there were, but so often (as with Lampião and many others) the original complaints hardly justified the consequences of the ever-escalating violence.

END OF THE CANGAÇO

The apex of the cangaço falls during the early 1920s, when several bands were roaming the most heavily afflicted region.[41] Activity centered at the Pajeú River area of Pernambuco, exactly where both Pereira and Lampião grew up and fell into outlawry. The story of the extinction of the cangaço there is pertinent to our discussion because it suggests that banditry was less deeply rooted than has usually been believed.

The cangaço had effectively ended in Pernambuco by 1928, and it ended there for the same reason that banditry changed in Porfirian Mexico: effective police action. Governor Estácio Coimbra and Chief of Police Eurico de Souza Leal jailed the low- and middle-level *coiteiros* (those who supplied the bandits and kept them informed of police movements) and forbade the high-level coiteiros— prestigious political chiefs—to cooperate with the outlaws any longer. At the same time they put the bandits under close pursuit. Within a few months only Lampião's band was left. Most bandits, including many of Lampião's, had surrendered, been captured, or changed their trade. In the summer of 1928 Lampião, too, realized that his career could no longer be maintained in his home state. He fled the area in August with only five men.[42]

Pernambuco and the states to its north were effectively free of organized rural banditry from then on. Lampião, it is true, survived another ten years. On the south side of the São Francisco, and now and again in Alagoas, the famed desperado rebuilt his band and achieved even greater notoriety.[43] But the cangaço consisted of only his band, and when he was killed in 1938, it was quickly brought to a halt. Banditry during those last years rested mainly on Lampião. By rights, the cangaço should have ended by the close of the twenties. The famed, feared, and seasoned veteran Lampião gave it an extra ten years.

In sum the most plausible explanations for the cangaço's rise center on the continuing tradition of private vengeance and increasing anarchy occasioned by the erosion of the power of traditional families. Such conditions did not make the cangaço inevitable, but they did make it possible. History, however, involves much of what appears to be chance, and without certain casual happenings, the rural criminality that we call the cangaço might have occurred at only a low level and attracted little attention beyond its own setting. What built it, gave it notoriety, and, in large measure, sustained it over a prolonged period was the participation of a few capable and colorful individuals. Without their attracting force many of those who followed would have lived their lives in peaceful anonymity or committed their criminal deeds in relative obscurity. Social forces may determine much of history, but at least along the margins where those forces converge, exceptional individuals, like the terrible, memorable cangaceiro chieftains, also make their marks.

Finally, what can be said about Brazilian cangaceiros as social bandits? It is unnecessary to argue that Hobsbawm's social bandit is entirely fictional. Over its heyday of more than half a century, the cangaço offers some limited evidence for social banditry drawn from both fact and legend. But in the main the cangaço occurred within a particular historical context—varied and complex in origin, as history commonly is—that is illuminated little and distorted much by the imposition of an unconscious class struggle.

Perhaps Hobsbawm, anxious to portray his bandits as incipient revolutionaries, drew his social bandit in too contrived a fashion. All banditry, after all, would seem to be social banditry, involving, as it does, relations between people.[44] Still another conceptualization, however, might be suggested: that social bandits are simply those who arise from conditions that make banditry more likely. The society of the backlands of northeastern Brazil during the late nineteenth and early twentieth centuries conforms to such a view. Yet a recognition of this fact in no way glorifies bandits or justifies their criminal careers; so many others, living under the same conditions, did not choose those paths. There is, thus, a concept of social banditry that does not make heroes of those who accepted pillage, torture, and murder as part of a day's work. Nor does it structure evidence in a highly selective and prejudicial manner. It has the merit, therefore, of interpreting the cangaço in a way that offends neither moral nor historical sensibilities.

NOTES

1. On Brilhante, see Raimundo Nonato, *Jesuino Brilhante, O cangaceiro romántico, 1844–1879* (Rio de Janeiro: Editora Pongetti, 1970); on Silvino, Linda Lewin, "The Oligarchical Limitations of Social Banditry in Brazil: The Case of the 'Good Thief' Antônio Silvino," *Past and Present*, 82 (Feb. 1979): 116–146, and Severino Barbosa, *Antônio Silvino, O rifle de ouro* (Recife, 1977); on Pereira, Ulisses Lins de Albuquerque, *Um sertanejo e o sertão*, 2nd ed. (Rio de Janeiro: J. Olympio, 1976), especially pp. 203–222; Luis Wilson, *Vila Bela, os Pereiras e outras histórias* (Recife: n.p., 1974); and Nertan Macedo, *Sinhô Pereira, o commandante de Lampião* (Rio de Janeiro: Editora Artenova, 1975).
2. On Lampião, see Billy Jaynes Chandler, *The Bandit King: Lampião of Brazil*

(College Station: Texas A&M Press, 1978), and references in the bibliography. Among the many books on Lampião published in Brazil, probably the best is Ranulfo Prata's *Lampião* (Rio de Janeiro: Ariel Editora, 1934).

3. A good rendering of the traditional bandit legend is Kent L. Steckmesser, "Robin Hood and the American Outlaw," *Journal of American Folklore*, 79, 312 (1966): 348–355.

4. 29 July 1938.

5. Maria Isaura Pereira de Queiroz, "Notas sociológicas sobre o cangaço," *Ciência e Cultura*, 77 (May 1975): 495–516, and Esmaregado de Freitas, *Diário de Pernambuco* (Recife), 12 March 1926, offer useful commentaries on the origins of the terms.

6. *Primitive Rebels* (Manchester: Manchester Univ. Press, 1959); *Bandits* was first published in 1969 but is now available in a second edition (New York, Pantheon: 1981) that includes a long "Postscript" in which the author adds afterthoughts and considers some of his critics.

7. See his confession of faith in *Bandits*, p. 164.

8. Ibid., p. 10.

9. Ibid., pp. 138–164.

10. The "noble robbers" are discussed in *Bandits*, pp. 41–56, the "avengers" on pp. 58–69. In *Bandits*, Hobsbawm refers to the cangaceiros in several places (pp. 58–59, 60–62, and passim) and in an interview he gave in Brazil, reported in *Veja*, 11 June 1975, pp. 3–5.

11. The circumstances of the entry into the cangaço of Brilhante, Silvino, and Pereira are generally not disputed and are covered in the works cited earlier. The case of Lampião is more complex; see Chandler, *Bandit King*, pp. 24–35.

12. Interpretations of the cangaço that emphasize class aspects tend to see the cangaceiros as victims of injustice, as in Rui Facó, *Cangaceiros e fanáticos*, 2nd ed. (Rio de Janeiro: Civilização Brasileira, 1965), pp. 65–66. Amaury de Souza notes that the desire for revenge was prominent but also suggests that many cangaceiros came from the most dynamic, daring elements of the lower classes. See his "The *Cangaço* and the Politics of Violence in Northeast Brazil," in Ronald L. Chilcote, ed., *Protest and Resistance in Angola and Brazil* (Berkeley: University of California Press, 1972), p. 112. Chandler discusses the social origins of Lampião's bandits in *Bandit King*, pp. 214–217.

13. Chandler, *Bandit King*, pp. 169, 202–204, and passim.

14. Ibid., pp. 205–206 and passim.

15. Ibid., pp. 208–213.

16. *Primitive Rebels*, p. 23.

17. Some recent inquiries into the nature of the cangaço emphasize the close ties that existed between the cangaceiros and society—ties that severely restrict consideration of the cangaço as social protest. Among them are Peter Singelmann, "Political Structure and Social Banditry in Northeast Brazil," *Journal of Latin American Studies*, 7,1 (1975): 59–83; Lewin, "The Oligarchical Limitations of Social Banditry." Chandler documents Lampião's extensive and often intimate ties with fazendeiros and political chieftains in *Bandit King*, pp. 48–49, 86–87, 116–117, 182–184, and passim, and describes his relation to the Prestes Column, pp. 61–73.

18. *Bandits*, p. 55.

19. A similar view of the American West is found in Werner J. Einstadter, "Robbery-Outlawry on the U.S. Frontier, 1863–1890: A Reexamination," in James A. Inciardi and

Anne E. Pottieger, eds., *Violent Crime: Historical and Contemporary Issues* (Beverley Hills, Calif.: Sage, 1978), pp. 22–23.

20. A good study of entire communities as participants in criminal activities is Y. C. Simhadri, *The Ex-Criminal Tribes of India* (New Delhi: National, 1979).

21. Chandler, *Bandit King*, pp. 70, 205.

22. Francesco Salvatore Romano, in *Storia della Mafia* (Milan: A. Mondadori, 1966), pp. 41–45, provocatively discusses the bandit myth and suggests the "superman" hypothesis.

23. Chandler, *Bandit King*, pp. 197–198.

24. Candice Slater treats this type of literature in *Stories on a String: The Brazilian "Literatura de Cordel"* (Berkeley, Calif.: Sage, 1982).

25. Most studies of the cangaço attempt to point to its origins. In addition to the ones already cited, such as Facó, Singelmann, and Lewin, the following are representative: Pedro Baptista, *Cangaceiros do nordeste* (Paraíba: Livraria S. Paulo, 1929); Adhemar Vidal, *Terra do homens* (Rio de Janeiro: Secção de Livros da Empresa Gráfica "O Cruzeiro," 1944); Maria Isaura Pereira de Queiroz, "Notas sociológicas," pp. 503–509.

26. Roger Lee Cunniff, in "The Great Drought: Northeast Brazil, 1877–1880" (Ph.D. diss., University of Texas, 1971), pp. 280–300, gives a factual and thoughtful evaluation of the effects of that disaster, concluding that although severe, the effects have usually been exaggerated.

27. Euclides da Cunha's *Os sertões* (translated into English by Samuel Putnam as *Rebellion in the Backlands*), first published in 1902, is the classic study of Canudos, but it should be balanced by a work such as Ataliba Nogueira, *Antonio Conselheiro e Canudos: Revisão histórica* (São Paulo: Companhía Editora Nacional, 1974). On Padre Cícero, see Ralph della Cava's *Miracle at Joaseiro* (New York: Columbia University Press, 1970) and its bibiliography.

28. Facó's *Cangaceiros e fanáticos* should be consulted on the Cariri.

29. Lewin, "The Oligarchical Limitations of Social Banditry," p. 120; Robert M. Levine, *Pernambuco in the Brazilian Federation (1889–1937)* (Stanford: Stanford Univ. Press, 1978), pp. 46, 29; Billy Jaynes Chandler, *The Feitosas and the Sertão dos Inhamuns* (Gainesville: University of Florida Press, 1972), pp. 137–142.

30. Many, if not most, of the prominent bandits who operated during the 1877–1879 drought, for example, were already bandits when the drought hit. See Lewin, "Oligarchical Limitations of Social Banditry," footnote 12.

31. Levine, *Pernambuco*, p. 46.

32. See Hobsbawm's interview in *Veja*, 11 June 1975, pp. 3–5.

33. Queiroz, "Notas sociológicas," p. 506.

34. Almost all students of the *cangaço* cite private vengeance as a major cause, and it obviously played the leading role in the fall of the cangaceiro chieftains into outlawry. A compelling study of this in another culture is Pasquale Secchi, *Per una sociologia del banditismo sardo* (Sassari, Sardinia: G. Dessi, 1972). Works amply illustrating the exercise of private vengeance in Brazilian history include L. A. Costa Pinto, *Lutas de famílias no Brasil* (São Paulo: Companhía Editora Nacional, 1949), and Chandler, *The Feitosas*.

35. For one case study over a long period, see Chandler, *The Feitosas*.

36. Ibid., pp. 125–130.

37. Ibid., pp. 77–78.

38. Souza, "The Cangaço," pp. 122–123.

39. Chandler, *Bandit King*, pp. 13–15.

40. Deciding why some areas had few or no bandits is about as difficult as deciding why others had relatively many. One suggestion that conforms to our analysis here is that where power remained in the hands of traditional families, banditry did not usually develop. At least, these two conditions—the persistence of considerable family power and the absence of banditry—existed together in several areas of the Northeast, including the Inhamuns area of Ceará (see Chandler, *The Feitosas*). In the Inhamuns, banditry never developed.

41. One researcher compiled a list of 25 bands that operated at least sometime or other between 1919 and 1927, some, of course, for only a short while. See Frederico Pernambucano de Mello, *Aspectos do banditismo rural nordestino* (Recife, 1976), pp. 25–26.

42. Chandler, *Bandit King*, pp. 85–111.

43. Ibid., pp. 112–237.

44. Anton Blok has made this point in his critique of Hobsbawm in *The Mafia of a Sicilian Village, 1860–1960* (New York: Harper & Row, 1975), p. 99.

7

Andean Banditry and Peasant Community Organization, 1882–1930

ERICK D. LANGER

Banditry has been common throughout the Andes, but brigandage affected certain areas more than others. It varied not only in frequency, but also in type, from cattle rustling and highway robbery to wholesale raids on hacienda houses. This variation has always presented a problem to those studying this phenomenon in the region. Enrique López Albújar, in his classic *Los caballeros del delito*, competently debunked the view of contemporary Peruvian criminologists that hot climates produced more criminals. The author argued that the severity of exploitation among the peasantry determined whether a particular area was infested by brigand gangs.[1] Although this insight helps to explain the existence of brigands in some areas, López Albújar did not account for the differences in behavior between the various regions of Peru in which these outlaws operated.

José Varallanos, who first attempted to put the study of banditry on a scientific footing and at whose prompting López Albújar wrote his work, was the first to distinguish systematically between bandit types in Peru. Varallanos saw differences between bandits of the coastal regions and of the highlands. The author showed that bandits in the highlands were primarily cattle rustlers, whereas those along the coast robbed travelers along the desolate highways. He attempted to explain this difference by positing that the highland bandit had few economic motivations, since most peasants possessed land. In contrast, coastal highwaymen needed money, since they had no independent means of subsistence.[2]

Although Varallano's differentiation between coastal and highland bandits is useful, the lack of socioeconomic information makes the author's theories regarding highland banditry tenuous at best. Not all peasants in the uplands owned lands, and Varallanos ignored changes in highland land tenure patterns. For example, hacienda expansion at the expense of Indian communities probably

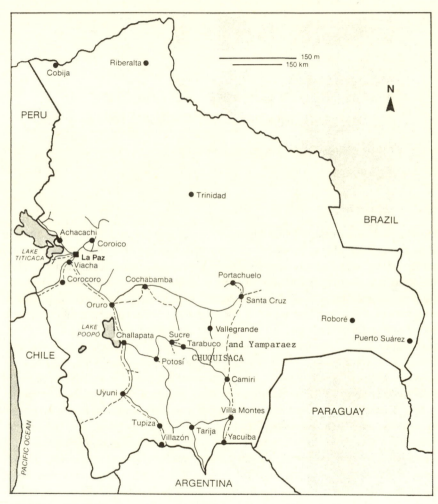

10. Map of Bolivia
From: *Maps On File*, © 1985 by Martin Greenwald Associates.
Reprinted by permission of Facts On File, Inc., New York.

increased the level of exploitation and thus might have had a significant impact on the extent and types of banditry.

Eric Hobsbawm relied heavily on both Varallanos and López Albújar for his information on Peruvian banditry. And given his attempt to synthesize material from all over the world, he did not account for the regional variations of banditry within the country.[3] Benjamin Orlove, an anthropologist who compared Hobsbawm's model with banditry in the Cuzco area (southern Peru) during the early 1970s, justified the lack of a national or Andean approach. According to Orlove, this perspective would have been futile, since landholding patterns and power relations differed markedly from region to region. Because these variables determined what, if any, banditry existed in a particular region, the phenomenon in the Andes was too diverse to analyze as a whole.[4]

However, as López Abújar and Varallanos demonstrated with their pioneer works, generalizations about brigandage are useful. They can help to define issues that go beyond Peru and the Andes. This study attempts to contribute to the analysis of regional differences in banditry by focusing on the internal organization of the peasantry throughout the Andes. An analysis through this perspective illuminates a central issue in Hobsbawm's analysis: which peasants are likely to become bandits and which are not.

Social banditry was only one of many possible responses to social and economic pressures on peasant society. Litigation or, at the other extreme, mass rebellions and mob actions were alternatives to banditry that peasants often used to resist changes in their way of life. How peasants reacted depended not only on the rural social structure, but also, more important, on the internal cohesiveness of peasant society.

In the case of the Andes many peasants maintained a strong corporate identity, which, at the community level, had been encouraged and exploited by the state to facilitate the collection of tribute. On many haciendas communal traditions predating the Spanish Conquest survived, albeit in altered form. On many Andean estates the organizational structure, with its hierarchy of officers, such as *jilakatas* or *alcaldes*, was preserved and performed many of the same functions as its counterpart in the communities. In addition, haciendas in Peru and Bolivia were often divided into sections founded on traditional criteria, such as the kinship-based division into moieties and *ayllus*.[5]

In pockets within the Andes, miscegenation, increasing economic differentiation, and other historical factors had virtually eliminated the Indian communities and many pre-Columbian traditions. Such was the case along the Peruvian coast, in the economically dynamic central highlands of Peru, in the Cochabamba valley in Bolivia, and along the eastern slopes of the Andes, where many Indian peasant villages had been wiped out by raiding jungle tribes. Without a communal structure to preserve Indian characteristics, the people in these regions became identified as mestizos, a social and cultural distinction more than a racial category. Mestizos also predominated in the many small Andean towns and their surrounding countryside.

It is in these mestizo areas, especially those far from centers of authority, that banditry flourished and that bandit attacks on property took their most virulent form. In more heavily Indian areas there was some cattle rustling, but on a much smaller scale than along the coast and in the mestizo pockets of the highlands. Why this difference? In the mestizo areas economic differentiation and the lack of communal traditions had taken their toll, making it virtually impossible for the rural population to organize on a large scale and manifest their sentiments through massive rebellions. At best, they protested through legal means and, if that failed, through banditry. In turn, among the communities and haciendas in the heavily Indian regions, rebellions were quite common and were the preferred mode of social protest.

These differences are clearly manifest in Yamparaez and Tomina, two adjacent provinces in the department of Chuquisaca (Bolivia). In predominantly Indian Yamparaez there was much small-scale cattle rustling. In contrast, in mestizo-dominated Tomina, banditry became endemic during the early twentieth century and presented the most serious problem faced by the province. A detailed comparison of cattle rustling and bandit activities between these provinces illustrates the varieties of rural criminal behavior found in the Andes and clarifies which peasants became bandits and why.

INDIANS AND RUSTLING IN YAMPARAEZ PROVINCE

The province of Yamparaez has always been culturally part of the Andean highlands. Two high plains, with their large level areas, ideal for growing barley and potatoes, dominate the province. The only two towns in the province, Yamparaez and Tarabuco, are located on the cold, windswept plains that are named after them. To the north and south the terrain becomes more rugged, descending into the subtropical river valleys of the Río Grande and the Pilcomayo, respectively.

Yamparaez province contained, according to the 1900 census, a plurality of Indians, 6,690 out of a total population of 16,009 (42%). Mestizos followed close behind with 6,506 (41%). The Indian figure is low because probably only Indian tribute payers and their families were counted. Other Indians who resided on haciendas but escaped paying the head tax were subsumed into the mestizo category. The 1950 census unfortunately only breaks down racial composition on a departmental basis, making it impossible to compare with the more detailed earlier census. However, the percentage of Indians in the department is much higher than in the 1900 census, reflecting racial criteria based on dress and ability to speak Spanish rather than tribute categories. For our purposes the 1950 indicators are probably more accurate. Thus the pattern common throughout much of the Andean highlands, that of a heavily Indian population living either on haciendas or in communities, prevailed in Yamparaez.[6]

Yamparaez haciendas and, to a certain extent, Indian communities benefited from a trade boom in the early twentieth century. This was exceptional for southern Bolivia because most of the region entered into a prolonged period of stagnation once the great Potosí silver mines were abandoned in the last years of the nineteenth century. Yamparaez temporarily escaped this fate because of geographical accident. Its towns straddled one of the main routes between the highlands and the recently colonized and economically flourishing Chaco region and so benefited from growing trade between the two points.

Cattle, which thrived on the virgin Chaco pastures, were driven through Tarabuco on their way to Sucre or the tin-mining centers in the department of Potosí. Likewise, hogs raised in the subtropical Andean foothills passed through Tarabuco and Yamparaez. Inhabitants of the town of Yamparaez dominated much of this livestock trade. Other goods, such as *ají*, a pepper used for flavoring many local dishes, brown sugar from Santa Cruz, wheat from the plains of Mojocoya, and wood from Padilla, traveled on donkeys and mules through the province.

Tarabuco, in particular, developed into an important regional, commercial entrepôt. Barley, one of the main crops of the Tarabuco high plains, became a valuable commodity because the grain was used as fodder for the many pack animals, hogs, and cattle passing through. The Sunday market in town attracted local hacendados and community Indians, who sold their barley crops to the long-distance traders. The inhabitants of Tarabuco, in large part mestizo, and some local hacendados, eager to take advantage of this prosperity, began buying much of the Indian community land in the plain surrounding the town. As a result some of the community organizations, or ayllus, were weakened as Indians lost their land base and had to become hacienda peons to survive.[7]

Although resistance to these measures seldom included banditry, there was much cattle rustling, as evidenced by the records of the Tarabuco court, in existence since 1900. The number of court cases involving this crime did not reflect the true amount of cattle rustling in the province. In many instances victims took matters into their own hands and reached some kind of accord with the perpetrator.[8]

According to Tarabuco court documents, rustling increased between 1900 and 1930. From 1900 to 1909 only 25 cases were recorded, but the next decade this figure doubled to 51. From 1920 to 1929 the number of rustling cases almost tripled over the previous ten years to 137. In 1930 the Tarabuco judge complained that half of all judicial complaints dealt with rustling, but only a handful were ever prosecuted. Thereafter rustling decreased, as strong government repression diminished the ranks of potential criminals.[9]

Cattle were by far the most popular targets. From 1900 to 1930, 434 cows, steers, and oxen were reported stolen. Donkeys, the second most rustled animals, lagged far behind at only 83 head. Only 39 horses, 19 mules, 18 sheep, and 8 hogs disappeared during the same period. The number of animals stolen correlates well with the relative value and marketability of each species, indicating that for some thieves, cattle rustling was a commercial venture.

But only a few men were repeat offenders; the majority of accused apparently did not live from cattle rustling. Those who appeared frequently in court documents rustled a disproportionate share of animals. Three men, all mestizos, accounted for twenty-five cases, or slightly more than 10 percent, of all recorded rustling instances during the first three decades of the twentieth century.[10] These individuals, especially active in the 1920s, presumably earned their living in this way. They usually participated in gangs ranging from two to seven members. Most of these professional rustlers worked with one or two other men. For example, in 1924 Ramón Lara teamed up with Nicanor Mollo and stole two steers from an Indian of Icla. Lara, a Tarabuco sandalmaker and notorious rustler, was accused ten times as a cattle thief between 1916 and 1930. He sold the cattle to a butcher in Tarabuco and split the proceeds with his partner.[11]

Most rustling activities were not elaborately organized commercial enterprises. The court records show that the vast majority of *abigeatistas* acted alone. Usually the rustler, at best, owned a yoke of oxen or a couple of donkeys. In a 1930 report the Tarabuco judge implied that many stole cattle to make ends meet rather than to supplement their income beyond the subsistence level. For example, Gaspar Salazar stole one steer and two oxen from a couple of Indian peons from Hacienda La Ciénega in Tarabuco. Salazar apparently took the animals to pay off debts to Samuel Gallardo, an accountant and prominent Tarabuco resident.[12]

An analysis of the accused rustlers' professions, a good indicator of social status, only partially confirms the 1930 report. In fifty-eight cases out of a total of ninety-five (61%) listing professions, defendants were categorized as *labrador* (laborer) or *tejedor/a* (weaver), both clearly peasant categories. The rest of the alleged rustlers were either mestizo artisans living in Tarabuco or, significantly, the provincial elites. Seventeen cases (18%) involved townsfolk such as butchers, sandalmakers, tailors, potters, and muleteers. Twelve (13%) of the accused cattle thieves were merchants, *proprietarios* (landowners), or housewives. Another eight (8%) were *agricultores*, or farmers, an ambiguous category that encompassed both large landowners and peasants. (See Table 7:1.)

The relatively high proportion of non-peasants among defendants suggests that rustling trials involved issues beyond simple livestock theft. In fact, many of these court cases were disputes over land and grazing rights, an endemic problem in Andean rural society. This problem was exacerbated because of the region's complex transhumance patterns. Many peasants owned livestock that they grazed in neighboring provinces because pastures were relatively scarce in Yamparaez. Pasture owners, often large hacendados or prosperous merchants, periodically held *rodeos*, or cattle roundups, to collect grazing fees from the owners of animals found on their properties. Peasants often disputed the right of the hacendados to collect the fees and accused the landowners of rustling their cattle as a countermeasure to have their livestock returned.[13]

Thus rustling charges were used as leverage against powerful individuals to gain some relief from what peasants considered exploitative exactions. In another frequent type of lawsuit, peasants accused their creditors of rustling in an effort to retrieve their animals taken as payment for an unpaid debt. In a typical action

Table 7:1
Alleged Rustlers in Tarabuco, by Profession

Peasants		Elite	
Laborer	52	Merchant	8
Weaver	6	Landowner	3
—TOTAL 58(61%)		Housewife	1
		—TOTAL 12(13%)	

Townsfolk		Ambiguous	
Butcher	12	Farmer	8
Sandalmaker	2	—TOTAL 8(8%)	
Tailor	1		
Potter	1		
Muledriver	1		
—TOTAL 17(18%)			

Source: Juzgado de Instruccion de Tarabuco, 1900–1930.

Federico Arancibia brought suit against Vicenta v. de Valencia, a merchant and shopkeeper of Tarabuco, alleging that she had stolen his five donkeys. In her defense Valencia asserted that Arancibia had given her the pack animals to use in return for canceling a 300-Bs (Bolivianas) debt.[14]

The Tarabuco judge's 1930 report also charged that most of the rustlers were Indians. To the contrary, Indians tended more often to be victims than perpetrators. Of seventy-three court documents stating ethnic origin, forty involved Indians as victims, whereas in only twenty cases were Indians inculpated as abigeatistas. In turn, of thirteen trials involving mestizos, all were listed as defendants.

It would be difficult to argue that cattle rustling in Yamparaez province represented social banditry in the Hobsbawmian sense. Peasants, rather than the better-off, were overwhelmingly victims of the abigeatista. Out of the 144 cases in which the victim's profession was noted, laborer, weaver, and *hilandera* (spinner) occured in 111 (77%). Other categories that implied a higher status (landowner, merchant, housewife, lawyer, butcher, and carpenter) constitute only 29 cases (20%). Agricultores, an ambiguous category, were victims in 4 instances (3%). (See Table 7:2.)

Why did the peasantry not resort to banditry? Although many rural inhabitants benefited from the trade boom around Tarabuco, many community Indians were slowly but surely losing their lands and being forced to become hacienda peons. In fact, if there were "professional" bandits in the province at all, they were a small number of mestizos, usually operating in small bands, who took from Indians as well as other folk.

But lack of bandit activity did not mean that Indians did not fight for their way of life. From 1918 onward, communities resisted the commissions sent out

Table 7:2
Rustling Victims in Tarabuco, by Profession

Peasants		Elite	
Laborer	100	Landowner	15
Weaver	9	Merchant	7
Spinner	2	Housewife	3
—TOTAL 111(77%)		Lawyer	2
		—TOTAL 27(19%)	

Townsfolk		Ambiguous	
Carpenter	1	Farmer	4
Butcher	1	—TOTAL 4(3%)	
—TOTAL 2(1%)			

Source: Juzgado de Instrucción de Tarabuco, 1900–1930.

to measure and parcel Indian land. By the 1920s they began to invade haciendas composed of former community lands. Hacienda peons were not quiescent either. From 1922 onward, labor disputes between landowners and peons erupted throughout the region and led to hacienda-wide revolts and even labor stoppages. Both rural movements, that of the community Indians and that of the hacienda peons, culminated in the great revolt of 1927. This important rebellion, which originated in northern Potosí and rapidly extended throughout much of Bolivia, effectively halted the further loss of Indian lands and in some cases led to better labor conditions on the estates.[15] Thus although social banditry did not exist, other forms of rural social protest did.

BANDOLEROS IN TOMINA

Even before the Spanish conquest, Tomina was a frontier.[16] Bordering Yamparaez on the east, the area formed a buffer zone between the sedentary highland cultures and the various tribes that migrated from the desolate Chaco. When the Inca empire weakened under the onslaught of the Spanish conquistadores, the Tomina region was overrun by fierce Chiriguanos, a number of warlike tribes that had recently migrated to the Chaco. Incan colonists were either slaughtered or fled to the relative safety of the highlands, leaving the province virtually depopulated.[17] Spaniards and their Indian servants subsequently resettled the land and created a predominately mestizo population.

Only the western fringe of Tomina (which later split off as Zudáñez province) held a significant Indian presence. According to the 1900 census, only in canton Presto, located in this western region, were Indians in the majority. Elsewhere, mestizos and whites maintained a large numerical superiority. In 1900, 28,174 residents, slightly more than half the total population, were categorized as mestizos. Approximately one-third (15,923) qualified as whites and only 16 percent (8,588) as Indians.[18]

Land tenure patterns also differed from those in Yamparaez. Rather than a division between haciendas and Indian communities, Tomina had a large number of small holdings interspersed with a few huge estates. These latifundios were located primarily along the western fringe, along the major east-west trade route, and on the sparsely inhabited eastern frontier. In most cases the haciendas along the eastern frontier were large only on paper. Because of the lack of labor and the distance to the main routes, landowners had little incentive to work or develop the estates there. Hacendados usually exploited only a small section close to the hacienda house and adjoining workers' huts. Those few peons living in the remote areas of the estates had little supervision, and the hacendado had little effective control over them. Thus peasants in the eastern part of the province acted more like smallholders, which is not what the official papers might suggest.[19]

During the last few decades of the nineteenth century, Tomina became one of the main suppliers of cattle to the burgeoning silver-mining industry in the highlands. This boom period, however, proved to be short-lived. The abrupt decline of silver mining after 1895 severely weakened the provincial economy, especially in remote areas, where cattle grazing among smallholders had been the main activity. Also, in the 1890s the Chiriguano Indians were finally subdued, and settlers from the frontier areas to the east of Tomina invaded the Chaco's fringes. The colonists' cattle multiplied rapidly in the virgin pastures and soon competed successfully with Tomina livestock in already reduced highland markets.[20]

These changes reduced much of the province's remote areas, in which small-holders predominated, to a subsistence economy. In contrast, the large estates, hugging the main east-west trade route that wound its way through Tomina, prospered. Proximity to the main trail lowered transport costs and made possible the commercialization of goods, such as wheat and ají, that were too expensive to haul from less accessible areas. The province experienced growing regional economic inequality by the early twentieth century. Despite increasing trade between the highlands and the Chaco, only a small proportion of provincial rural society was able to profit. While cattle traders and large landowners thrived, the rest of the province languished. It is in this context that banditry became rampant throughout Tomina.

The judicial archives in the provincial capital of Padilla are fragmentary, but surviving annual indexes describing all trials heard give some indication of the frequency of banditry and cattle rustling.[21] Between 1882 and 1888, 211 instances of cattle rustling and 5 armed bandit attacks came to the attention of the court. By 1905 these numbers had increased tremendously. In that year alone 296 cases of livestock theft and 28 armed attacks were reported. This crime wave reached its height in 1930, when the Tomina subprefect reported that he received, on the average, two to three cattle rustling denunciations daily. If this number is correct, the incidence of abigeato had doubled or tripled in the twenty-five intervening years.[22] Only in 1930 were authorities able to contain outlawry in the province. A military regime, briefly in power between 1930 and 1931, sent out a commission that executed any suspected bandit who was unfortunate enough to be in prison at the time. Military recruitment for the rapidly escalating conflict with Paraguay in the Chaco later removed many of the young male peasants who were most likely to join in bandit activities.

Banditry in Tomina was different from cattle rustling in Tarabuco. Most obviously, armed robbery, common in Tomina, virtually did not exist in Tarabuco. Abigeato was also different. Gangs of profit-minded rustlers took livestock to the neighboring province of Vallegrande, in the department of Santa Cruz. There they sold the animals to merchants for resale in Argentina or, less commonly, the Santa Cruz market. By the early twentieth century the trail through sparsely populated canton Pescado to neighboring Vallegrande was an important funnel for the ever-increasing trade in stolen cattle. As a result, outlaw gangs from Pescado and Vallegrande virtually took over the canton and established small fiefdoms that controlled the illegal trade through their territory.

Efforts by local authorities to capture the brigands in Pescado proved fruitless. In 1914 the subprefect of Tomina led a force of twenty police to clean up the canton. They attacked a stronghold at Salto, from whence the strongest band had launched raids on the main east-west trade route. However, the outlaws, better armed than the police, forced the subprefect to retreat. Police commissioner Adolfo Ampuero tried to organize another invasion. However, unwilling to fight against superior forces, all but two of his deputies fled into the countryside. Undaunted, Ampuero mounted another campaign with seven men collected from the town of Pescado. This time the brigands had been forewarned and melted into the hills. The hapless commissioner found only a few women who had been unable to retreat with the men. Such well-armed gangs made formidable enemies. A band of at least six attacked the estate of Silvestre Rocha, well-to-do landowner of Mosocllacta, in Padilla province. They shot at the hacienda house and then took all of Rocha's livestock, including 29 cattle, 150 sheep, and 25 goats.[23]

These bandits were mostly peasants from the lowest strata of society. Labrador was by far the most common profession of those brought to trial in Padilla. Unfortunately, the term was used indiscriminately for both smallholders and hacienda peons, making it impossible to differentiate between the two. Only a few other professions were mentioned. One bandit described himself as a carpenter, and another, according to the victim, "has no profession other than robbery." One defendant, Cirilo Garnica from Villar, stated that he was a proprietario. Described as one of two chiefs of a gang of highwaymen, he seems to have been an exceptional case. In no other trial was a landowner accused of banditry.[24]

For most brigands, banditry was not a full-time activity. Most outlaws had close ties to the land and possessed a plot somewhere in the province or were hacienda peons on some estate. Even the most renowned bandits with long criminal records kept usufruct rights over some plot. The infamous Olegario Cabrera, described in 1922 as having been in jail three times for various misdeeds, was a peon on the hacienda of a Spanish merchant, Manuel Monterde. Although it was unlikely that Cabrera completed all the usual obligations of a hacienda worker, apparently the bandit did not bother Monterde. According to the Spanish merchant's son, who met the brigand in his childhood, Cabrera left him alone because the merchant "was a good *patrón* and all the peons liked him."[25]

Unlike in Tarabuco, women in Tomina often participated in robber bands. They even took part in the beatings and slayings that often accompanied the assaults. In 1924 police surprised a group of three women and three men beating up two couples to find out where they had hidden the money earned selling some livestock. Two of the women were sisters and related to another one of the attackers. Relatives often formed the nucleus of a group, and in most cases women were probably sisters, wives, or lovers of the male participants.[26]

Not surprisingly, given the small number of Indians in the province, virtually all bandits were mestizos or perhaps whites. Only in one case was an Indian associated with a gang of highwaymen. A defendant implicated an Indian named Saturnino as the informant in an attack in canton Tomina. The suit alleged that four or more bandits armed with pistols and knives assaulted the house of an Indian, murdered him, raped his daughter, and took an undisclosed amount of money. Other than serving as the source of information, Saturnino did not participate in the attack. As in Tarabuco, Indians more often were victims than robbers.[27]

There were no Robin Hoods among Tomina bands; brigands attacked rich and poor alike. One hacienda peon, the target of an unsuccessful attack, described graphically the fear felt by much of Tomina's rural population. In 1928 bandits used Hacienda Punilla as their base. They "sowed terror among all the inhabitants of the districts; [the local residents] have not felt safe a single instant, especially at night, passing cruel moments of fear until the light of day has dissipated with the shadows the feared danger." The items stolen in some assaults record the poverty of the victims. Santusa Sanchez, a weaver from Sopachuy, was assaulted in 1922. After beating the woman, the highwaymen stripped the habitation, taking a newly woven poncho, a blanket, saddlebags, two bridles, and a few coins.[28]

But merchants and wealthy hacendados also suffered bandit attacks. Because assaults on the rich yielded more, brigands favored these targets. In 1903 four men raided the house of two cattle merchants in Villar, netting more than 7,000 Bs cash, a Winchester rifle, and other items. However, the wealthy were often better protected, making attacks on them more risky. In another instance, seven brigands (including two women), traveling with some stolen livestock from Vallegrande, raided the hacienda house of Eulogio Carvajal Urcullo in Pescado. Carvajal Urcullo, a prominent landowner with holdings in Pescado and Padilla, repulsed the attack after the gang had penetrated the house. With the help of houseguests, he captured the leader, Filemon Coronado, an escaped convict from Vallegrande.[29]

Although bandits often murdered peasants, they only threatened or beat land-

owners and merchants. It appears that bandits could no less escape the predominant value system than any other member of Andean rural society. In only one
instance did robbers trangress this invisible line and murder one of their social
betters. Aniceto Reyes, a prominent Liberal and scion of an old established
Padilla family, was attacked and killed in 1915 on his estate. The uproar this
incident created in the provincial press clearly demonstrated that the bandits had
gone too far. The outlaws apparently recognized this themselves. Although the
culprits were never caught, no other important personage in Tomina was
murdered.[30]

Despite this aversion to murdering members of the elite, most bandits did not
work under the protection of landowners. When hacendados caught alleged
troublemakers, punishment could often be swift and brutal. In 1919 four men
kidnapped Rafael Santos, hung him from a harness, and beat him. Later he was
taken to a makeshift prison in the hacienda house of Roman Rivera, a local
priest and landowner. Rivera also abused Santos, charging that the now severely
injured man had stolen a steer from his estate and killed one of his peons.
Although Santos later brought suit against Rivera, apparently no action was taken
against the priest.[31]

At best, landowners helped to mitigate the punishment meted out to their
workers once they were caught by authorities. Mariano Alvarado, a hacienda
peon of Adrian Montero, participated in the robbery and beating of a modestly
wealthy farmer. Unfortunately for Alvarado, he was the only one captured and
brought to justice. Rather than spend time in jail, the usual sentence for such a
case, he was freed, thanks to Montero's considerable influence. In return, Alvarado signed a contract with Montero, promising to return his part of the booty
(clothes and some furniture). In effect, restitution to the farmer was minimal,
since the gang had numbered between eleven and twenty members and had stolen
500 Bs in cash as well as other items. Montero's interest in preserving his labor
force apparently triumphed over the will to punish criminal behavior.[32]

Although evidence from the judicial archives does not point toward widespread
social banditry, local folklore contains elements that Eric Hobsbawm pinpointed.
These stories do not correspond to reality as reflected in the judicial archives;
rather, they exhibit a selective memory that emphasizes only certain traits among
bandits. No tale deals with robbing other peasants. All involve some act against
either merchants or landlords, and in many cases they emphasize the terror in
which the local elites held the outlaws. On the other hand, the stories celebrate
the sense of honor among the outlaws and revel in their ruthlessness.

Two stories about Pio Romero, perhaps the most famous and feared bandit,
illustrate this point. Romero was a peon of Hacienda Torrecillas who had a
remarkable career over a period of at least ten years.[33] According to one tale,
Romero entered the tiny town of Pescado with his forty men. He went directly
to the store of a Spanish shopkeeper and forced him to open up despite the late
hour. The bandit demanded forty suits for his men, a request with which the
terror-stricken merchant complied. When Romero left he exclaimed that he would

repay the Spaniard in a month. Precisely one month later Romero returned and paid the hapless shopkeeper in full.

Another legend concerned Pio Romero's demise. It not only celebrates the brutality and guile of the infamous brigand, but also shows the limits beyond which the rural elite would not tolerate the highwaymen's actions. The outlaw made a trip to Vallegrande to rob a hacendado who had sold many cattle and so had much cash on hand. Arriving late one evening at the hacienda, Romero posed as a cattle trader and purchased fifty animals from the unsuspecting landowner. Because it was dark by the time they concluded their deal, the brigand was offered a bed in the hacienda house. Once all were asleep Romero unlocked the gates and let in his accomplices, who had been hiding outside. The gang took the money and, in a violent fit, cut the throats of all the hacienda's occupants, including the dogs. The next morning the brother of the hacendado discovered the massacre, organized a well-armed posse, and rode to Romero's residence. There they ambushed and killed the outnumbered bandits.

Curiously, while many of the older inhabitants of the province remember these stories, none has been put to paper. Younger Bolivians apparently have little, if any, interest in these colorful figures. Instead, as evidenced by the ubiquitous image peering from many bus mirrors and the like, they seem to admire a more recent hero, Che Guevara. During his brief Bolivian campaign, Guevara briefly traveled through parts of Tomina, in what is now Belisario Boeto. Since his death, the guerrilla leader has acquired many traits associated with older bandit-heroes and perhaps has become a suitable substitute for those who need a champion to fight injustice and give hope to the poor.

CONCLUSION

The legends that still persist indicate that Tomina bandits, to a certain extent, acquired the status of social bandits. Does this mean that these bandits really were the type that Hobsbawm so eloquently described? There are some striking congruences with the model elaborated in *Bandits*. Tomina bandits were, for the most part, peasants and, at least in Pescado, maintained some support from their social equals. However, it is difficult to distinguish between support given under duress and genuine voluntary aid.

Although brigands often used violence against their peers and probably robbed fellow peasants as often as landlords or merchants, they did, in a sense, redistribute wealth in the province. Given the fact that a large proportion of Tomina's rural population participated in or abetted cattle rustling or robberies, many peasants, at least temporarily, improved their living standards by brigandage. Moreover, the most lucrative targets, the wealthy few who benefited from east-west trade, almost certainly contributed a much larger proportion of the total loot than hapless peasant victims. In this way the inhabitants of the remoter frontier sections of Tomina benefited from the Chaco highlands trade even after they had lost their position as cattle exporters. For this reason perhaps the folklore that grew up around some of the most famous Tomina bandits gives these individuals more traits of social bandits than they deserve.

Criminal activity in Yamparaez and Tomina shared some characteristics. In both provinces banditry and cattle rustling increased in the early twentieth century and reached a peak in the 1920s and early 1930s. Although it is difficult to state with certainty for Tomina, peasants, and especially Indians, suffered more from the depredations of abigeatistas and bandits than did other strata of provincial society. Both these similarities were due to larger socioeconomic changes. In Yamparaez the increase of criminal activity reflected a general social malaise, perhaps touched off by the rapid fall of southern Bolivia from a political and economic center to a stagnating backwater. In Tomina the relative powerlessness of the peasantry, especially the Indians, a legacy of the Spanish conquest and the ensuing social order, made these groups easy targets for the unscrupulous, including bandits.

Despite these similarities the overwhelming sense is that criminal activity in Yamparaez was quite different from that in Tomina. Although cattle rustling was common in the two areas, in Tomina it was more frequent and much more highly organized. Gangs controlled an extensive illicit cattle trade circuit through canton Pescado to Vallegrande merchants. In contrast, few rustlers in Yamparaez organized into groups or made much money. Most Tarabuco cattle thieves acted alone, taking a cow or two to pay off a debt.

Tomina bandits often used violence to achieve their goals. Brigands were able to operate with virtual impunity because, in many cases, they owned weapons that were superior to those of the police. Yamparaez rustlers seldom used weapons; in most cases livestock was stolen surreptitiously from deserted pastures. The former province's penchant for violence perhaps reflects a frontier heritage from the colonial period, when the area constantly had to be defended from the attacks of fierce Chiriguano warriors.[34]

Although most rustlers in Yamparaez were one-time offenders, in Tomina it is possible to speak of a large group of outlaws who formed a type of criminal underclass that committed the vast majority of illegal acts. Unlike in Argentina, where many real or potential bandits were condemned as criminals to supply needed ranch hands or cannon fodder for the army, Tomina elites did not take advantage of these individuals to fill their labor needs. Thus the elites' salient economic interests were not the underpinning of the criminal justice system in Tomina as they were in Buenos Aires province.[35] In Yamparaez, in fact, just the reverse was true. Peasants at times accused landowners of rustling in the hope of avoiding grazing fees or acknowledging disputed land rights. The Yamparaez peasants, not the landlords, used the criminal justice system as a weapon in their struggle to maintain their position in society.

Why were these differences between adjacent provinces so marked? It might be argued that divergent economic conditions played a large role. Yamparaez, especially the town of Tarabuco, thrived on the trade between the highlands and the Chaco region during the early twentieth century. In contrast, trade in Chaco cattle marginalized the important Tomina livestock sector and created an increasingly unequal distribution of wealth in the province. This led to banditry, as those excluded from the prosperity engendered by the trade boom attempted to take some of the profits for themselves.

But the economic argument is difficult to sustain. In Yamparaez certain groups benefited more from increased trade than did others. Hacendados, town mestizos, and merchants undoubtedly earned more from Tarabuco's strategic position than did either hacienda peons or Indian community members. Nevertheless, there was no corresponding change from petty cattle rustling to widespread highway robbery and armed assaults on haciendas.

Differences in criminal behavior did not lie primarily in economic conditions, but in the divergent makeup of peasant society in the two provinces. Ethnic composition and, closely related to this, the level of organization among rural inhabitants, determined the forms of protest. In Yamparaez the predominantly Indian population, whether on haciendas or in communities, had maintained a high level of cohesion. Threatened by unfavorable laws or economic conditions, they acted collectively to protest change. As a result the many protests that shook the Yamparaez countryside encompassed entire haciendas or communities. The countryfolk only acted individually when using the judicial system. Banditry, a form of protest requiring only primitive forms of organization, never became a weapon in the struggle against landlord or merchant domination.

In contrast, mestizo-dominated Tomina lacked the cultural and social cohesiveness of Yamparaez. This was reflected in its landholding patterns, where smallholders controlled the majority of provincial lands. Also, other than the far western fringe, the territory had been a frontier region repopulated with a diverse populace shorn of their ties with highland culture. Therefore, even on haciendas, no communal tradition existed to foster ties among members of the labor force. It was in this area that banditry became endemic, especially after the turn of the century, when economic conditions deteriorated severely for the majority of Tomina's population.

Why did the Indians of Yamparaez not resort to widespread banditry as well? Cattle rustling existed there but never reached the proportions or showed the same characteristics as in Tomina. The difference lies in the results achieved by different types of peasant resistance. Hobsbawm was correct in arguing that banditry is in fact an inefficient type of social movement incapable of stemming the tides of change.[36] The Indians of Yamparaez understood this and instead used the judicial system to their advantage or took collective action that, as in 1927, could be successful. The inhabitants of Tomina lacked the option of large-scale rebellion. Banditry was the last rearguard effort to ameliorate their condition and escape the rural crisis that structural changes in the twentieth-century Bolivian economy engendered.

This theme can be extended to the rest of the Andes and perhaps to Latin America in general. Rural inhabitants chose the most efficacious means to resist what they considered detrimental social and economic change. In areas where the population was organized into corporate units (which in many areas included haciendas), they often chose to revolt en masse. Only where social and economic forces had destroyed communal traditions or in areas where such traditions never developed did countryfolk resort to banditry, a less effective alternative. This was the case along the Peruvian coast, in the predominantly mestizo areas, and along the eastern Andean frontier. This might also help to explain why banditry throughout much of Latin America is found primarily in sparsely populated frontier areas rather than in densely settled peasant strongholds.

NOTES

1. Enrique López Albújar, *Los caballeros del delito*, 2nd ed. (Lima: Editorial Juan Mejía Baca, 1973).

2. José Varallanos, *Bandoleros en el Perú: ensayos* (Lima: Editorial Altura, 1937), especially pp. 35–71.

3. Eric J. Hobsbawm, *Bandits*, rev. ed. (New York: Pantheon, 1981), especially pp. 21, 170.

4. Benjamin S. Orlove, "The Position of Rustlers in Regional Society: Social Banditry in the Andes," in Benjamin S. Orlove and Glynn Custred, eds., *Land and Power in Latin America: Agrarian Economies and Social Processes in the Andes* (New York: Holmes & Meier, 1978), p. 179.

5. See Erwin P. Grieshaber, "Hacienda-Indian Community Relations and Indian Acculturation: An Historiographical Essay," *Latin American Research Review*, 14,2 (1979): 107–128. On community and hacienda cultural institutions, see William E. Carter, *Aymara Communities and the Bolivian Agrarian Reform* (Gainesville: University of Florida Press, 1964).

6. Republica de Bolivia, Oficina de Inmigración, Estadística y Progaganda Geográfica, *Censo de la población de la república de Bolivia según el empadronamiento de 1 de setiembre de 1900*, 2nd ed., (Cochabamba: Editorial Inca, 1973), pp. 4–5; República de Bolivia, Ministerio de Hacienda y Estadística, Dirección General de Estadística y Censos, *Censo demográfico 1950* (La Paz: Editorial Argote, 1955), pp. 100–101. For a comparison of racial categories between the two censuses, see Erwin P. Grieshaber, "The Changing Definition of an Indian: A Comparison of the Bolivian Censuses of 1900 and 1950," unpublished ms. (1984).

7. See Erick D. Langer, "Rural Society and Land Consolidation in a Declining Economy: Chuquisaca, Bolivia 1880–1930" (Ph.D. diss., Stanford University, 1984), pp. 97–105.

8. "Informe del Sr. Torres Goitia, Juzgado de Instrucción en Tarabuco," in General Simón Aguirre, *Informe del Prefecto de Chuquisaca* (Sucre: Escuela Tip. Salesiana, 1930), p. 70, Biblioteca Nacional de Bolivia, Sucre, Bolivia. (Hereinafter all *informes prefecturales* are cited IP, followed by the date and page number.)

9. Juzgado de Instrucción de Tarabuco, 1900–1930 (hereinafter cited as JIT); IP 1930, p. 69.

10. These men were Pedro Loaiza, with ten trials; Ramón Lara, with ten; and Mariano Navarro, with five denunciations. Significantly, two of the three rustlers (Lara and Navarro) needed cattle in their professions. Lara was a sandalmaker and Navarro a butcher. Loaiza identified himself only as a *labrador*. See JIT 1914:115 (court cases are organized

by year and case number); 1914:389; 1916:68, 1921:no number (hereinafter n.n); 1922:n.n., 13; 1923:20, 24; 1924:37, 40, 45, 48; 1925:64, 70, 74; 1926:61; 1928:6; 1929:8, 12; 1930:23, 27, 29, 30, 32.

11. JIT 1924:37.

12. IP 1930, p. 70. See JIT 1922:4.

13. For transhumance patterns, see IP 1928, pp. 121–144. Examples of disputes resulting from rodeos are found in JIT 1901:7; 1921:n.n.; 1924: 41; 1929:7.

14. See JIT 1927:89; also 1921:n.n.; 1922:4, 13; 1923:17; 1930:32.

15. For a fuller description of these revolts, see Langer, "Rural Society," pp. 108–115.

16. Tomina refers to the province as it existed before 1917, consisting of the present provinces of Azurduy, Belisario Boeto, Tomina, and Zudanez.

17. See "Descripción de la Villa de Santiago de Tomina y su distrito, sacada de la relación que por mandado del consejo se hizo y envió de aquella ciudad en el año de 1608," in Luis Torres de Mendoza, *Colección de documentos inéditos relativos a la conquista y organización de las antiguas posesiones españolas de América y Oceania sacados de los archivos del reino y muy especialmente del de Indias* (Madrid: Imprenta de Frías y Cia, 1868), 9:339.

18. Bolivia, *Censo de 1900*, pp. 4–5.

19. See José L. Havet, "Rational Domination: The Power Structure in a Bolivian Rural Zone" (Ph.D. diss., University of Pittsburgh, 1978), pp. 80–100. On conditions along the eastern border, see Alcides D'Orbigny, a French naturalist who visited the region shortly after independence. Conditions had not changed significantly by the early twentieth century. See D'Orbigny, *Viaje a la America meridional*, trans. Alfredo Cepeda (Buenos Aires: Editorial Futuro, 1945), pp. 1472–1477.

20. On changing economic conditions, see Langer, "Rural Society," pp. 241–246.

21. In the late 1960s, when Ché Guevara operated in neighboring Vallegrande, the Bolivian army took over all of Padilla's governmental buildings, including the courthouse. According to witnesses, soldiers used old papers from the judicial archives as bedding and fuel. A significant portion of these valuable documents was lost and the remainder of the archive completely disorganized.

22. See Archivo Judicial de Padilla (hereinafter AJP), "Inventario de los espedientes que el Actuario Roberto Rua ha entregado al igual Mariano Civera con asistencia del Fiscal del Partido Doctor José Luis Carvajal (1889?)," and "1905: Juicios criminales." For 1930, see IP 1930, p. 100. The number of rustling incidents in Tomina is much larger than in Yamparaez partly because the territory under the jurisdiction of Padilla was substantially larger than the former.

23. See IP 1914, pp. viii-x for the running battle between authorities and bandit gangs that year; AJP 1924:n.n.

24. AJP 1920:139; AJP 1920:68.

25. Alberto Monterde, interview with author, Padilla, 20 January 1982.

26. AJP 1924:n.n.

27. Ibid.

28. AJP 1928:85; AJP 1922:n.n.

29. AJP 1903:66; AJP 1924:n.n.

30. See *El Deber*, No. 8 (Padilla, 1915), Archivo Rudy Miranda (hereinafter ARM), Padilla. This did not mean that Tomina bandits did not kill landowners in their forays outside of their native province. See, for example, IP 1926, p. liii; and IP 1928, p. 172.

31. AJP 1919:445.

32. AJP 1926:11.

33. These stories are based on interviews held in Villa Serrano, 19 January 1982, with Arcil Noyes, a longtime resident of Villa Serrano and at the time subprefect of the province of Belisario Boeto. The first notice I have found of Romero comes from "1905: Juicios criminales," in which the bandit appeared twice as a defendant. The last mention comes from an article in *El Deber*, 1,8 (April 1915): 1.

34. Silvio Duncan Baretta and John Markoff suggest that the frontier legacy was one of violence. See their important article, "Civilization and Barbarism: Cattle Frontiers in Latin America," *Comparative Studies in Society and History* 20 (Oct. 1978): 587–620.

35. For Argentina, see Richard W. Slatta, "Rural Criminality and Social Conflict in Nineteenth-Century Buenos Aires Province," *Hispanic American Historical Review*, 60,3 (Aug. 1980): 450–472.

36. Eric J. Hobsbawm, *Primitive Rebels: Studies in Archaic Forms of Social Movements in the Nineteenth and Twentieth Centuries* (Manchester: Manchester University Press, 1959), pp. 26–28.

8

"La Chambelona": Political Protest, Sugar, and Social Banditry in Cuba, 1914–1917

LOUIS A. PÉREZ, JR.

POLITICAL REVOLT BECOMES SOCIAL PROTEST AND BANDITRY

On the morning of February 10, 1917, government authorities in Havana discovered a far-flung conspiratorial network involving key officers of the army and ranking members of the Liberal party. From this inauspicious beginning Cuba plunged directly into the third revolutionary upheaval of the island's young republican experience. Historians placing the February revolution solely within the context of national politics have moved competently, often eloquently, through the course of events of that Cuban spring, detailing at some length the vicissitudes of the short-lived Liberal revolt. Prepared, if not predisposed, to see the February revolt as a function of partisan struggles in Cuba, historians have interpreted the insurrection of 1917 wholly as a political phenomenon. To be sure, powerful political currents ran through the movement. The political origins of the February revolution, however, have effectively obscured its social content. What began as a political revolt developed quickly into a social protest of considerable significance and lasting impact in twentieth-century Cuba.[1]

The Liberal plot to overthrow the Conservative government of Mario G. Menocal was conceived as a response to the president's illegal imposition of a second term. The conspirators organized the planned coup around a swift seizure of military installations in Havana, seconded by army takeovers of provincial capitals.[2] Liberal hopes for a quick seizure of power depended entirely on winning the support of the armed forces. Organized less than a decade earlier under the

Reprinted from *Inter-American Economic Affairs*, Spring 1978, with permission of Inter-American Affairs Press.

Liberal government of José Miguel Gómez (1908–1912), the national army continued in 1917 substantially under the command of Liberal appointees.[3] In all, the Liberal plotters fully expected some 75 to 85 percent of the regular armed forces to join the party against the Conservative government.[4]

The conspiracy also secured the endorsement of party functionaries at both the appointed and elective levels of government. Several members of the Liberal delegation in the national congress pledged to abandon Havana to join the party leadership in the field. At the provincial and municipal levels elected Liberal officeholders ratified the conspiracy.[5] The governor-elect of Camagüey, Enrique Recio Agüero, coordinated party directives in the province. In total, one governor and some thirty mayors placed the resources and authority of their offices at the service of the Liberal plot.[6]

So confident were the Liberals in the success of the movement that the conspirators conferred on the insurrectionary movement a distinctive festive quality. "La Chambelona," as the revolt was to become known, was seen as something of a musical jamboree, in which street dancing, strolling musicians, and minstrel orchestras would lead the triumphant Liberal advance on Havana.

The need to set the conspiracy into motion prematurely on February 10, however, represented only the first of a series of disasters for the disgruntled Liberals. To be sure, Liberals enjoyed some success in eastern Cuba. In Oriente province mutinous army chieftains seized command of the provincial regiment and arrested pro-government officers. Insurgent army commanders moved on Santiago de Cuba, displacing Conservative government officials and organizing a new Liberal de facto administration under military control. Within hours the pro-Liberal forces had seized control of the province.[7] Army mutinies in smaller interior cities, supported by municipal authorities, resulted in Liberal seizures of Campechuela, Guantánamo, Bayamo, Holguín, Mayarí, and Baracoa. The uprising in Camagüey province enjoyed similar success. The majority of the province's military posts fell to Liberal partisans without struggle.[8] By February 14 Camagüey had joined Oriente under Liberal authority.

The Liberal effort in Las Villas province experienced mixed results. Municipal authorities in Abreus, San Juan de las Yeras, Camajuaní, and Corralillo followed the party leadership into rebellion. Military subposts and rural guard stations, moreover, defected in sufficient numbers to allow José Miguel Gómez to establish the insurgent field headquarters in central Cuba. The regimental command in the provincial capital, however, remained loyal to the government.[9]

In the west the uprising failed almost as completely as it had succeeded in the east. Alerted to the Liberal conspiracy in Havana, the government moved swiftly against suspected plotters. Outside of a scattered number of short-lived mutinies, largely rural guard posts, military stations in Pinar del Río, Havana, and Matanzas provinces remained securely under government authority. By February 12, by which time the eastern third of the island had passed almost entirely under insurgent control, the American legation in Havana could report "perfect quiet" in the west.[10]

The stillborn uprisings in the west had far-reaching repercussions for Liberals nationally. The failure to capture Camp Columbia and La Cabaña military fortress in Havana ended all Liberal hopes for a quick transfer of power. The axis of the conspiracy had passed through the capital's military garrisons; on the seizure of Camp Columbia and La Cabaña had rested the taking of Havana and, ultimately, the ouster of the Conservatives. Within forty-eight hours it had become apparent that the Conservative government had survived the initial conspiratorial thrust intact, retaining, in varying degrees, control over the western two-thirds of the island and in apparent command of the allegiance of the bulk of the armed forces. The failure to take Havana, moreover, persuaded many Liberal co-conspirators, committed to but not yet compromised by the conspiracy, to delay active participation pending subsequent developments. Failure in the capital ended among many Liberals all hopes for success; for many, events in Havana signaled the collapse of the movement, thereby serving to discourage any further participation of Liberals committed earlier to the conspiracy.

Liberal politico-military reversals in Cuba were compounded by setbacks abroad. In the wake of the abortive coup in Havana, many Liberal leaders hoped that the news of the revolt in the United States would force Washington to intervene in the dispute in their behalf.[11] Instead, the Wilson administration denounced the Liberal assault on constitutional government. On February 13 Secretary of State Robert Lansing expressed the "greatest apprehension" over the news of the revolt in Cuba. "Reports such as these of insurrection against the constituted Government," Lansing warned, "cannot be considered except as of the most serious nature since the Government of the United States has given its confidence and support only to Governments established through legal and constitutional methods."[12] In a second note five days later the State Department reiterated in some detail its support of the Menocal government and its view of the insurgency:

1. The Government of the United States supports and sustains the Constitutional Government of the Republic of Cuba.

2. The armed revolt against the Constitutional Government of Cuba is considered by the Government of the United States as a lawless and unconstitutional act and will not be countenanced.

3. The leaders of the revolt will be held responsible for injury to foreign nationals and for destruction of foreign property.

4. The Government of the United States will give careful consideration to future attitude towards those persons connected with and concerned in the present disturbance of peace in the Republic of Cuba.[13]

The American notes had immediately a far-reaching effect. Indeed, for a movement reorganizing after February 10 around the expectation of a favorable hearing from the United States, the two notes proved devastating. Many Liberals who earlier had delayed their decision to join Gómez now abandoned their plans to support the movement altogether. Publicity of American support of Menocal, moreover, contributed to arresting the deterioration of the government's position nationally. A considerable number of insurgent chieftains in the field, now convinced that Washington's position ended the movement's only remaining hope of success, surrendered to government authorities.[14] Other Liberal leaders, weighing personal political aspirations in the future, pondered the meaning of the fourth clause of the February 18 note; given the nature of U.S. control over the Cuban national system, few political leaders in the field, thinking into the future, could receive such a warning without pausing to reexamine the wisdom of their actions in 1917. Many yielded to the future. Two days later members of the Liberal congressional delegation caucused under the leadership of Juan Gualberto Gómez and declared themselves "pacifists."[15] A number of insurgent Liberal mayors surrendered immediately. In perhaps the most demoralizing defection of all, the 1916 Liberal presidential candidate, Alfredo Zayas, disassociated himself from the rebel leadership and surrendered to Conservative authorities in Havana.[16]

Two weeks after the American note of February 18, moreover, Conservative forces scored their most important military victory over the insurgent Liberals. On March 7, in Caicaje, Las Villas, government troops defeated one of the main bodies of the insurgent army, taking prisoner some 200 Liberal soldiers and virtually the entire field command of the revolution, including José Miguel Gómez, his son Miguel Mariano, and Governor Enrique Recio Agüero.[17]

LIBERAL REVERSALS

As the rebellion faltered forward into the second month, the hopelessness of the Liberal cause increased. Indeed, by mid-March the Liberal armed challenge no longer constituted a direct threat to the Conservative government. Politico-military setbacks in Cuba and diplomatic reversals in the United States had convinced many national Liberal leaders in the field of the futility of further armed opposition to the Menocal government. The protest had earlier lost the active support of a considerable number of civilian party leaders who, in response to the American notes of February 13 and February 18, refused to mortgage their political careers to a movement opposed in Washington and apparently doomed in Cuba. The long-range repercussions of Caicaje, moreover, transcended the immediate effects of the loss of Gómez and the insurgent general staff. Civil and military chieftains, demoralized by the capture of the *jefe máximo* of the insurrection and now convinced that Caicaje signaled the final collapse of the movement, felt relieved of any further obligation to support the Liberal protest. After mid-March individual insurgent leaders in increasing numbers reached private peace settlements with government representatives. Some Liberal chieftains surrendered in exchange for guarantees of personal safety; others chose to abandon the field of armed struggle for exile abroad. By early spring hundreds of key figures of the Liberal uprising had found safety in the United States, Jamaica, Mexico, Haiti, and the Bahamas.[18]

Through capture, death, and exile the Liberal protest had been deprived of most of its nationally important chieftains. Civilian leaders who had originally organized the movement, together with army officers who had seconded the party leadership in mid-February, gradually disappeared from the field. When, in April, Menocal followed Washington's lead in declaring war on Germany, several more prominent leaders, including General Gerardo Machado, abandoned the field as an expression of solidarity with the homeland in the moment of the international crisis. In New York, Orestes Ferrara, the Liberals' public relations agent in the United States, announced that Cuba's declaration of war made Liberals "understand that our duty was to maintain internal peace above any other cause."[19]

REGIONAL SOCIAL PROTEST AND BANDITRY

The collapse of the insurgent national leadership deprived the movement of central direction. With the capture or death of ranking political and military leaders, and the flight, defection, and exile of others, direction of insurgent forces continuing to operate in the field passed to unknown subaltern commanders. Indeed, after mid-March the quality of the insurgency had undergone a radical transformation. However effective the combination of American diplomacy and Cuban military measures may have been in suppressing the Liberal political challenge, by early spring Havana had still failed to put an end to the insurrection. In the interior countryside of Oriente and Camagüey, the insurgency had acquired a new meaning and purpose. The collapse of central insurgent authority had decentralized the leadership of the armed struggle and transformed a national movement into a protest that was largely regional and local. By early April the insurgency had reorganized around scattered field units distributed throughout the eastern provinces. The organized political challenge had come to an end without a cessation of the insurgency.

In mid-March, in the wake of Liberal reversals, the main bodies of organized insurgent forces in Oriente and Camagüey had dispersed into mobile guerrilla units. The establishment of guerrilla columns had necessitated the organization of new commands destined to survive in the field long after the ranking Liberal leaders had deserted the armed struggle. The main body of insurgent Liberal armies in Santiago de Cuba, Baracoa, Mayarí, Songo, Guantánamo, and Manatí retired into the interior reorganized into irregular units.[20] Estimates of the total number of rebels operating as guerrillas in late March and early April varied. In Camagüey some 3,000 to 4,000 armed men remained in the field.[21] In Oriente various estimates placed guerrilla forces between 5,000 and 7,000 men.[22]

As the leadership of the insurrection decentralized the social base of the insurgency broadened. In addition to—and increasingly, in the course of the spring, independent of—the original political grievances the armed protest embraced a variety of local issues. The populist appeal of the Liberal party and flamboyant leadership had early attracted to the insurgent banner workers, farmers, and peasants in virtually all the eastern provinces. The "ignorant and incapable class," the American consul in Havana reported, made up the majority of the Liberals' support.[23] In the Guantánamo valley the revolutionary move had widespread support among sugar workers in the region. As late as May observers speculated that there would be a "continued increase in the drift of the laboring classes to the ranks of the bandits and revolutionary force."[24] Throughout the spring Afro-Cubans in increasing numbers joined the partisan bands operating in the East.

Local social and economic grievances, independent of national political issues, gained increasing prominence as the rebellion entered the third month, now without national direction. In 1917 a way of life was coming to an end in eastern Cuba. Throughout the latter half of the nineteenth century the eastern provinces had remained largely impervious to the currents then transforming sectors of western Cuba into the bastion of the sugar latifundios. Sugar estates in the East, by comparison, were primitive family enterprises, without the capital and technological resources of the West, and singularly incapable of participating in the modernization impulse of the nineteenth century.[25] Thirty years of intermittent warfare in the course of Cuba's struggle for independence, moreover, during which Oriente and Camagüey had served almost uninterruptedly as the central theater of military operations, ended any reasonable likelihood of the sugar estates in the East overtaking their counterparts in the West; the scorched-earth tactics of contending armies, Valeriano Weyler's reconcentration program, and the subsequent flight of both labor and capital dealt the final body blows to the production capabilities of the eastern estates.

By the turn of the century Oriente contained the largest number of independent farms with the smallest average acreage.[26] A variety of different communities and economic enterprises survived into the twentieth century intact. The sugar estate continued to coexist forbearingly with the coffee plantation, the cocoa field, the single independent farm, and the innumerable unincorporated rural communities.[27] To be sure, the sugar latifundio occupied an important place in the eastern landscape. Typically, however, the latifundio in Oriente was more traditional than commercial, more family than corporate. Life on the *oriental* estate was turned inward, isolated, and largely self-contained; estates conferred on their owners more prestige than profits. In 1899 only one-half of 1 percent of the farms in Oriente was more than ten caballerías (330 acres), constituting some 26.9 percent of the area under cultivation.[28] At about the same time Oriente province claimed the highest number of individual land proprietors.[29] For generations much of the land in these backwater rural areas was held in common, frequently without formal title; family land claims, after reaching back to the century of conquest and settlement, rested on little more than local tradition and simple occupancy. Few had hardly more than a vague notion of the size or value of their land.[30]

The collapse of European beet sugar production and the rise of sugar prices early in World War I forecast a profound transformation of the economic purpose of land in Oriente and Camagüey. Soon after August 1914 the drive to subdue eastern Cuba under the regime of the corporate sugar latifundio gained increasing momentum. Cane fields spilled out of the traditional sugar regions in western and central Cuba and advanced implacably eastward; miles of imposing timber forests succumbed to the expanding fields of frail stalks of cane. Teresa Casuso recalled many year later:

I remember, in Oriente, the great impenetrable forests that were set aflame, whole jungles that were fired and razed to the ground to make way for the sugar cane. My parents were in despair for that lost wealth of beautiful, fragrant tropical wood—cedar, mahogany, and mastic, and magnificent-grained pomegrante—blazing in sacrifice to the frenzy to cover the country-side with sugar cane.[31]

Newly organized sugar conglomerates, representing enormous sums of American capital, appeared throughout eastern Cuba. Old estates, traditional holdings, and family farms passed under new foreign management; larger sugar producers absorbed smaller estates. Consolidation of sugar properties placed more and more land under increasingly fewer owners. As early as 1912 the Atlantic Fruit Company launched major sugar operations throughout Camagüey and Oriente. The Santa Cecilia Sugar Company expanded its holdings of 10,000 acres in the area of Guantánamo. The Manatí Sugar Company, incorporated in 1912 and completed in 1914, acquired in Oriente some 76,500 acres of sugar and the supporting rail infrastructure. The Guantánamo Sugar Company secured ownership of some 55,000 acres in southeastern Oriente. The Cuba Cane Sugar Corporation launched by far the most ambitious enterprise of the period. Organized in 1916, Cuba Cane did not establish new mills, but assumed direction of existing estates. Within a year Cuba Cane had acquired seventeen fully equipped mills, owning outright 353,000 acres and leasing on a long-term basis an additional 194,000 acres. Some 500 miles of rail, together with 400 locomotives and 2,500 cane cars, passed under the control of Cuba Cane.[32]

Older established American operations in Cuba modernized and expanded the acreage under sugar cultivation. In 1916 the Cuban-American Sugar Company acquired some 325,000 acres, eight sugar mills, two refineries, 500 miles of telephone, and 225 miles of railroad. The United Fruit Company cultivated sugar on some 127,000 acres of recently acquired land on the north coast of Oriente. In Niquero, Oriente, the New Niquero Sugar Company rounded out its expansion at 28,000 acres while leasing an additional 9,000.[33] The Atkins family, residents of Cuba since the latter half of the nineteenth century, modernized its operations in Camagüey and in 1915 organized the Punta Alegre Sugar Company.[34] Between 1914 and 1917 some twenty new sugar mills inaugurated operations in Cuba, largely all in Camagüey and Oriente. Visiting Cuba in early 1917, assistant secretary of the navy Franklin D. Roosevelt confided to his diary that the "development of the Eastern end of Cuba was marked and of course sugar for two years has been a gold mine."[35] By 1920 American investment in Cuban sugar had reached some $400 million and had come to dominate almost half of sugar production on the island.[36]

The expansion of the zones of sugar cultivation into eastern Cuba adversely affected other agricultural enterprises in Camagüey and Oriente. In Oriente coffee and cocoa planters lost their workers and, ultimately, their lands to sugar. By 1919 coffee and cocoa production had ceased in nine Oriente *municípios*, including Santiago, Mayarí, Holguín, Banes, Gibara, Puerto Padre, Victoria de las Tunas, Campechuela, and Niquero. Several coffee plantations, such as El Olimpo and others in Songo and Palma Soriano, were converted directly into sugar plantations.[37]

Much to the bewilderment and confusion of the people of Camagüey and Oriente, in less than a decade scores of small landowners, farmers, and peasants were transformed into a rural proletariat. Those who resisted the pressures to abandon the soil found themselves driven to search for new land deep in the inhospitable mountain reaches of the Baracoa and Sierra Maestra ranges, far away from traditional transportation routes and distant from local agricultural markets.[38] The concentration of land into the sugar latifundio uprooted the farmer, destroyed the rural landowning and independent farming class, impoverished the rural population, and converted the countryside into a satellite of foreign capital.[39]

Dislodged as an independent property-owning class, moreover, an entire sector of eastern Cuba's population found itself further displaced as a labor force. The coefficient vital to the success of the new sugar conglomerates arising in eastern Cuba necessarily involved the availability of a plentiful supply of cheap labor. For this the sugar companies turned to Haiti and Jamaica. Starting as early as 1913 increasing numbers of Antillean laborers arrived in Cuba to work in the newly organized cane fields of Camagüey and Oriente. In 1917 a record number of Jamaicans and Haitians arrived in Cuba.[40] Between 1913 and 1921 some 180,000 workers were contracted legally in Haiti and Jamaica to cut cane in eastern Cuba.[41] Many thousands more were suspected to have entered the island illegally.[42]

The arrival of West Indians in such numbers in less than a decade further contributed to the general disruption of Oriente society. Between 1907 and 1919 the population of Oriente showed an extraordinary increase of some 60 percent, from 455,086 to 730,909.[43] A community largely beyond the main reaches of the twentieth century and, by virtue of isolation and temperament, for generations impervious to outside influences was suddenly subjected to a wave of foreign immigration totally without precedent. Foreign languages, strange customs, and new religions swept through the province, undermining the region's long tradition of cultural stability and local isolation.

The increase of the provincial population in Oriente, however, although consistent with population trends across the island generally, concealed an entirely different demographic drama occurring at the local level. Sugar not only appropriated the land, but also displaced the people. Considerable numbers of *barrios* in those municípios experiencing the severest socioeconomic dislocations suffered sharp losses of population. Indeed, between 1907 and 1919 at least five barrios situated in the new sugar districts of eastern Cuba disappeared altogether.[44] Former coffee- and cocoa-producing municípios, most notably Gibara, Mayarí, Holguín, Puerto Padre, and Baracoa, suffered the greatest losses. Fully one-third of the twenty-three barrios of Baracoa experienced a decline in population; more than half of the fourteen barrios in Cobre lost population. Similar developments were experienced in Alto Songo, Bayamo, Guantánamo, and Jiguaní.[45]

In early 1917, as the Liberal party plotted against the Menocal government, eastern Cuba found itself in the throes of a socioeconomic upheaval. The traditional world of generations of *orientales* was crashing suddenly in their midst, in full view, without warning, without apparent reason. By displacing farmers and peasants, thereby ending self-sufficiency, and depressing wages through the importation of cheap labor from neighboring West Indian islands, the new sugar latifundios contributed powerfully to reducing living standards throughout eastern Cuba. A society made up in the main of self-sufficient farmers was reorganized into a community consisting largely of dependent farm workers, frequently working for foreign corporations, eating foreign-produced foods, living often in company towns, and buying from company stores.[46] Land in eastern Cuba ceased to produce for the local population and became, instead, the preserve of products destined for foreign markets. The loss of control over the economic purpose of land further increased Cuba's dependency on foreign food imports. Between 1914 and 1916 food imports increased in dramatic terms[47]:

Meat	$11,269,163	$18,427,137
Cereals	15,393,569	26,151,554
Fruits	722,057	1,247,812
Vegetables	5,602,017	10,362,443

"The small Cuban population," one observer commented, "cannot produce $300 or $400 worth of sugar per capita and at the same time produce their own food."[48] The loss of self-sufficiency occurred, moreover, almost simultaneously with the first of a series of relentless price increases, especially in food. Between November 1916 and October 1917 the price of rice increased 75 percent in one typical company store in Oriente; flour increased by 46 percent and beans by some 50 percent.[49]

A growing mood of resentment and indignation well anticipated "La Chambelona" in Camagüey and Oriente. Rage among the peasants, farmers, and small landowners mounted; popular reaction against the bewildering disruption of Oriente society increased. As early as October 1914 some 4,000 peasants marched angrily against local government authorities in Baracoa, protesting the loss of their land. A confrontation of tragic proportions between the demonstrating peasants and the armed forces was avoided only after local authorities pledged to seek legal means through which to recover the lost lands.[50] In July 1917 peasants in Santiago protested maneuvers designed to dispossess them of their lands.[51]

In February 1917 the prevailing mood in eastern Cuba was very much predisposed to rebellion. Indeed, the Liberal revolt found virtually an entire province poised at the brink of revolution. Supporters of "La Chambelona" in Camagüey and Oriente brought to the insurgency a complexity of grievances that went well beyond the political dimensions of the Liberal protest. That the insurgency survived well after the collapse of central political direction was in no small measure due to the socioeconomic nourishment that the Liberals' political protest received locally in Camagüey and Oriente. The disappearance of Liberal chieftains facilitated this process and served to invigorate the politically bankrupt insurgency with local socioeconomic issues.

The autonomy passing on to local insurgent forces after the disappearance of national leadership permitted partisan bands to turn their attention increasingly to local grievances, thereby generating local support. Three months after the Liberal coup stalled in Havana, the armed protest in Camagüey and Oriente had fully acquired characteristics of large-scale social banditry. The men and women who turn to social banditry, Eric Hobsbawm wrote, are products of the imposition of capital by external forces, "insidiously by the operation of economic forces which they do not understand and over which they have no control."[52] Bandits, Hobsbawm wrote elsewhere, tend to reflect the "disruption of an entire society, the rise of new classes and social structures, the resistance of entire communities or people against the destruction of its way of life."[53]

Well before the outbreak of the February revolution, acts of individual rebellion and personal revolt were on the increase in Camagüey and Oriente. Displaced from the land, deprived of a livelihood, many orientales channeled their rage into banditry. The livestock and wares of the large latifundios and foreign estates, together with company stores, were subjected to increasing attacks. Several rural rebels quickly distinguished themselves and acquired province-wide reputations as popular symbols of oriental resistance to foreign technology and capital. Such personalities as José "Cholo" Rivera and Rafael Valera became the scourge of the estates. As early as November 1914 banditry had reached sufficient proportions to prompt secretary of gobernación Aurelio Hevia to pledge publicly new energetic measures to combat the prevailing wave of "lawlessness."[54]

In the early spring of 1917 a political rebellion conceived by the national directors of the Liberal party had reorganized around local issues under the direction of provincial bandits. As early as February 28 the French consul in Santiago reported the interior "filling with guerrillas difficult for the insurrection leaders to control."[55] Almost from the outset insurgent bands enjoyed the protection of the provincial population. "In the great part of the country," the American consul in Caimanera reported in mid-April, "the rebels find welcome shelter among the inhabitants."[56] Protected, sheltered, and supported by the local population, armed partisans attacked sugar estates, seized livestock, and made off with food and supplies; goods seized from estates and company stores were often redistributed among communities in the interior.[57] By the spring the protest in eastern Cuba had evolved into a peasant cry for vengeance on the propertied, a fury of energy directed toward curbing the estate and the righting of individual wrongs. One observer remarked of the revolt in late March:

The Liberals do not want to fight, they do not want to kill or destroy, but being under-officered the men who have private grievances against some of the plantation owners or managers have avenged them in spite of the influence of their officers. The destruction of property is done a great deal by private individuals not by the revolutionists.[58]

The decentralization of the insurgent command, and the subsequent dispersals of Liberal armies into local guerrilla units, converted a difficult situation into an impossible one for Conservative authorities in Havana. The widened social base of the protest had pushed the insurgency beyond the limited political objectives inherent in the original Liberal plot. "The revolutionary forces operating in this province," the American consul in Caimanera reported in late May, "have now degenerated into groups of bandits headed by notorious characters having no political significance."[59]

Nowhere did the compelling undercurrents of the insurrection in Oriente and Camagüey in early spring emerge in such relief as in the relationship between armed bands and American property owners. The decentralization and dispersal of the rebel forces increased the difficulty of the sugar estates to negotiate private settlements with local insurgent units. No single commander exercised complete and effective authority over the far-flung bands located throughout the sugar districts of eastern Cuba. "The great difficulty in which I find myself," one estate manager wrote, "is that there is no one single chief, or head with whom I can treat, there being present in our neighborhood seven men acting as Captains, Colonels and Generals, constantly giving unintelligible orders and counter orders and always finding a group ready to obey."[60] In the absence of adequate protection from Havana, planters in the eastern interior had on several earlier occasions successfully negotiated settlements with insurgent Liberal chieftains in which the estates offered food, supplies, and shelter in exchange for assurances guaranteeing the security of estate property and personnel. By early spring these informal arrangements were becoming increasingly unworkable. "We did not ask for any [government] protection before," the assistant manager of the Miranda Sugar Company cabled the New York office, "while the Liberals were organized and under recognized leaders, but now the situation is different—for the rebels are scattered throughout the country and we fear the small bands that come across our property may do us some damage."[61]

The inability of government forces to act either adequately in the protection of property or decisively in the suppression of the armed bands assumed a new urgency in April and May as past informal pacts between planters and rebels proved increasingly ineffective. One group of American citrus colonists in Oriente petitioned Washington for assistance in the face of new developments in the province:

For nearly two months the rebel forces were held in restraint by rebel chiefs that were in our neighborhoods, and we owe it to their efforts that our colonies were left undestroyed at the time. After the government "successes" in the Southern part of the Province, large hordes of rebels invaded our territory. The leaders lost control and our business places, farms, and homes have been raided or burned, our horses and cattle have been carried away or killed.[62]

The attack on property served to alienate the insurgents from the Liberal organizers of the revolt. Key party leaders looked with horror at the force they had contributed to unleashing in the eastern third of the island. The revolt had acquired social dimensions never intended by its architects. In early May congressional Liberal leaders caucused in Havana and ordered all party members still under arms to surrender to government authorities.[63] Too many ranking members of the Liberal party held substantial interests in the very sugar properties under siege in eastern Cuba. With sugar profits peaking in the early spring, the persistent insurgency, beyond the control of the organized political parties, threatened both the completion of the 1917 harvest and, more important, the planting of the 1918 crop. Antonio de Sánchez Bustamante, a Liberal senator from Havana, sat on the board of directors of the Cuba Cane Sugar Corporation. Miguel Arango, the Liberal vice-presidential candidate in 1920, managed the Mantatí Sugar Estate. In New York, Orestes Ferrara, a member of the board of directors of Cuba Cane, quickly disassociated himself from the insurgency after mid-March. The revolt, Ferrara declared through his attorney in New York, Martin W. Littleton, had "gone crazy and was destroying property right and left."[64] As long as the revolution was "purely political," Littleton informed the State Department, Ferrara did not disguise his sympathy and support for the Liberal cause. "Now that the revolution has come to a point where it will end in anarchy," Littleton explained, "he is very much opposed to it because anarchy means the ruin of individual rights and property, and he is a large holder of property himself."[65]

SEND IN THE MARINES?

Growing attacks on property involved American interests much more directly in the Cuban insurrection. Throughout the early spring the protracted rebellion impinged increasingly on American economic interest in Cuba. Confidence in Havana's ability to restore order in the East gave way in Washington to apprehension and official skepticism. In mid-May the State Department concluded that Havana was incapable of ending the protest in Camagüey and Oriente without armed assistance from the United States. Sugar planters in eastern Cuba clamored for protection against local bands.

In Santiago de Cuba, American consul Henry H. Morgan concurred. The revolt no longer posed a serious political threat, Morgan conceded. The unwillingness of planters in eastern Cuba to clear burned areas in preparation for the 1918 crop, however, owing largely to a general lack of confidence in Havana's ability to guarantee the security of future sugar production, posed the largest single threat to the next year's harvest. The only certain means through which to inspire confidence among the planters and provide minimum assurances of safety to the sugar crop, Morgan counseled, involved the sending of "American Marines to the province to cooperate with Cubans but with authority to pursue and destroy rebel bands where ever located."[66] Several weeks later Morgan again reassured Washington that the protest no longer posed a political threat to Conservatives in Havana. The small quantity of arms and ammunition recovered from the insurgent forces, however, raised speculation among the planters that behind the hidden and unretrieved weapons stalked another revolution planned for the 1918 harvest season. A repetition of the 1917 disorders, Morgan warned, threatened to destroy not only the 1918 crop in Santa Clara, Camagüey, and Oriente, but also all future sugar production in eastern Cuba. "I am of the opinion," Morgan wrote, "that the only way to forestall such an uprising will be to send an armed force into the country as it is the only force the rebels respect and fear."[67] In late June, Morgan issued a third request for American armed forces. "No confidence whatever," the consul general insisted, "can be placed in the Cuban troops, for they are not competent to control the situation." U.S. troops would act in conjunction with Cuban forces; the joint operations would receive maximum publicity throughout the island, Morgan suggested, and serve to inspire confidence among the planters.[68]

THE DECLINE OF BANDITRY

Widespread social banditry in eastern Cuba diminished somewhat by the summer of 1917. In August the first contingent of Marines arrived in Cuba and established camps in Camagüey and Oriente. For the rest of the year Marine "practice marches" were organized around the pursuit of armed bands in the eastern interior.[69] In July 1917 Menocal suspended constitutional guarantees. This, the president explained to the American minister, enabled the government to "imprison persons believed to be German intriguers when under ordinary conditions they can be held only three days unless there is proof of the lawlessness."[70] In fact, the suspension of constitutional guarantees announced the inauguration of a systematic government campaign of selective terror and intimidation in Camagüey and Oriente. As early as April a reign of terror had descended on rural communities in the eastern interior. Between April 2 and April 5 some fifty persons were summarily executed by an army patrol on the property of the Elia and Jobabo estates.[71] Throughout the summer government agents moved against suspected rebels and rebel sympathizers; assassinations reached near epidemic proportions. "A large number of murders are being perpetrated in this province and Camagüey by hired assassins," Consul Morgan reported from Santiago de Cuba on August 31, "the victims being members of the Liberal party who took part in the last revolution."[72]

Not all insurgent bands disappeared, however. In June the *New York Times* correspondent in Havana reported learning that the armed protest continued unabated in the "mountainous regions of Oriente province."[73] As late as July 31 the American vice-consul in Antilla reported the existence of "mountainers" near the Oriente towns of La Maya and Songo, well armed, some with new rifles, and all with plenty of ammunition.[74] Many survivors receded deeper into the mountain folds of the eastern wilderness, there to remain as a community of outcasts and fugitives in much the same fashion as the *palenques* and bandits of the nineteenth century.[75] Periodically, in the years that followed, the capital press published brief back-page accounts of the results of army encounters with the bandit veterans of "La Chambelona." In December 1917 the bandit chieftain "Nando" Guerra eluded a government ambush in San Jerónimo, Camagüey. In January 1918 Justo and Enrique Hernández were captured and summarily executed by a rural guard patrol in Céspedes, Camagüey. In January 1920 Augusto Puente Guillot met his end at the hands of the rural guard unit in Boniato, Oriente. Ultimately, the capital press lost interest in reporting the fate of the bandit survivors of "La Chambelona."[76]

The landscape of Camagüey and Oriente remained, nevertheless, irrevocably changed. Sugar in the East was no longer a way of life; traditionally one out of many, it had become virtually the only way. At an enormous cost eastern Cuba had finally overtaken the West. Economic and social subjugation to the regime of the corporate sugar latifundio was only one aspect of the new order. Along with the corporate estate went, in increasing numbers, the repressive forces of the state. An expanded network of rural guard posts descended on the eastern provinces to provide protection for the sugar estates.[77] Abusive, arbitrary, and high handed, the rural guards would come to terrorize the next generation of farmers and peasants.[78]

Orientales would never fully reconcile themselves to the new order of their universe. What Fidel Castro found in the Sierra Maestra mountains some forty years later were the descendants of many of the irreconcilable first-generation *montuno* families. For many of the early peasant converts to *fidelismo*, the decision to support the embryonic guerrilla columns was very much a function of the legacy of 1914–1917.[79] More important, the survivors of "Granma" stepped unwittingly into a local revolutionary tradition, however vague and ill-defined. The rage of 1917 quickly transformed itself into an enduring enmity against the sugar latifundios, the foreigners that owned them, and the rural guards that protected them. Nowhere else on the island was land as impassioned an issue and as powerful a longing as it was among the dispossessed montuno families of eastern Cuba.[80] From this point, it was a short and natural step to secure the participation of the primitive rebels of 1917 in the revolutionary struggle of the 1950s.

NOTES

I am grateful to José Keselman and Steven F. Lawson for their helpful advice and criticism.

1. The corpus of literature varies only in detail in its treatment of the February revolution. See Charles E. Chapman, *A History of the Cuban Republic* (New York, 1927), pp. 362–385; Russell H. Fitzgibbon, *Cuba and the United States, 1900–1935* (Menasha, 1935), pp. 155–165; Hugh Thomas, *Cuba, the Pursuit of Freedom* (New York, 1971), pp. 525–532; Leo J. Myer, "The United States and the Cuban Revolution of 1917," *Hispanic American Historical Review* 10 (Feb. 1930): 138–166; Bernardo Merino and F. de Ibarzabal, *La revolución de febrero. Datos para la historia*, 2nd ed. (Havana, 1918); José Navas, *La convulsión de febrero* (Matanzas, 1917); Herminio Portell Vilá, "La Chambelona en Camagüey," *Bohemia*, 53 (8 May 1960): 12–13, 199; and Herminio Portell Vilá, "La Chambelona en Oriente," *Bohemia*, 53 (24 April 1960): 12–13, 124. Nor have Cuban historians since 1959 made any significant historiographical advance. See Dirección Política de las F.A.R., *Historia de Cuba*, 3rd ed. (Havana, 1971), pp. 566–570; Julio Le Riverend, *La República* (Havana, 1973), pp. 126–129; and Pedro Luis Padron, "La sublevación liberal de 1917," *Granma*, 25 October 1969, p. 2.

2. Matías Duque, *Ocios del presidio*, 1917 (Havana, 1917), pp. 23–25.

3. Horacio Ferrer, *Con el rifle al hombro* (Havana, 1950), pp. 218–219; Raimundo Cabrera, *Mis malos tiempos* (Havana, 1920), p. 187; Luis Solano Alvarez, *Mi actuación militar. Apuntes para la historia de la revolución de febrero de 1917* (Havana, 1920), pp. 19–41.

4. Carlos Guas, "¿Quién ordenó el levantamiento de febrero?" *El Mundo*, 17 June 1919, p. 16; William E. Gonzales to secretary of state, 15 February 1917, 837.00/1489, General Records of the Department of State, Record Group 59, National Archives, Washington, D.C. (hereinafter cited as DS/NA, RG 59).

5. Fernando Inclán Lavastida, *Historia de Marianao* (Marianao, 1943), pp. 138–139; Navas, *La convulsión de febrero*, pp. 19–23.

6. Merino and Ibarzabal, *La revolución de febrero*, pp. 101–103.

7. Lus Moret de Mola, "Sobre la guerra civil de 1917: Memorandum," *Boletín del Archivo Nacional*, 60 (Jan.-Dec. 1961): 179–181. P. Merrill Griffith, "City Taken by Military Forces," 12 February 1917, File (1917) 800, Miscellaneous Correspondence, American Consulate, Santiago de Cuba, Records of the Foreign Service Posts of the Department of State, Record Group 84, National Archives, Washington, D.C. (hereinafter cited as FSP/NA, RG 84).

8. Portell Vilá, "La Chambelona en Camagüey," p. 13.

9. Wilfredo Ibrahim Conseugra, *Hechos y comentarios. La revolución de febrero en Las Villas* (Havana, 1920), pp. 19–30.

10. William E. Gonzales to secretary of state, 12 February 1917, Department of State, *Foreign Relations of the United States: 1917* (Washington, D.C., 1925), p. 355 (hereinafter cited as *FRUS*).

11. See Raimundo Cabrera and Orestes Ferrara to secretary of state, 12 February 1917, 837.00/1066, DS/NA, RG 59, and Orestes Ferrera, *Memorias: Una mirada sobre tres siglos* (Madrid, 1975), pp. 204–208.

12. Robert Lansing to William E. Gonzalez, 13 February 1917, *FRUS*, p. 356.

13. Robert Lansing to William E. Gonzales, 18 February 1917, ibid., p. 363.

14. *Diario de la Marina*, 20 February 1917, p. 1.

15. "La guerrita de febrero de 1917," *Boletín del Archivo Nacional*, 61 (Jan.-Dec. 1962): 232.

16. William E. Gonzales, "Revolution and History—As Mr. Ford Sees It" (unpublished ms., William E. Gonzales Papers, South Caroliniana Library, University of South Carolina, Columbia).

17. Waldemar León, "Caicaje: Batalla final de una revuelta," *Bohemia*, 59 (30 June 1967): 100–102.

18. Herminio Portell Vilá, "La Chambelona en Occidente," *Bohemia*, 52 (22 May 1960): 82; Miguel de Marcos Suárez, *Carlos Mendieta* (Havana, 1923), p. 117.

19. Orestes Ferrara to Woodrow Wilson, 13 May 1917, 837.00/1480, DS/NA, RG 59.

20. Merino and Ibarzabal, *La revolución de febrero*, pp. 220–248.

21. Ferrer, *Con el rifle al hombro*, p. 239.

22. P. Merrill Griffith to secretary of state, 15 May 1917, 837.00/1361, DS/NA, RG 59.

23. Gaston Schmutz to secretary of state, 26 February 1917, 837.00/1165, DS/NA, RG 59.

24. H. M. Wolcott, Caimanera, to secretary of state, 1 May 1917, 837.00/1375, DS/NA, RG 59.

25. Franklin W. Knight, *Slave Society in Cuba During the Nineteenth Century* (Madison, 1970), pp. 41–43, 156–157.

26. U.S. Department of War, *Informe sobre el censo de Cuba: 1899* (Washington, D.C., 1900), p. 554.

27. See, for example, property patterns in the *Municipio* of Holguín, in José A. García y Castañeda, *La municipalidad holguinera. Comentario histórico, 1898–1953* (Holguín, 1953), pp. 102–102.

28. Robert B. Hoernel, "Sugar and Social Change in Oriente, Cuba, 1898–1946," *Journal of Latin American Studies*, 8 (Nov. 1976): 233.

29. In 1902 proprietors numbered at some 16,900. Oriente province contained, moreover, the largest number of renters—some 43,721. See Victor S. Clark, "Labor Conditions in Cuba," *Bulletin of the Department of Labor*, 41 (July 1902): 688.

30. Enrique Lavedián, "Los ladrones de tierras en Oriente," *Gráfico*, 3 (7 Feb. 1914): 10. See also Robert B. Batchelder, "The Evolution of Cuban Land Tenure and Its Relations to Certain Argo-Economic Problems," *Southwestern Social Science Quarterly*, 33 (Dec. 1952): 241. For a discussion of the varieties of property ownership in eastern Cuba, see Francisco Pérez de la Riva, *Origen y régimen de la propiedad territorial en Cuba* (Havana, 1946), pp. 24–148.

31. Teresa Casuso, *Cuba and Castro*, trans. Elmer Grossberg (New York, 1961), p. 9. "If things go on like this," *El Mundo* editorialized in April 1916, "we will be planting cane in the patios of our homes." In León Primelles, *Crónica cubana, 1915–1918* (Havana, 1955), p. 182.

32. John Moody, *Moody's Analyses of Investments. Part II. Public Utilities and Industrials: 1917* (New York, 1917), pp. 997, 1174, 1280, 1644, 2029.

33. Ibid., pp. 1225, 2038.

34. Edwin Atkins, *Sixty Years in Cuba* (Cambridge, Mass., 1926), p. 342; Benjamin Allen, *A Story of the Growth of E. Atkins and Company and the Sugar Industry in Cuba* (New York, 1929), pp. 32–33.

35. Franklin D. Roosevelt, Longhand Diary, Trip to Cuba, January 21–25, 1917, Papers as Assistant Secretary of the Navy, Franklin D. Roosevelt Papers, Hyde Park, New York.

36. Robert W. Dunn, *American Foreign Investments* (New York, 1926), pp. 212–222. The rapid expansion of American-owned sugar estates between 1914 and 1916 alarmed many Cubans. As early as 1915 a number of congressmen advocated legislation designed to curtail foreign ownership of land in Cuba. See Wilfredo Fernández, *Problemas cubanos. Vendiendo la tierra se vende la República* (Havana, 1916); Luis Fernández Marcané, *La nacionalización de los ingenios cubanos* (Havana, 1921); and Primelles, *Crónica cubana*, pp. 64–65, 183–184.

37. Cuba, *Census of the Republic of Cuba, 1919* (Havana, 1920), p. 950.

38. Juan Jerez Villarreal, *Oriente (biografía de una provincia).* (Havana, 1960), p. 307; Antonio Núñez Jiménez, *Geografía de Cuba*, 2nd ed. (Havana, 1959), pp. 253–255.

39. Ramiro Guerra y Sánchez, *Sugar and Society in the Caribbean: An Economic History of Cuban Agriculture* (New Haven, Conn.: Yale University Press, 1964), pp. 85–93; Alberto Arredondo, *Cuba: Tierra indefensa* (Havana, 1945), pp. 246–248.

40. Some 18,000 Jamaicans and Haitians arrived in eastern Cuba to participate in the 1917 sugar harvest. See Cuba, Secretaría de Hacienda, Sección de Estadística, *Inmigración y movimiento de pasajeros en el año de 1917* (Havana, 1918), p. 5.

41. Cuba, Secretaria de Hacienda, Sección de Estadística, *Inmigración y movimientos de pasajeros en el año . . . 1913–1921* (Havana, 1914–1922).

42. Evelio Tellería Toca, "Mas de un cuarto de millón de braceros importados," *Granma*, 14 April 1970, p. 2; "El jamiquino y el haitiano," *La Lucha*, 19 October 1919, p. 12. J. Pérez de la Riva, "La inmigración antillana en Cuba durante el primer tercio del siglo xx," *Revista de la Biblioteca Nacional "José Martí,"* 18 (May-Aug. 1975): 74–88.

43. Cuba, *Census of the Republic of Cuba, 1919*, p. 392.

44. These included Nuevas de Jobosí and Santa Gertrudis in Camagüey and Aguarás, Cuaba, and La Plata (Puerto Padre) in Oriente.

45. This information is compiled from data in the Cuban censuses of 1907 and 1919.

46. Hoernel, "Sugar and Social Change," p. 235.

47. In H. H. Morgan to Herbert C. Hoover, 4 August 1917, 837.50/13, DS/NA, RG 59.

48. *New York Times*, 23 December 1917, p. 7.

49. Hoernel, "Sugar and Social Change," p. 235.

50. *Diario de la Marina*, 11 October 1914, pp. 1, 5.

51. *La Lucha*, 2 July 1917, p. 2.

52. Eric Hobsbawm, *Primitive Rebels* (New York, 1959), p. 5.

53. Eric Hobsbawm, *Bandits* (New York, 1969), p. 18.

54. Guillermo Rubiera, "Mario García Menocal y Deop," in Vicente Báez, ed., *La enciclopedia de Cuba*, 9 vols. (Madrid, 1975), 9: 137.

55. In William E. Gonzales to Robert Lansing, 28 February 1917, 837.00/1155, DS/NA, RG 59.

56. H. M. Wolcott to secretary of state, 20 April 1917, 837.00/1374, DS/NA, RG 59.

57. Loló de la Torriente, *Mi casa en la tierra* (Havana, 1956), pp. 89–93; statement

of N. Arthur Helmar, Division of Latin American Affairs, "Memorandum," 28 March 1917, 837.00/1315, DS/NA, RG 59.

58. Statement of N. Arthur Helmar, Division of Latin American Affairs, "Memorandum," 28 March 1917, 837.00/1315, DS/NA, RG 59.

59. H. M. Wolcott, "Political Conditions in Oriente Province," 22 May 1917, File (1917) 800, Miscellaneous Correspondence, American Consulate, Santiago de Cuba, FSP/NA, RG 84.

60. Diary of John R. Bullard, Jobabo, Cuba, 8 March 1917, 837.00/1472, DS/NA, RG 59.

61. L.M.A. Evan to C. Warner, 8 April 1917, 837.00/1788, DS/NA, RG 59. A. H. Lindelie, president of the Bayate Sugar Company, described the insurgent chieftains in mid-March as "neighbors and friends of ours." See A. H. Lindelie to A. J. Gronna, 16 March 1917, 837.00/1308, DS/NA, RG 59.

62. Andrew Kobler et al. to American consul, Santiago de Cuba, "Petition," 20 April 1917, File (1917) 800, Miscellaneous Correspondence, American Consulate, Santiago de Cuba, FSP/NA, RG 84.

63. *Diario de la Marina*, 7 May 1917, p. 12.

64. Martin W. Littleton to Frank L. Polk, 17 March 1917, File 228, Drawer 77, Frank L. Polk Papers, Sterling Memorial Library, Yale University, New Haven, Conn.; *New York Times*, 15 March 1917, p. 4.

65. Martin W. Littleton to Frank L. Polk, 7 May 1917, 837.00/1358, DS/NA, RG 59.

66. Henry H. Morgan to secretary of state, 30 May 1917, 837.61351/12, DS/NA, RG 59.

67. Henry H. Morgan to secretary of state, 16 June 1917, 837.61351/17, DS/NA, RG 59.

68. Henry H. Morgan, "Situation in Oriente Province, Cuba, and the Necessity for Sending One Regiment of U.S. Troops to that Part of the Island," 28 June 1917, 837.00/1394, DS/NA, RG 59.

69. Colonel M. J. Shaw, commanding officer, Seventh Regiment, to Major General Commandant, "Report of Operations," 3 November 1917, 837.00/1398, DS/NA, RG 59.

70. William E. Gonzales to secretary of state, 14 July 1917, 837.00/1396, DS/NA, RG 59.

71. Rubiera, "Mario García Menocal y Deop," p. 157. The Elia estates was one of the newly organized sugar properties in eastern Cuba, established in 1915 in the município of Guaimaro, Camagüey.

72. Henry H. Morgan to secretary of state, 31 August 1917, 837.00/1415, DS/NA, RG 59. See also J. Buttari Gaunard, *Boceto crítico histórico* (Havana, 1954), p. 377, and Vincente Méndez Roque, *Otros días* (Havana, 1962), pp. 117–118.

73. *New York Times*, 2, 3 June 1917, p. 4.

74. American vice-consul, Antilla, "Post-Revolution Conditions in Oriente Province, Cuba," 31 July 1917, 837.00/1408, DS/NA, RG 59.

75. See Francisco López Leiva, *El bandolerismo en Cuba (Contribución al estudio de esta plaga social)* (Havana, 1930), pp. 20–36. When, in 1958, Raul Castro established a second guerrilla front in the Sierra Cristal range in northeastern Oriente, he encountered some 200 bandits (*escopeteros*) operating in the region; these forces were promptly incorporated into the rebel army. See Euclides Vázquez Candela, "El Segundo Frente

Oriental 'Frank País': Pequeña república insurgente," *Revolución*, 11 March 1963, p. 8.

76. These accounts are found in *La Lucha*, 28 December 1917, 11 January 1920, and 25 December 1918, and in *Diario de la Marina*, 11 January 1920.

77. See Cuba, Congreso, Cámara de Representantes, Octavo Período Congresional, *Memoria de los trabajos realizados durante las cuatro legislaturas ordinarias y las dos extraordinarias del octavo período congresional, comprendido del dos de abril de mil novecientos diez y siete y siete de abril de mil novecientos diez y nueve* (Havana, 1919), p. 816; José González Valdés, "La Guardia Rural," *Boletín de Ejército*, 4 (Feb. 1919): 783–785; Oscar Pérez Vega, "El frente interior y la Guardia Rural," *Boletín del Ejército*, 6 (May-June 1955): 83–91.

78. Louis A. Pérez, Jr., *Army Politics in Cuba, 1898–1958* (Pittsburgh, 1976), pp. 142–143.

79. For a social profile of some of the early peasant recruits, see Luis Rolando Cabrera, "Baldomero, el montuno que salvó a seis expedicionarios del 'Granma,' " *Bohemia*, 51 (22 Mar. 1959): 46–47, 128; Vicente Cubillas, " 'Yo fuí el primer guía de Fidel al Illegar el Granma,' " *Revolución*, 2 December 1959, p. 8; Juan Hidalgo, "Guillermo García: El primer campesino que se unió a Fidel en la Sierra Maestra," *Hoy*, 2, 21 June 1963, pp. 6ff.; Regino Martin, "Charla con el comandante Crescendio Pérez: Un héroe de leyenda," *Carteles*, 40 (8 Feb. 1959): 38–40, 82. Hugh Thomas described Crescendio Pérez, one of the first peasants to join Castro, as "a bandit more than a radical, a common criminal." Thomas, *Cuba, the Pursuit of Freedom*, p. 901.

80. The first territory occupied by the rebel army, Ernesto Che Guevara later recalled, was

inhabited by a class of peasants different in its social and cultural roots from those that inhabit the regions of extensive, semi-mechanized Cuban agriculture. In fact, the Sierra Maestra, locale of the first revolutionary column, is a place that serves as a refuge to all the peasants who struggle daily against the landlord. They go there as squatters on the land belonging to the state or some rapacious landlord, searching for a new piece of land that will yield them some small wealth. They struggled continuously against the exactions of the soldiers, always allied with the landowning power. . . . The soldiers who made up our first guerrilla army of rural people came from that part of this social class which was most aggressive in demonstrating its love for the land and its possession.

Ernesto Che Guevara, "Cuba: ¿Excepción histórica o vanguardia en la lucha anticolonialista?" in Ernesto Che Guevara, *Obra revolucionaria*, ed. Roberto Fernández Retamar, 2nd ed. (Mexico, 1968), pp. 517–518.

9

Political Banditry and the Colombian *Violencia*

GONZALO G. SÁNCHEZ and DONNY MEERTENS

translated by Edna Gutiérrez de Moolick

The *Violencia* brought to Colombia a horrifying period of brutality and terror from the late 1940s to the early 1960s. The powerful dynamics of partisanship, regionalism, and class conflict gave rise to movements for armed struggle. But beginning with the first National Front government of Alberto Lleras Camargo in 1958, political legitimacy was denied to those engaged in armed struggle. Thereafter, in the Colombian countryside, and particularly in the coffee regions, political banditry appeared and in some cases grew out of previous movements for armed struggle. Political bandits formed alliances with peasants, merchants, and local elites. But they suffered defeat during the 1960s for several reasons: their contradictory bases of support (peasant and elite), their own tactical blunders, and effective national military and political mobilization against them.

Political bandits share some characteristics with classic social bandits. And their activities and social composition invite comparison with groups in Spain, Italy, Brazil, Mexico, and Peru. But ultimately, political banditry in Colombia represents a distinctive response to the national trauma of the Violencia and stands apart as yet another of the varieties of Latin American banditry.

CONTEXT: THE *VIOLENCIA*, 1946–1958

The dominating factor of the first two governments of the *Violencia* (1946–1953) was official terrorism. The impact of this at the urban level was the silencing of the working class that allowed capital to gain, without obstacles, economic success and accumulate wealth after the war. Then that terrorism became generalized at a rural level as an anti-liberal and anti-communist crusade that uprooted the democratic aspirations of the peasants and denied them their share of land and power taken from the landowners. The silencing of the working

11. Map of Colombia
    From: *Maps On File*, © 1985 by Martin Greenwald Associates.
       Reprinted by permission of Facts On File, Inc., New York.

class had practically been achieved by 1948, and the anti-liberal and anti-communist crusade became a conservative cause from 1949 on.[1] In order to continue this crusade the repressive machinery of the state—such as the somber, dangerous police who came from the Boyacá region—was complemented by the action of paramilitary organizations, such as the "*pájaros*" (paid assassins) in Valle and Caldas.[2]

But there would be other visible effects of the countryside terror: the plunder of land and goods, after the murder of the owners or the use of threats that ended in forced sales; the appropriation of crops and cattle; the burning of houses, sugar refineries, and coffee-processing plants; the destruction of seed plots; the physical pressure on discontented rural workers; the massive migrations to cities; or the displacement of peasants to other areas controlled by their own party until regions were homogenized politically. And at the bottom of all this came a profound reorganization of rural social classes and regional leadership.

The dilemma of the pursued was to perish or resist, and although in many areas of the interior there appeared elementary mechanisms of defense and support, it was almost impossible to structure resistance organically. Resistance became concentrated, in fact, in more or less defined areas that served as great poles of attraction and organization.

The first large guerrilla nuclei were formed in areas like the Llanos that combined certain characteristics: political homogeneity; open frontiers for colonization capable of absorbing productively an unlimited number of fugitives from the interior of the country; considerable distances from the central government that rendered repression difficult; and proximity to neighboring Venezuela, whose government was supposedly friendly to the resistance. Toward the end of 1952 there were an estimated 20,000 fighters in the Llanos, a bastion of the guerrillas in the fifties, which had experienced the most significant ideological transformations and gained the broadest national perspective in its development.

Other important guerrilla fronts were those of the southwest of Antioquia (the Pavón-Urrao Comando), of Carare-Opón in Santander, and of Yacopí-La Palma in the northwest of Cundinamarca. The liberal guerrillas of the south of Tolima, the most directly manipulated by merchants and coffee growers, showed little interest in national coordinating efforts and were noticeably absent from most important meetings of this type held in 1952.

In the area of Sumapaz, a stronghold of peasant movement allied with Jorge Eliéser Gaitán during the thirties, and with a solid tradition of organized struggle for the land, it was possible to transform old peasant leagues into an ample and disciplined guerrilla movement that, in the long run, was victorious. It forced the government during the sixties to treat the problems of the region, not as a question of public order, but as conflict over land.

The Communist party initially proclaimed tactics of self-defense in its areas of greatest influence in Tequendama and to the south of Tolima. In Tolima the Communist party joined the guerrilla fight relatively late (compared with the Liberals), whereas in Tequendama and more so in Viotá, it took advantage of the fears of Liberal landowners of the spread of war to establish with them a "diplomatic front." They could then negotiate with the government a relative peace that allowed them to extend logistical support to those areas in which war was inevitable.

In this context the resistance appears as a combination on a large scale of various political expressions and different levels of class-consciousness that vary historically not only from one region to another, but also within each one of them. Its social components are equally varied, on the level of common soldiers as well as that of leadership. Among the latter are to be found, for example, migrants (Eliseo Velásquez in the Llanos), army deserters (Saúl Fajardo in Yacopí and Dumar Aljure in the Llanos), old agrarian leaders (Isauro Yosa in Chaparral and Juan de la Cruz Varela in Sumapaz), small landowners (Leopoldo García "El Capitán Peligro" in the south of Tolima), ex-policemen who had participated on the popular side during the "9th of April" upheaval after Gaitán's assassination in 1948, jailbirds who escaped from prison during the same events, and poor peasants, like Guadalupe Salcedo, who became the national symbol of the resistance during the period.[3]

LIBERAL FRAGMENTATION AND BANDITRY

The resistance suffered fragmented, sometimes conflictive relations (as happened between Liberals and Communists in the south of Tolima) and difficulties in projecting broadly social, rather than sectarian, goals to their programs, ideology, and actions. Furthermore, some of their developments created great uneasiness among the ruling classes, including those who had joined the liberal banner.

There were three main divisive factors. First, guerrillas broke with Liberal landowners in the Llanos over the pact that the latter made with the army against the armed peasants. In this pact, for the first time, the epithet of "bandits" was applied to the rebels by their own party (declaration of Sagamoszo, 1952). Thus "banditry" as a label, an epithet, preceded the social reality of bandit activity.

Second, a national coordinating plan of the main fronts of armed resistance came out of the "First National Conference of the Popular Movement of National Liberation" that took place in August 1952 (Conference of Boyacá). A "National Coordinating Committee" made up in its majority by members of the urban "petit bourgeoisie" emerged from that meeting. The third reason of alarm was the change in the correlation of forces produced in early 1953, when the guerrilla movement, at least in the Llanos, assumed the military offensive.

It was then that the national liberal leadership found a hearing among the *ospinista* faction of the Conservatives, followers of Mariano Ospina Pérez. Together they formulated a new pact of the ruling classes that encompassed not only the basic aspects of national economic orientation, but also those concerning the general direction of the state and the political process itself. The union alienated those who saw in it an unheard of oligarchic pact as well as those who considered it an expression of reprehensible conciliation. The antagonisms within both parties hindered the formalization of a direct pact with immediate effectiveness, but a formula for transition was found: the arbitration of the armed forces that, in the person of General Rojas Pinilla, took power in June of 1953. For all intents and purposes the major political leaders, excepting the defeated sector, were not disposed to run any more risks from the revolutionary potential or the uncontrollable anarchy that was incubating behind the Violencia. Their support made the transition to military rule possible.

Rojas represented a political solution to the crisis and not a dictatorship in the usual sense. His intervention was received as a "coup of opinion." With a simple but deeply felt motto, "Peace, Justice, and Liberty," followed by an offer of unconditional amnesty, Rojas achieved almost immediately a resounding triumph and general approbation. Such accolade doesn't cease to arouse a certain wonder, for "he was, strangely, a military man without great merit who, without the force of arms, succeeded in the political objective which one of the most sophisticated politicians in the country failed to achieve by military means. The amnesty seemingly constituted a concession to the [guerrilla] movement, but in truth it meant its worst defeat."[4] The military estimated that once the fighting was stopped in the Llanos and Tolima, the rest was simply a matter of time. Later events proved that they were not entirely wrong; but it is also true that once the initial euphoria was over, the military repression would be felt in a selective manner and with special acuteness in those areas where the guerrillas had been clever enough to wait before surrendering.

Rojas was an arbiter, not the principal actor, and he attempted to resist, on the economic plane, the multiple and contradictory pressures from the entrepreneurial associations. He achieved a transitory equilibrium that was impossible to maintain over a long period, especially when the end came to the coffee bonanza that had buoyed the beginning of his government.

The ruling classes attempted to limit the military government by making it a subordinate force rather than an autonomous political body. Nevertheless, in his role of mediator, Rojas should have had to rely on political strength and his own social bases. In their absence he attempted to create them by establishing a third force that would find support from the union of the people and the armed forces. The contradiction was inevitable: when Rojas increased his efforts to gain autonomy, the unification of the ruling classes became stronger. Colombia is, after all, a country in which the two-party monopoly seems to be integral to social stability.

The direct pact was now made fully legitimate. Alberto Lleras Camargo and Laureano Gómez, representing the Liberals and Conservatives, respectively, in 1956 came to an accord about the pact's fundamental issue: the alternation of the parties in power every four years during a minimum period of sixteen, the same as the equal distribution between the two parties of all the bureaucratic scaffolding of the state. Opposition to Rojas became concentrated around a civil front, and in May 1957 he had to leave power in the hands of a military junta because of the irresistible pressure of a general strike instigated by industry, the banking system, merchants, and the church, with ample popular backing.

The junta's commitment was to call a general plebiscite that would ratify the bipartisan accords and hand over power in mid–1958 to the first president of the National Front, Alberto Lleras Camargo. The Violencia had formally come to an end.

NATIONAL FRONT AND THE RISE OF BANDITRY, 1958–1965

In reality the Violencia had not come to an end. During the first stages of the National Front the Violencia simply changed character and initiated a new phase that covers the period from 1958 to 1965. The particular and dominating expression—although not the only one—was political banditry.

This banditry, because of its dimensions, has no parallel, at least in Western history of the twentieth century. It is estimated that by 1964, when the crisis had already begun, there were more than 100 active bands made up of armed peasants. The bands ignored the peace treaties between official directorates of the two traditional parties and thereby prolonged the struggle between them. Bandits gained the militant or passive support of rural communities of their own party and the protection and assistance of local leaders, who, making use of them for electoral reasons, pushed them into wars to exterminate, weaken, or contain political adversaries in the local or regional power structure.[5] Many bandit chiefs had previously enjoyed Liberal party support as guerrilla fighters from 1949 to 1953.

The decisive element in the loss of this precarious legitimacy was the rejection of the proposals of amnesty, initially in 1953–1954, under the military government of Rojas Pinilla and later, in 1958, under the first government of the National Front. Some refused to accept amnesty because they considered the proffered guarantees insufficient, suspect, or misleading. Others, having temporarily submitted to them, found that the constant harassments to which they were exposed and the burden of so many years of irregular living kept them from readapting to the routine of country life. Besides, they were all influenced not only by the lesson of the assassination of Guadalupe Salcedo, the most prestigious commander of the resistance against the dictatorial government of Laureano Gómez, but also by the memory of many other ex-guerrillas who were reincorporated to civilian life and, after some time, shot down by the state security apparatus. Under these circumstances a good number of the old guerrillas found no other secure way out than that of returning to the hazardous jungle life, burdened with the label of banditry that their own party now proffered in reprisal for what was considered unacceptable insubordination and treason.

Clearly, then, amnesty exerts in each stage a particular and fundamental function. The objective of the first, in 1953–1954, was to disarm the guerrillas.

That of the second, in 1958, had a double purpose: to legitimate the bipartisan armed struggle against Rojas' "tyranny" and, in the name of the National Front pact, to condemn the continuance of that struggle.

By then the guerrillas' anti-government contest, that is, the struggle against the central power that had been the unifying force in their first war, became rather confused as a consequence of two disintegrating factors. The first was the massive incorporation of adolescents into the armed struggle. These young men had grown up in an atmosphere of terror, watching their houses being burned down, their families massacred, their plantations destroyed, their properties abandoned. For them their violent actions of retaliation and vengeance were explicable and justified when measured by the official criminality that was sanctioned or promoted during the first years of the Violencia.

The second factor of disintegration was growing regionalism. The armed struggle shifted from dependence on national political directives to dependence on local leaders who provided bandits with a measure of legitimacy. This subordination to provincial interests precluded national political projection, no matter how extensively the bands might be spread over the country. Regionalism, then, appears as one of the defining characteristics of the phenomenon of political banditry.

Banditry cannot be considered, therefore, simply a leftover from the Violencia. It was an armed expression distinctive from the earlier stage. As a particular historical product, it resulted from the changing relationship of those up in arms with the state, the political parties, and the holders of local and regional power.

To be a "bandit" means, above all else, to have lost political legitimacy, as also happened to Brazilian *cangaceiros*. Having had their political protectors defeated, cangaceiros found themselves with all the state, police, and judicial power against them.[6] But the social contexts are very different. Banditry in the sertão developed in a milieu of dynamic alliances between feuding families and disputing political factions that provided a range of options for political "status" and a minimum possibility of independence.

On the other hand, in Colombia, bipartisanship introduced a much more static element into relations between armed bands and their protectors. The affiliation of both stemmed practically from birth, from "hereditary hatreds." Who should be termed a "bandit" was a question that was decided in the course of a long process, whose crucial moment was determined by the installation of the National Front.

Looking back, what is observed is a continuous narrowing of the political space of the rebellious peasant, even within the lines of his own party. During the first years of the 1950s he was labeled a "bandit" only by the opposing Conservative party and its government regime. After the establishment of the military government of Rojas Pinilla, the rebel was considered a bandit by the army. And once the National Front was constituted, rebels lost the support of their national political leadership and were forced to look to local politicians.

The prolongation of the tactical alliance between local leaders and bandits and the hostility of both to a new centralizing policy are reminiscent of the role played by the Sicilian Mafia during the nineteenth century. In reality, the *mafiosi*, which at that time were hard to tell from bandits, opposed tenaciously at the beginning of the century the Bourbon occupation of Sicily. They became the spearhead of caciques and landowners who saw in Bourbon policy a dangerous undermining of landholdings as well as of electoral fiefs. After 1860, during the Risorgimento and the Garibaldian Revolution, which dislodged the Bourbons, they upheld Sicilian landowners who saw in national political unification a real danger that would dislocate the well-rooted local structures of power and property. The expansion of banditry during this period was a response just as much to economic crisis as it was to the efforts of the Garibaldian Revolution to resolve by purely repressive methods a central question, the status of the peasant from the south of Italy.[7]

Although certain parallels thus exist in the Brazilian and Italian cases, there is something more in the Colombian experience. In the Colombian countryside an essential continuity existed. Peasant support was given to bandits in their zones of operation. There they would invariably be alluded to as "guerrillas," that is, as rebels with a cause or, in a more familiar tone, as "the boys from the bush." In similar fashion Sandinista rebels were termed "los muchachos."

This combined support of peasants and local leaders is what provides the internal tension so characteristic of Colombian banditry. On the one hand, banditry represented a vague local expression of insubordination to national political policies of the ruling classes. But it also served as a point of departure of those same ruling classes to avoid the nonconformists' adoption of a revolutionary form.

It was the recognition of this contradiction and the expressed purpose of meeting with one of its poles that prompted the dissident tactics of the MRL (Movimiento Revolucionario Liberal), a Liberal splinter group led by Alfonso López Michelson, to penetrate the rural zones and create campaigns of peasant balloting. They offered the shelter of their banner to the nonconformist sectors of the National Front, including bandits and their rural bases of support. According to López:

> There would be no advantage to Liberalism in creating a mechanical union in the present circumstances, and, on the other hand, it would surely mean a desertion of other factions to non-liberal camps which at present are welded to the MRL [Revolutionary Liberal Movement]. I have not launched a personal dissidence movement against the Liberal Party in order to injure it, but a doctrinal dissidence in order to save it. . . . If the requested union with officialdom were to take place, a great many of the nonconformists would feel justified in taking shelter under the communist banner or other groups distinct from the Liberal Party.[8]

In contrast, the left, with sectarian blindness, antagonized bandit chiefs by overestimating their role as agents of the regime. The left understood, after it was too late, that it was also possible to act on the other pole of the contradiction and to win bandits over to the revolutionary cause, or at least to neutralize them in areas where there was a conflictive coexistence between banditry and revolutionary movements.

What all this suggests is that banditry cannot be understood in isolation either as a static relationship between peasants and the ruling classes or as a historical aberration in the national political process. In its inherent fragmentation and within the broader social and political development of the country, banditry reflects the success of the ruling classes in disorganizing the dominated classes. The Colombian masses engaged in a series of struggles and suffered a succession of defeats: political defeats and disillusionment of the popular front regarding the "Revolution on the March" of Alfonso López Pumarejo; decapitation, with Jorge Eliécer Gaitán's murder, of an ascending bourgeois democratic movement; and a sense of impotence after the heroic but miscarried national insurrection of April 9, 1948. Finally came the unexpected annihilation of the guerrilla movement of the 1950s, which, despite its military effectiveness and popular support, succumbed under the government's double play of amnesty and repression.

In this context of continued reversals of popular movements, and faced with the vigorous recomposition of the ruling classes in the National Front, banditry broke out in wide rural zones as an agrarian, anarchic, and desperate response. And for the desperate the only program that made any sense was destruction for the sake of destruction. Terror became not only an integral part, but also, in most cases, the dominating element in their actions.

To this "negative program" of the frustrated and the desperate—to use Hobsbawm's expression—another element was added to the so-called generation of "the sons of Violence": vengeance. Cruelty is inseparable from vengeance and is made legitimate by it. Where the peasants, victims of the official *Violencia* of the first phase, could not collectively organize a resistance, unmeasurable cruelty and massacre appeared as extreme manifestations of primitive power, the only power available to the humiliated, frustrated peasant. This thirst for killing and destruction has more rational roots that were, in some measure, consciously manipulated by bandit chiefs: the need to inspire admiration as much as fear, two key elements in gaining peasant adherence. The success of the bandits depended on the accurate management of these two components of peasant reaction.[9]

Such works as those of Camilo Torres, priest-turned-guerrilla fighter, who perceived in rural Colombia before the Violencia an archetypal society of submissive peasants, static, closed, and undifferentiated, could help to generate false interpretations of the Colombian case.[10] But recent investigation has made evident the dynamics of the agrarian and political mobility in which the country lived during the period before the Violencia and, more concretely, after the decade of the twenties, which, in a certain sense, had been its golden age. Banditry in Colombia was not based on the prior absence of agrarian class organization. It emerged as a result of its disappearance or annihilation under the counteroffensive of the ruling classes. As fruit of this historical process, banditry in Colombia cannot be considered a pre-political phenomenon.

Banditry served to substitute for or supplant autonomous pre-existent organizations of the land recovery struggle. However, banditry in Tequendama, Sumapaz, and the south of Tolima, three of the principal bastions of the agrarian struggle during the twenties and thirties, represents a partial exception to this process. In these regions, despite errors, vacillation, and failures, the continuity of the agrarian democratic movement was maintained until the beginning of the 1960s.

Mass movements (agrarian syndicates, peasant leagues, democratic fronts) alternated with guerrilla warfare. This is not to say there was no banditry, but it was comparatively uncommon. Yet those regions provided a great number of bandit leaders and bands to other areas. "Chispas," the guerrilla fighter from the south of Tolima during the early fifties, only found favorable support in the region of the Quindío.

Banditry in the areas mentioned, to whatever degree it existed, accomplished a different role than it did in other parts of the interior—a role that resembled that of the pájaros, or assassins at the service of politicians and landowners, precisely against organized peasants. This had something to do, obviously, with the old antagonism and incomprehension of the Communist party toward *gaitanismo* (the movement of Jorge Eliéser Gaitán), which were reproduced in the quarrels between *limpios* (Liberals) and *Comunes* (Communists) during the fifties.

GEOGRAPHY OF BANDITRY

Political banditry arose in almost all the areas that were shaken by official persecution or guerrilla fighting during the first stages of the Violencia, but it spread with unequal intensity according to certain political or economic variables. It did not find fertile ground, for example, in the great bulwarks of guerrilla struggle at the beginning of the fifties: the Llanos (plains), where Eliseo Velásquez and the famous Guadalupe Salcedo fought; the Sumapaz and the south of Tolima (strongholds of the legendary peasant leader Juan de la Cruz Varela and "General Mariachi," respectively); the west and southwest of Antioquia of Captain Juan de J. Franco; and the province of Santander, battleground of the former revolutionary Mayor of Barrancabermeja during the 9th of April uprising, Rafael Rangel.

On the other hand, political banditry prevailed where peasants in the countryside felt the effects of government terrorism but failed to create their own form of resistance: north of Valle, north of Tolima, and Viejo Caldas. Within this triangle are concentrated, in effect, the most renowned bandit-leaders of the period: "El Mosco" (the Fly), "Zarpazo" (Whack), "La Gata" (the Cat), "Chispas" (Sparks), "El Capitán Venganza" (Captain Vengeance), "Desquite" (Revenge), and "Sangrenegra" (Black Blood). It was also there that banditry reflected with the greatest clarity its character as a loose counteroffensive by the oppressed classes and where its avenging nature became most visible. Through banditry, rural communities expressed their rejection of a state and a central power that in all the preceding decade they had identified with destruction, terror, and cruelty.

Banditry was not most profoundly rooted in those zones that were dominated by large landholdings. It reproduced like a hydra head where large, medium-sized, and small properties coexisted, particularly in coffee-producing regions. It might be said that the case of Dumar Aljure, an old companion-in-arms of Guadalupe Salcedo who found political protection in the remote Llanos Orientales, is exceptional. But considering the dimensions of this extensive region of immense landholdings, and the fact that it was the main center of resistance during the fifties, the case appears marginal. Besides, Aljure, as an old army deserter, could not be amnestied, a disability that played a determinant part in his decision to continue his irregular life.[11]

Another equally significant characteristic is the scarcity of banditry in those areas that contained, in terms of relations of production, more or less consolidated structures, whether they were archaic or capitalistic in their forms of social organization. For instance, Boyacá and Nariño represent the first case, and the sugar territory of Valle and the agriculturally mechanized area of Espinal and Guamo (Tolima) illustrate the second. In those areas where a process of capitalistic development had been started before the Violencia, the ruling classes prevented, at whatever cost, political interference (the case of Espinal-Guamo), or they used private forms of violence that actually reinforced the process already begun. Such was the case of Valle, where bandits were less common than pájaros, paid delinquents who played a clear function of expropriation and agrarian plunder at the service of powerful sugar entrepreneurs.

COFFEE AND BANDITS

The coffee-growing regions, the privileged sanctuaries of the bands, deserve to be treated in greater detail. The counties that became the bases of operation for one or another band stand out significantly for their high rate of coffee production. Sevilla and Caicedonia in Valle, Armenia and Calarcá in the Quindío, and Chaparral and Líbano in Tolima were all centers of coffee production (although Líbano suffered a decline precisely because of the Violencia).[12]

These areas (with the exception of Chaparral) consisted of small plots but also felt the domination of the great coffee haciendas. Characterized by an intermediate level of development, they had been subjected, at least since the 1930s, to a destabilizing cycle of decomposition and restoration of different sorts of pre-capitalist exploitation. In fact, in some areas large coffee haciendas dominated local production in spite of being numerically insignificant compared with the small and medium holdings. Such was the case of Líbano (Tolima) and the region of Montenegro and Quimbaya (Quindío).

Many factors created the crisis of the hacienda system, which began even before the Violencia. The agrarian struggles of the 1920s and the agrarian laws of the 1930s led landowners to abandon the system of pre-capitalist sharecropping and tenant farming and to substitute contractual and wage labor. But those changes in the system, instead of raising the level of productivity, furthered its decline. The new system generated shortages of food and labor that could not be countered by major technological development, still nonexistent at that moment.[13]

The impact of the Violencia on the old and weakened hacienda structure is evident. In one form or another it finished off the hacienda as a system, although seldom as a property. Actually, the downfall of the coffee plantations came as a result of abandonment or owner absenteeism. In some cases a new distribution of power between the hacendado and the peasants who were up in arms placed the old landowners at a disadvantage compared with the dynamic middle class, which exerted itself to introduce new technological advances in the cultivation of coffee.

Even more vulnerable, however, were the small and medium-sized holdings that changed hands frequently or contributed to the patrimony of the new beneficiaries of the altered public order. In this regard the role of the sharecropper (*agregado*) in the medium-sized properties deserves special attention, for not only did he retain his importance, but, as in Quindío, he also formed 24 percent to 28 percent of the economically active population in 1954. This was the case of "La Mina" and "Los Juanes" in the county of Pijao, favorite areas of the bandits "Melco" and Efraín González.[14]

The rise of banditry in the densely populated and highly integrated coffee region contradicts, at first glance, the tendency of bandits to settle in relatively inaccessible frontier areas. For instance, Antônio Silvino, the forerunner of Lampião in the Brazilian northeast, opposed by every means within his reach the integration of Pernambuco into the railroad system. He also expressed a permanent hostility to the mail service within his area of operation. In the expansion of communications bandits see, not without reason, an enemy as dangerous as repression itself. It has been said that Andalusian bandits were finished off by the Guardia Civil and by the wire, that is, the telephone and the telegraph.[15]

But Andalusian bandits carried out their activities under geographical and demographic conditions that were very different from those of Colombian bandits. In Andalusia they not only operated in areas of extensive landholdings (considered by Quirós as the main cause of the phenomenon), but also in regions where the workers of the land—day laborers, renters, sharecroppers, and even owners of small and medium-sized properties—lived in more or less large towns. In short, open country, lacking population centers other than isolated farmhouses with a few workers or the manager, made up the environment in which bandits and highwaymen operated until the first half of the nineteenth century. Similar conditions presented themselves in the north of Peru. The region of Piurá, with great landholdings and extensive deserts, was also the land of the *Caballeros del Delito*.[16]

In the Colombian coffee zone, despite the development of communications, there are almost impenetrable areas, such as the inhospitable peaks of the Cordillera Central, that serve as centers of refuge. The zone also offered many conditions that compensated for the dangers of persecution and that impeded repression. The network of roads, for example, made possible the easy supply of provisions, clothing, and munitions for the band. Dense, shady coffee groves provided physical camouflage when bandits eluded the authorities. They also made it possible, particularly during the harvest season, to perform what Jaime Arocha has called "social camouflage," that is, the scattering of the pursued bands among the workmen of the plantations.[17]

BANDIT ENTREPRENEURSHIP

Besides such technical and tactical advantages, the area provided clear economic incentives. Beginning in 1954–1955 two characteristics of the coffee-Violencia interplay began to crystallize. The first was the plundering of peasants or the purchase of their land at ludicrous prices exactly when a bountiful crop was expected. The second was the theft or confiscation of their coffee after it had been collected and processed by the peasants. The first action would be the usual practice of hacendados, other peasants, and above all, merchants who used the current anxiety to intimidate producers. The second became the typical means of support for bandits.

In both cases the agregado (tenant farmer) played a key role, since he was the only person who continued to be a permanent physical presence on the property when the "boss" had been forced to flee or had been murdered. For absentee owners the only guarantee of obtaining a minimum part of their harvests, or at least of not losing their property immediately, was to have an agregado who was accepted by "those who dominated the zone." The tenant had control, therefore, of all the means of production and made key decisions about the disposition of the crop. But merchants pressured and manipulated him, on the one hand, because he usually was indebted to them. On the other hand, bandits threatened him or simply convinced him of the advantages of complicity.

Sharecropping thus constituted a profitable system under which the bands could appropriate part of the crops without ruining the cooperative peasant. Both the sharecropper and his tenants understood that cooperation with the bandits meant less involvement by the owners in the daily activities of production. It also meant a greater share of the crops for the accomplices or the possibility, which many of them perceived, of taking over the property. From coerced complicity to an explicit agreement was only a short step.

The "Jefes de Vereda" ("Road Bosses"), closely linked to the gangs in Quindío, offer clear evidence of this phenomenon. With coffee as a booty easily expropriated and marketed, banditry not only survived, but also became profitable. It was not surprising, then, that joining the bands should become a strong temptation for part-time coffee workers. Their semi-employed condition, the growing disparity between the price of coffee and daily wages,[18] and, later on, the dire results of the crisis in real wages toward the end of the 1950s provided powerful economic stimuli for peasants to join various armed groups. In fact, although the heads of the bands were predominantly the sons of small property owners, members of bandit gangs were mostly day laborers.

Behind the sharecropper and the bandit was the complicitous merchant who would buy stolen or "confiscated" coffee. He speculated with prices and altered weights, and his knowledge of the community and location of the plantations put him in an excellent position to take over lands and crops. As in Argentina, Mexico, Brazil, and elsewhere, bandit-merchant cooperation benefited both parties.

Besides the economic interests of many layers of agricultural society in tolerating, or even encouraging, banditry, there existed another reason that prevented Colombian bandits from developing too much hostility toward cities or highly urbanized areas. From these political power centers came the bandits' source of protection and legitimacy, and therefore their guarantee of impunity.

POLITICAL AND SOCIAL BANDITRY

Colombian political banditry developed characteristics that distinguish it clearly from banditry elsewhere. In Andalusia, Argentina, and up to a certain point in Peru the bandit was marginal to society. He was an "outlaw" who operated in sparsely inhabited places. Having left his agrarian community as a fugitive or avenger of injustice, he was considered a popular hero worthy of protection. His permanent physical absence from the community helped to spawn myths around him and his adventures.

On the other hand, the political bandit of Colombia retained his political affiliation and counted on protection from well-known figures of higher social class during most of his career. He wove within the rural population an extensive, specialized network of collaborators. He functioned as an integral part not only of rural society, but of all society. He developed multiple links with the local power structure. And he maintained ties with the city that he did not fear as did the social bandit. There was so little hostility to urban contact that the band of "Chispas" set up an urban network that operated in the towns of Armenia and Calarcá.

The profit inducement offered by the rich coffee areas created the peculiar class composition of Colombian banditry. Liberal bandits, initially antagonistic to both rich and poor Conservatives, began to attack or weaken the economic interests of property owners of their own party. However, in so doing they did not enlarge their social base, nor did they win the approval of Conservative peasants. They only narrowed their relationships and network of support within the Liberal party. The same occurred with bandits of the Conservative party.

Bandits arrived at a pragmatic recognition of the division of classes within their own party but not within society as a whole. This failure produced a fragmented class consciousness as social antagonism conflicted with party dependence.

Here the political bandit meets with the social bandit, and elements of both are mixed in the same persons. "Chispas" as well as Lampião typify this process. What Pereira de Quiróz remarks about the cangaceiro is also valid for Chispas, the Colombian bandit.

There was in Antônio Silvino and in Lampião a certain recognition of social justice and they proclaimed that they defended the poor, dividing with them the product of their depredations. There was no element, however, which denoted any ideal regarding equality of goods; rather the concept of helping the poor which was the same as that of the colonels [landed elite]: a paternalism that caused them to divide with the poor the leavings from the tables of the rich. Many a colonel took pride in being a protector of the poor. But in this case, as in the case of Lampião, they meant *their* poor primarily, that is, those who helped them and suppported them.[19]

Given his evolution, racked by party hatred, does the Colombian bandit evoke the image within the peasantry of the social bandit, the myth of the invulnerable fighter for a common cause? The answer is as complex as the historical development of the protagonists. Actually, personalities such as "Chispas," Efraín González, or "Capitán Venganza" represent in fact, if not as clearly as in legend, fundamental aspirations of the peasantry that move them closer to the classic social bandit: an ideal of justice and liberty, the possibility of an ephemeral moment of wealth and power that places them on the side of those "who make themselves respected," an example of social mobility that arouses peasant admiration.

Despite the fact that the Colombian bandit and the social bandit share common characteristics, they do not exhibit the same urgency to cultivate an attractive public image. Many of the classic bandits developed a certain ability to manipulate their public image. The elegant mastery with which the Andalusian bandits of the Romantic age, the Mexican highwaymen, or the Peruvian "Sambambé," organizer of gangs in Piurá and Lambayaque, "lived their own myth" has never been surpassed. They managed not to be involved personally in murders, they shared some booty with the poor, and they introduced into their "profession" the chivalrous form of demanding tribute: the courtly robbery, or the assault with hat in hand, elegant phrases, and gallantries with the ladies.

The bloody ambience and terror of the Violencia, on the contrary, did not lend itself to this type of romantic frivolity. Political bandits, even when they evolved toward a more social role, did not attempt to give an air of moderation to acts of violence, nor did they hide atrocities committed. Acts of violent terrorism were justified as righteous vengeance against representatives of the opposing party, even though these might be peasants from the same region. Retaliation was a fundamental component not only of practice, but also of image.

The myth of the social bandit (to whatever degree he might actually exist)—defender of the poor, heroic, invincible, and with the gift of ubiquity—was not shared by all of the same peasant class.

LIMITS OF POLITICAL BANDITRY

Having arrived at a certain fragmentary class consciousness, Colombian bandits began to experience an internal contradiction between their original role as political bandits and the trajectory toward new options that clashed with the role they had played previously.

Simultaneously, the army, bolstered by counterinsurgency arms and training from the United States, wove a complex network of positive and negative relationships with the rural population: of gratification or punishment; of arms for peasants in whom they had confidence and jail for those who were bandit accomplices; rewards in cash for those who became informants and accusers and harassment, inspections, torture, and extortion for those accused of complicity with bandits.[20]

The other side of the coin was that of the relationship of gangs with their zones of support. Peasant solidarity had its basis in the identification of Liberal bandits of the first phase of the Violencia with vague ideals of democracy, liberty, or simply the legitimacy of defensive action and retaliation against government persecution. Later gangs of bandits, derivative factions from the first period or their legitimate heirs, now anathematized by the National Front, were portrayed once more as protectors or avengers. But these bandits faced difficult circumstances because their struggle no longer included a dictatorship as antagonist. The government now wore a mask of democracy.

When the increasing autonomy of bandits became a threat to the local leaders who had earlier encouraged them, the sectarian character of political bandits conflicted with the social orientation they now tried to give to their deeds. Only in exceptional cases did they succeed in extricating themselves from this dilemma. Hacienda owners no longer perceived them as partners in a common partisan cause or as the armed expression of political rivalry. Landowners joined the army in declaring bandits to be enemies of all principles, especially of the one that they prized most highly, private property. Increasingly less tied to the local and regional power structure, bandit fortunes became determined mainly by what Hobsbawm noted as the special relationship between the peasant and the social bandit.

All this explains why, during the last phase of military action, the army's main objective was to break the social tie between the peasant and his bandit "protector." And it was precisely there that the political and ideological limits of banditry as a political tactic emerged. Desertion, the buying of informants by the army, offers of immunity to prisoners in exchange for information, and the harassment of support networks were factors that weakened both the offensive and the elusive capabilities of bandit gangs.

But the decisive factor in their elimination was not so much the military element as the political one—the bandits' inability to accommodate changing sociopolitical conditions. When bandits most needed the sympathy and direct support of the peasantry, they acted in such a way that the peasants lost the perception of them as an expression of class malaise and misery or as natural allies against the oppressive army. Bandits failed to distinguish whether an informant acted voluntarily or whether he acted under torture or intimidation. Bandits did not understand that peasants could tire of providing permanent, economic contributions. They failed to develop alternative sources of income to ease the heavy responsibilities that weighed on their peasant supporters. They did not develop successful methods to sift information and neutralize government propaganda and psychological warfare. Finally, the abuses of isolated renegade groups who exploited the disorder for selfish gain further undercut popular support and political legitimacy.

Kidnapping and extortion provided some additional income, according to the importance that each band assigned to it. But the growing shortage of economic contributors dictated that most of the daily support of bandit groups eventually fell on the shoulders of the peasants. Small groups of the dismembered large bands often committed indiscriminate depredations. Bands increasingly relied on terror instead of loyalty to the "cause."

The step from gay and enthusiastic rural bazaars supervised by the "commandos" to forced individual quotas was unsuccessful, perhaps because a vast gulf existed between the political consciousness and commitment of some of the chiefs and their peasant supporters. In any case, to the degree that the economic relationship took on a coercive coloring, the delicate balance between admiration and fear so characteristic of the backing by the peasantry for bandits tended toward fear and, finally, opposition.

Peasant ambiguity became open rejection when bandits committed a final and decisive error out of desperation: harassment and indiscriminate punishment in their own zones of refuge. Retaliations against real or presumed traitors in their old bases of support, accompanied by sexual violence—which had a profound impact in rural society—provoked on a wider scale what the gangs were trying to neutralize: treason, a growing reluctance to offer hospitality, and unwillingness to provide information about troop movements. To many peasants, moreover, bandits became vengeful executioners and common criminals. The bandits' own actions helped to create a climate favorable to the success of government psychological warfare and the flowering of the "informer industry."

In reality, the objective course of events had placed before the bandits several options: to break with traditional bipartisanship, to design a new strategy against the army, to become revolutionary guerrillas siding exclusively with the peasants, or to strike out blindly on all sides. They could suffer a disorganized and anarchic retreat, face certain death with a grim fatalism, or desert to the enemy against their old companions. But those who faced this intricate web of alternatives with the greatest clarity, like "Chispas" and "Pedro Brincos," became the main targets of military persecution and fell. Most of the bandits were not ideologically or politically prepared to understand the complexities of the situation. Consequently, they selected the worst tactic, to antagonize the peasantry, their most loyal protectors.

To define the bandits, under those conditions, simply as agents of reaction or as allies of the army (as the Communist party had done in January 1964),[21] when the final battle was being unleashed against them, shows a lack of understanding of the knot of contradictions that engaged them. The vascillation of the ruling classes about the course of their struggle, the ruptures of old partisan molds, the fear of seeing their immense local and regional power at the service of a new cause—all this surged up, with all its ambiguities, as the unacceptable challenge of banditry to the established order. That is why the "tactical dissident" wings of the parties and the caciques, using the power base created by banditry, negotiated their incorporation into the national political system and started, from their new governmental positions, the great official crusade of extermination.

This historical contradiction also produced an apparently enigmatic and ambivalent peasant attitude. After having contributed to the extermination of the bandits, the peasants then grieved for them. The disappearance of men like "Chispas," "Desquite," and Efraín González left among the peasantry a profound sense of orphanage and defeat. Peasants missed political bandits not because of what they had been, but because of the changes and aspirations that bandits symbolized after they were dead.

Perhaps, except for the idealized memory that the peasants still hold in their old zones of support, the "social bandit" had also been defeated as a mythical character. In his place the anti-myth, so many times instilled by the military through psychological warfare, gradually won over public opinion. What took place in Colombia was the opposite process from that of the Brazilian cangaço. Over time, the cangaço lost much of its characteristic ambiguity and developed toward an image of the ideal social bandit. The cangaceiro ended up as a national symbol of native virtues and the embodiment of national independence at a time of massive foreign immigration and the expansion of imperialist domination over the economy, culture, and politics of Latin America.

In Colombia, on the contrary, the bandit personifies a cruel and inhuman monster or, in the best of cases, the "son of the Violencia," frustrated, disoriented, and manipulated by local leaders. This has been the image accepted by public opinion, an expression, naturally, of the unequal struggle between the representatives of the new political centralization and the peasant class, defeated for the present.

The growth and decline of political bandits and their tottering evolution toward a more social role point to the impossibility of the massive transformation of banditry into a revolutionary movement. They also illustrate the impossibility of classifying bandits rigidly and narrowly as a group. Neither paradigms of contemporary revolutionary movements, agents of reaction, nor basely inhuman criminals, they were, in fact, "trapped with no way out!"

NOTES

1. Studies on the *Violencia* include James D. Henderson, *When Colombia Bled: A History of the Violencia in Tolima* (University: University of Alabama Press, 1985); Germán Guzmán, Orlando Fals Borda, and Eduardo Umana Luna, *La Violencia en Colombia* (Bogotá: Punta de Lanza, 1977); Darío Fajardo, "La Violencia 1946–1964: Su desarrollo y su impacto," *Estudios Marxistas*, 21 (1981); Paul Oquist, *Violence, Conflict and Politics in Colombia* (New York: Academic Press, 1980); Camilo Torres, "La Violencia y los cambios socio-culturales en las áreas rurales colombianas," *Memorias del Primer Congreso Nacional de Sociología* (Bogotá: Universidad Nacional, 1963; Gonzalo Sánchez and Donny Meertens, *Bandoleros, gamonales y campesinos: El caso de la Violencia en Colombia* (Bogotá: Ancora, 1983). For a review of the literature, see Gonzalo Sánchez, "La Violencia in Colombia: New Research, New Questions," *Hispanic American Historical Review*, 65 (Nov. 1985): 789–807.

2. Pájaros was the name given to hired murderers. The best known of them was "El Cóndor," who operated in Valle. "Aplanchadores" (lit. Ironers) and "penca ancha" (lit. broad leaf) were bands organized by political bosses or landowners to terrorize the peasants.

3. The popular reaction to Gaitán's assassination, April 9, 1948, took the form of a great upheaval, not only in the capital (known as "El Bogotazo"), but also in the provinces. As a matter of fact, it exhibited its most organized and revolutionary character in the provincial towns, where "Juntas Revolucionarias," popular governments, and peasant militias were created. See Gonzalo Sánchez, *Los días de la revolución: Gaitanismo y 9 de Abril en provincia* (Bogotá: Centro Cultural Jorge Eliécer Gaitán, first ed. 1983; second ed. 1984).

4. Carlos Gabler, "La lucha de clases y la Violencia," mimeo (Bogotá: Universidad de los Andes, Department of Political Science, n.d.), p. 249.

5. Political banditry, considering its institutional or semi-institutional connections, tends to be expressed in more massive terms than social banditry. Risorgimento Italy is particularly illustrative. In the struggle of the Bourbon crown and the pontifical state against the Unitarian current, a real duality of powers in conflict, the *brigantaggio* that acted as a military arm of the crown came to constitute true regular armies. Those of Crocco and Borjes came to include something like 3,000 men at their peak and were able to impose control over vast regions. See Franco Molfese, *Storia del Brigantaggio dopo l'Unita*, 5th ed. (Milan: Feltrinelli, 1979), p. 103.

6. The cangaceiro was considered independent, unlike the *capanga*, who worked directly for a landowner. For this reason the capanga was also referred to as a cangaceiro *manso*. In practice, the distinction was rather vague and fluctuated with the political fortunes of their respective protectors. See Peter Singelmann, "Political Structure and Social Banditry in Northeast Brazil," *Journal of Latin American Studies*, 7, 1 (May 1975): 59–83; Linda Lewin, "The Oligarchical Limitations of Social Banditry in Brazil: The Case of the 'Good' Thief Antonio Silvino," *Past and Present*, 82 (Feb. 1979): 116–146.

7. See Anton Blok, *The Mafia of a Sicilian Village, 1860–1960* (New York: Harper & Row, 1975), and Molfese, *Storia del Brigantaggio dopo l'Unita*, p. 35.

8. *El Espectador*, 11 May 1965 (Bogotá). The same attitude on a local level is found in *Estrella Roja*, no. 6, Nov. 1962 (Líbano).

9. See Eric Hobsbawm, *Bandits* (New York: Pantheon Books, 1981), and his "Social Banditry," in *Rural Protest Peasant Movements and Social Change*, ed. Henry Landsberger (London: MacMillan, 1974).

10. Torres, "La Violencia y los cambios socio-culturales," passim.

11. See Richard L. Maullin, "The Fall of Dumar Aljure, Colombian Guerrilla and Bandit" (Pamphlet, Santa Monica: Rand, Nov. 1968).

12. The production of Líbano went down from 125,000 "cargas" (250 kg.) before the *Violencia* to 25,000 in 1957, *Tribuna*, 14 Dec. 1957 (Ibagué); Soledad Ruiz, "La fuerza de trabajo en la zona cafetera del Tolima," mimeo (Bogotá: DANE, 1972).

13. Gonzalo Sánchez, *Las ligas campesinas en Colombia* (Bogotá: Tiempo Presente, 1977).

14. Figures taken from the Colombian Ministry of Labor, *Caldas: Estudio de su situación geográfica, económica y social* (Bogotá, 1956), pp. 207, 343–344; see also Tito Alba, *Vida, confesión y muerte de Efraín González*, 2nd ed. (Bogotá: Bermúdez, 1971).

15. Maria Isaura Pereira de Queiróz, *Os cangaceiros* (São Paulo: Livraria Duas Cidades, 1977), pp. 76–77; Constancio Bernaldo de Quirós and Luis Ardila, *El bandolerismo andaluz* (Madrid: Turner, 1973), p. 210; see also Lewin, "Oligarchical Limitations," passim; and María Cristina Matta Machado, *As taticas de guerra dos cangaceiros*, 2nd ed. (São Paulo: Brasiliense, 1978).

16. Quirós and Ardila, *Bandolerismo*, p. 228; Enrique López Albújar, *Los Caballeros del Delito*, 2nd ed. (Lima: Juan Mejía, 1973), p. 329; see also Benjamin S. Orlove, "The Position of Rustlers in Regional Society: Social Banditry in the Andes," in Benjamin S. Orlove and Glynn Custred, eds., *Land and Power in Latin America* (New York: Holmes & Meier, 1980), pp. 179–194.

17. Jaime Arocha, *La Violencia en el Quindío* (Bogotá: Tercer Mundo, 1979), pp. 173–174, 177.

18. This situation was repeatedly denounced in the local press; see *Tribuna*, 3 Mar and 1 Apr 1954 (Ibagué).

19. Pereira de Queiróz, *Cangaceiros*, p. 207.

20. On counterinsurgency tactics, see Russell W. Ramsey, *Guerrilleros y soldados* (Bogotá: Tercer Mundo, 1981); and Colombia, Comando del Ejercito, *Casos tácticos de guerra de guerrillas en Colombia*, 3 vols. (Bogotá: Imprenta de las Fuerzas Armadas, n.d.).

21. *Voz Proletaria*, 23 Jan 1964.

10

Hollywood Bandits, 1910–1981

ALLEN L. WOLL

Perhaps the most common image of Latin Americans in American popular culture is the bandit. From political cartoons to television commercials ("The Frito Bandito") the bandit stands bedecked in bullets with a rifle nearby. A huge sombrero caps this disturbing image of hulking random violence. Hardly a new invention of filmmakers and advertising executives, this image can be traced to a variety of nineteenth-century printed sources.[1] Yet movies and, later, television have given the bandit a new and powerful life in the American repertoire of ethnic stereotypes. The prevalence of this image in recent years has caused a plethora of boycotts, pickets, and lawsuits in an attempt to eradicate this singularly derogatory image of the Hispanic.

Although the Hollywood bandit has maintained a uniform "look" throughout the twentieth century, his behavior has been less predictable. At times the bandit is depicted as a common criminal of the rudest sort. No social bandit is he, merely a bloodthirsty and uncontrollably violent sort who commits the most heinous deeds of filmic villainy. Nevertheless, the bandit occasionally has another side. Although wearing the same attire as the violent bandit, this character has a romantic quality. Often the subject of injustice in his early life, the noble bandit attempts to redress his grievances and win land, food, or power for himself and his brothers.

It may seem odd that the view from Sunset Boulevard could produce a character with such schizophrenic qualities, a bandit with both noble and vile instincts.[2] Yet, in order to understand the evolution of such a seemingly contradictory character, the social and political context of Hollywood moviemaking must be examined. The silver screen's bandits, like their real-life counterparts, do not exist in a vacuum.

Early silent films often played to immigrant and working-class audiences.

These relatively short films, which were shown at local nickelodeons, emphasized action and violence.[3] Although various ethnic characters populated these early efforts, the Hispanic bandit, usually a Mexican, swiftly became a stock figure in fast-paced action dramas. Indeed, one critic proclaimed the Mexican "the convenient villain."[4] Many of these ethnic characters perpetrated acts of violence, but Mexican bandits were clearly identified as the vilest. They robbed, murdered, plundered, raped, cheated, gambled, lied, and displayed virtually every vice that could be shown on screen.

The Mexican bandit became such an identifiable character that a dubious stereotype developed in a series of films produced between 1910 and 1916. The Mexican bandit became "the greaser" in such films as *Tony the Greaser* (1911), *Broncho Billy and the Greaser* (1914), and *The Greaser's Revenge* (1914).[5]

Whereas the ordinary villain would murder or steal, the Mexican greaser often carried his occupation to excess. More often than not, he reveled in excesses of violence. A bandit in *The Cowboy's Baby* (1910) throws the hero's child into a river. The "greaser" in *A Western Child's Heroism* (1912) attacks the Americans who saved his life. In *Broncho Bill's Redemption* (1910) a vile Mexican is given money to buy medicine for a dying man. Instead he steals the money and tosses away the prescription. *The Greaser's Revenge* (1914) finds José, "the evil half-breed," trying to kill Fred by throwing him into a deserted mine shaft.

To a certain extent the Mexican bandit image flourished in fictional films because of a nonfictional event: the Mexican Revolution.[6] Newspapers and documentary films thoroughly covered the events occurring south of the border and emphasized violence and bloodshed instead of political subtleties. A well-known "fictional" character, the Mexican bandit, seemed to be carrying out similar events in real life.

The notion that there may have been political, social, or economic motivations for revolution seldom was presented in the documentary views of a nation at war. For example, consider the following advertisement from *Moving Picture World*:

> To the victor belong the spoils and if you want to share in the fruits of Villa's conquests get control of the . . . right to exhibit . . . War pictures made by the Mutual Film Corporation under special contract with Villa himself! Villa is getting more famous every day. There is three times more about him in newspapers than about any other man alive. . . . The picture introduces hundreds of scenes taken during the Battles of Torreón, Chihuahua, and other famous conflicts and other scenes showing the tragic early life and adventures of the wonderful warrior, the greatest military genius since Napoleon.[7]

The "documentary" films, created from newsreel footage, were as violent as this advertisement suggests. The *New York Times* praised *Barbarous Mexico* (1913) after its premiere, noting that "there are many scenes in which General Villa is seen directing the movement of his troops and artillery, and cavalry battles are shown with remarkable clearness. Other views show the burning of dead bodies on the battlefield.''[8] In this fashion real images of violence reinforced fictional images of Mexican banditry and painted the bandido as a common criminal bent on violence. Explanations of logical causes for this revolution remained irrelevant to films of the day. The stereotypes were no doubt reinforced by cameramen and technical personnel who told tales of horrible encounters with ''real'' bandits to the movie magazines of the age.[9]

There was a brief hiatus in the film career of the Mexican bandit after 1917. With the ending of the Mexican Revolution and the beginning of World War I, Hollywood found a new ''convenient villain'' for its fictional films: ''the Hun.'' The respite was brief, for the violent bandit began to return to films by 1919.[10] Although earlier Hollywood ventures in the world of Mexican banditry brooked few complaints, the newly consolidated Mexican government began to object. Officials were irritated that Mexico was presented to the world as a nation of bandits. A high official of the government explained: ''The usual portrayal of the Mexican in moving pictures is as a bandit or a sneak. Ill will toward Mexico has been inflamed by these pictures to such an extent, that the Mexican government has found it necessary to make . . . a protest.''

In late 1919 the Mexican government sent a formal letter to film producers protesting their emphasis on ''films of squalor.'' The pronouncement explained that ''these films do not portray the average conditions in the country.'' Rather, the government contended that ''photographers travel about, seeking the worst conditions they can find, and compose their films entirely of such pictures.''[11] The letter ended with a subtle warning, as the government threatened to restrict motion picture photography in Mexico.

This warning did little to change Hollywood practices, so in February 1922 the Mexican government decided to ban all films that portrayed Mexicans unfavorably. By itself this action would have done little to restrict Hollywood productions that cast Mexicans as bandits. The offending film could still be distributed to other countries and little profit would be lost. Therefore, the Mexican government decided that, in addition, it would ban *all films* of the company that produced the offensive motion picture. This was a strong ultimatum delivered at the height of the American film industry's expansion southward. The Famous Players-Lasky offices, which had just completed a 100-film deal with Mexican distributors, was shaken by the ruling and issued a statement saying that ''the wishes of the government would be respected.''[12]

The threat of economic boycott proved a potent weapon in dealing with Hollywood. A variety of methods were swiftly used to calm the Mexican government. One technique involved the shifting of locales, as movies began to look to Argentine and Brazilian settings, ignored earlier in the century. Another pundit suggested the creation of fictional countries so that no one would be offended by the bandit image. Thus the 1928 film *The Dove*, set in Mexico in its original Broadway format, was relocated to Costa Roja, supposedly situated on the Mediterranean Sea! This ruse fooled hardly anyone. Mordaunt Hall, critic for the *New York Times*, explained: ''Taken by and large, José is perhaps a screen character to which the Mexican government might have objected, for he is greedy, sensuous, boastful, cold-blooded, irritable, and quite a wine-bibber."[13] Nevertheless, the Costa Roja subterfuge diffused any possible criticism, since José was not a resident of any specific Latin American country.

Hollywood's most common response to the complaints of Mexico and other Latin American countries was the elimination of the bandit throughout the 1920s. When he resurfaced by the 1930s, he seemed a totally different (and perhaps reformed) individual.

A significant change in the depiction of the Latin American bandit began by 1930. Words that were never used in conjunction with bandit suddenly appeared in film reviews and advertisements. *Captain Thunder*, a Warner Brothers film released in December 1930, described the hero as "a handsome and reliable Mexican bandit." A summary of the 1930 First National Film, *The Lash* (originally titled *Adios*), presented the following plot line: "Anger drives Francisco to stampede a herd of cattle he is delivering to Peter Harkness, the crooked land commissioner, and still obtain his money—thus earning him the name 'El Puma.' Don Francisco and others start making Robin Hood-type bandit raids, one of which leads to Francisco's rescue by Sheriff David Howard, their subsequent friendship, and David's love for Francisco's sister, Dolores." *The Arizona Kid*, a 1930 film from Fox starring Warner Baxter, described "The Kid" as a "bandit-hero."[14]

This stark change in the presentation of the bandit lasted throughout the 1930s and can be traced to two causes, one external and one internal, in Hollywood. First, threats of Latin American boycotts of American film companies accelerated during the 1930s. A respite in the late 1920s (thanks to the "Costa Roja subterfuge") ended with the coming of sound. Despite the settings of amorphous or non-existent countries, Spanish accents clearly pointed to the real-life homes of the screen's bandits. Interestingly, the "Costa Roja" setting was abandoned when the silent version of *The Dove* was remade as a "talkie" (*Girl of the Rio*) in 1932. With Dolores Del Río and Leó Carrillo, both of Mexican heritage, in leading roles, it became futile to pretend that the plot occurred anywhere but in Mexico. Violence greeted the film's premiere in Mexico City, and the Mexican chargé d'affaires in Washington, D.C., requested that the film be banned.[15]

Whereas complaints of the 1920s emanated mainly from Mexico and Central America, criticism during the 1930s was more widespread. Brazil requested a ban on *Rio's Road to Hell* (1931), while Cuba objected to *Cuban Love Song* (1931). After the furor over *Girl of the Rio* several Latin American countries agreed to ban offensive films in concert. Spain signed a treaty with El Salvador in 1935, which agreed to:

regard as disparaging to and to prohibit the trade and circulation and exhibition in both countries of cinematographic films or reels, sound or silent, produced by any process whatsoever, which attack, slander, defame, or ridicule, insult, or misrepresent directly or indirectly, the uses, institutions, habits, characteristics, or pecularities of or incidents occurring in Spain and Salvador.[16]

They also agreed that repeated offenses would warrant an embargo of all future films by the offending companies. This treaty became a model for other Latin American countries as well. Spain concluded similar agreements with Nicaragua, Peru, and Chile in 1935 and 1936. Peru also signed treaties with Chile and Argentina in the same period. Each country agreed to prohibit films offensive to the other contracting party.[17]

In this fashion the increasing pressure from Latin American countries forced Hollywood to tone down its image of the violent Hispanic in order to maintain its revenues south of the border. Yet certain domestic factors also forced the stereotype of the despicable Latin bandit in its new directions. A renewed emphasis on the Latin bandit in a sense mirrored the renewed interest of film companies in crime and banditry in the United States.

From 1930 to 1933 portrayals of American bandits or gangsters were among the most popular on the screen. These memorable characters include Rico (Edward G. Robinson) of *Little Caesar* (1930), Tommy Powers (James Cagney) of *The Public Enemy* (1931), and Tony Camonte (Paul Muni) of *Scarface* (1932). These films revealed a curious mixture of condemnation and admiration that elevated the gangster to a heroic plane. Although the gangster-hero would inevitably receive his just rewards at the end of the film, motion pictures now presented the audience with the social and economic factors that forced individuals onto the road to crime.[18]

In a similar manner the Latin American bandit came to be seen as a product of his environment. He often became a bandit because he was wronged by another. The violence of the bandit was no longer random or bloodthirsty; rather, it was determined by the logic of circumstances. The bandit of the 1930s became an admirable figure, struggling to right the wrongs committed against him or his fellow men. In the latter situation he approaches a Robin Hood characterization.

Perhaps the film that best illustrates the changing notions concerning the bandit in the 1930s is *The Robin Hood of El Dorado* (1936). Warner Baxter portrays Joaquín Murrieta, a "romantic figure whom tradition, fact, and fancy have made legend. Of him much has been written, many tales told." Joaquín's wedding is interrupted by the discovery of gold in a California valley. A humble farmer, he ignores the rush and retreats to his abode with his family. Prospectors discover that Joaquín's home sits atop the mother lode, and they try to drive him off the land. His wife is raped and murdered, and his mother is blinded. He vows to kill the prospectors for revenge and, in the process, becomes a notorious outlaw. Joaquín resents the fact that his "wanted" poster is placed next to that of Three-Fingered Jack, since "he kills to steal while I kill for justice." Joaquín completes his vengeance and once again retreats to his farm.

Yet harsh reality intrudes on his quiet life once again, when he and his brother are framed in the theft of a mule. Joaquín is whipped and his brother killed. Joaquín again vows to take revenge, and he returns to the bandit life. At first he robs from everyone, but then (after an encounter with his former hacendado's daughter) he realizes that the true villains are the North Americans who are changing the face of the Mexican land. He then decides to rob only Americans and distribute the wealth to his fellow Mexicans. In this manner he becomes an overnight hero to Mexicans in the area. Joaquín refuses to kill in his raids, but an associate's bullet accidentally kills a little girl. Joaquín is deeply moved by this event ("We fight Americans, this is good—but when we kill little girls, it is bad"), and he decides to quit and return home. A posse arrives and Joaquín is mortally wounded, but he drags himself to his wife's grave before he expires. This is then the new heroic Mexican bandit who is revered in the 1930s.

The sudden reversal of film images of the bandit is succeeded by another abrupt change in the 1940s. The new romantic bandit-hero suddenly disappears. This is an ironic shift, since films using Latin stars, locales, and historical heroes began to flood American screens. Such eminent leaders as Benito Juárez and Simón Bolívar were immortalized on film. Talent scouts brought planeloads of Latin Americans to Hollywood, and viewers discovered Carmen Miranda, Desi Arnaz, and Cesar Romero. Films allowed audiences to spend a *Weekend in Havana* (1941) or *Midnight in Mexico* (1948) or travel *Down Argentine Way* (1940). In all these filmic jaunts south of the Río Grande, a bandit was nowhere to be seen. Instead, all Latin Americans appeared basically the same as North Americans, as Hollywood presented its version of the Good Neighbor Policy.[19]

Hollywood's newly enlightened view toward South America was dictated by a variety of motives, many related to the threat of Nazism in Europe. Government policy directed filmmakers to avoid offending our neighbors and potential allies to the south. The Office of the Coordinator of Inter-American Affairs established a Motion Picture Section, headed by John Hay Whitney, to advise studios on the "basic job of spreading the gospel" of American unity during the critical war years.[20] Although patriotism and government policy led Hollywood to offer a rosier view of Latin America, economic motivations also played a major part. As the war continued, European film markets became increasingly unavailable to motion picture distributors. By late 1940 only Central and South America remained as major importers of American films. It would have been economic suicide to offend or alienate Hollywood's major foreign markets.

The one filmic casualty of this wartime economic and political situation was the bandit. The violent staple of the 1920s and the bandit-hero of the 1930s virtually disappeared during the 1940s. Whitney's office (as well as the Hays' office) took the lead, advising studios not to portray Latin Americans as being involved in any criminal behavior. As a result the use of a bandit character, whether heroic or not, became exceedingly difficult, since it might offend Latin American audiences.

After the war Europe again became Hollywood's major film importer, but legacies of the war years remained intact. The Motion Picture Association of America established an International Information Center in Los Angeles, charged with effecting "the deletion from motion pictures of any elements which might reasonably be expected to offend the sensitivities of foreign peoples." Two Latin

American specialists, one Cuban and one North American, were hired to assist screenwriters, directors, and producers in the preparation of scripts dealing with Latin American characters. One of the targets of this office was, again, the bandit. One script that was reviewed featured a Mexican bandit, "El Sombre," and after several discussions it was decided to make him a North American disguised as a Mexican in order to avoid offending Mexican audiences.[21]

But not all unfavorable views of Hispanics were eliminated in a reasonable and pacific manner. Mexico seized footage from *The Treasure of Sierra Madre* (1948) until John Huston agreed to reshoot some introductory scenes. Nevertheless, the lessons of the war years seemed to have been learned well, and the Hispanic bandit slowly disappeared from the screen.

As a result of the continual improvement in the Latin American image on the screen between 1940 and 1960, the return of the "greaser" was a major and unexpected surprise. By the mid–1960s, as violence returned to the screen, an old villain was resurrected. In the "spaghetti westerns" of Sergio Leone and the domestic versions of Sam Peckinpah, the murderous, treacherous, violent Latin American reappeared on the screen. With new heights of filmic savagery presented on the screen, violence by Latin bandits became excessive and widespread. Whereas during the silent era the "greaser" might vent his wrath on individuals or small groups, modern screen technology allows the Mexican to destroy mass portions of the population. In *Duck, You Sucker* (1972) Rod Steiger, portraying a peasant during the Mexican Revolution, is prone to throwing bombs every few minutes in order to destroy trains, munition dumps, and the like. Similar characters appear in *Butch Cassidy and the Sundance Kid* (1969), *Two Mules for Sister Sara* (1970), and *Bring Me the Head of Alfredo García* (1974).

While the return of the villainous bandit might have been unexpected, it need not have been a surprise. All the factors that led to the amelioration of the Latin image on film and the virtual elimination of the character of the bandit had disappeared by 1960. Latin American countries had once played a major role in forcing Hollywood to change its ways. But after 1945 a variety of changes in motion picture marketing patterns lessened the clout of Latin American countries. As Europe once again became a major source of revenue, Hollywood had less to fear from threats of boycotts.[22] At the same time the dependence of Latin American countries on Hollywood products had lessened considerably. Mexico, Argentina, and Spain churned out Spanish-language films, which, by the mid–1950s, began to rival American films in quality and production values.[23] Brazil accomplished a similar task for the Portuguese-language market. These domestic cinema movements were given an added boost by the fact that several governments recognized the massive drain of foreign currency reserves in the rental of Hollywood films. Brazil, Chile, and other South American countries have, at various times, established import curbs on Hollywood films and have set exhibition quotas for local film productions. The net result of these changes in the market structure has considerably lessened the ability of Latin American governments to effect change in Hollywood.

By the same token the factors that brought about Hollywood's Good Neighbor Policy had become less important by the 1960s. It is interesting to note that the bandit image returned shortly after the Cuban Revolution. Films gradually assumed Washington's Cold War saber-rattling stance, and sympathy toward Latin American characters, whether bandits or guerrillas, swiftly vanished.

The return of the traditional bandit stereotype has been of somewhat less concern to Hollywood's new Hispanic audience: Hispanic-Americans. Although the bandit remains a continuing concern of groups that protest Hollywood's use of stereotypes, other problems have moved to the forefront. The bandit character, while certainly Hispanic, remains a foreigner. But as Hollywood has shifted to dramas of American life to lure Hispanic audiences, a domestic version of the bandit evolved. The violent and anarchic "greaser" of the early silent films has been transplanted to American cityscapes. The bandit character has thus become urbanized, but remains just as violent, in such films as *Badge 373* (1973), *Boulevard Nights* (1979), and *Fort Apache, the Bronx* (1981).

Hispanic-American organizations have as yet been unable to wield the clout that Latin American nations mustered between 1920 and 1945 in dealing with Hollywood. There have been some successes, to be sure. *Nosotros*, an organization founded by Ricardo Montalban (himself a victim of Latin stereotyping during the 1950s), has implemented changes in several films and television shows (including the elimination of the Frito Bandito). Nevertheless, Montalban also noted an unexpected and unhappy irony. As stereotypes disappeared from the screen, film roles for Hispanic-Americans vanished as well.

As a result the violent bandit remains a thriving Hollywood icon, a hearty monument to an earlier age. Although he may have undergone a brief personality change in the 1930s, he remains the violent "greaser" of the early silent films. His character and perseverance remain a tribute, not to Hollywood's ability to represent reality, but to the changing play of market forces throughout the twentieth century. As a result the "convenient villain" remains as strong as ever.

NOTES

1. Mark Reisler, *By the Sweat of Their Brow: Mexican Immigrant Labor in the United States, 1900–1940* (Westport, Conn.: Greenwood Press, 1976), Ch. 6, and John J. Johnson, *Latin America in Caricature* (Austin: University of Texas Press, 1980).

2. See Benjamin Stein, *The View from Sunset Boulevard: America as Brought to You by the People Who Make Television* (New York: Basic Books, 1980).

3. Garth Jowett, *Film. The Democratic Art.* (Boston: Little, Brown, 1976), Chs. 1–4.

4. Blaine P. Lamb, "The Convenient Villain: The Early Cinema Views the Mexican-American," *Journal of the West*, 14 (Oct. 1975): 75–81.

5. Allen Woll, *The Latin Image in American Film* (Los Angeles: UCLA Latin American Center, 1981), Chs. 1–2.

6. Kevin Brownlow, *The War, the West, and the Wilderness* (New York: Alfred A. Knopf, 1978), pp. 87–106.

7. *Moving Picture World*, 21 (18 July 1914): 440.

8. *New York Times*, 10 May 1914.

9. Kevin Brownlow, *The Parade's Gone By* (New York: Ballantine Books, 1968), Ch. 18.

10. *New York Evening Sun*, 20 May 1918.

11. *Moving Picture World*, 40 (26 Apr. 1919): 532.

12. *New York Times*, 11 February 1922.

13. Ibid., 3 January 1928.

14. Kenneth W. Munden, ed., *The American Film Institute Catalog of Motion Pictures Produced in the United States (1921–1930)* (New York: R. R. Bowker, 1971), F2.0171, F2.0781, F2.2959.

15. *New York Times*, 9 May 1932.

16. League of Nations, *Treaty Series*, 165:3818 (1935).

17. John Eugene Harley, *World-Wide Influences of the Cinema: A Study of Official Censorship and the International Cultural Aspects of Motion Pictures* (Los Angeles: University of Southern California Press, 1940), Ch. 5.

18. Andrew Bergman, *We're in the Money. Depression America and Its Films* (New York: Harper & Row, 1971), pt. 1.

19. Allen L. Woll, "Hollywood's Good Neighbor Policy: The Latin Image in American Film, 1939–1946," *Journal of Popular Film*, 3 (Fall 1974): 278–293.

20. Donald W. Rowland, ed., *History of the Office of the Coordinator of Inter-American Affairs* (Washington, D.C.: Government Printing Office, 1947), pp. 3–77.

21. *Américas*, 1 (Oct. 1949): 3–5.

22. David Charles Botting, "History of the Motion Picture in Latin America" (Ph.D. diss., University of Chicago, 1950).

23. See E. Bradford Burns, *Latin American Cinema: Film and History* (Los Angeles: UCLA Latin American Center, 1975).

11

Latin American Banditry and Criminological Theory

DRETHA M. PHILLIPS

Latin American banditry poses a number of challenges for criminological theory. Like any body of substantive theory,[1] criminological theory is charged with explaining the "facts" of a phenomenon such that knowledge is generated and understanding enhanced. Substantive criminological theory, then, addresses itself to the question of *why* the facts of crime stack up as they do. It is on this level that Latin American banditry initially confronts the theorist.

To which of many "why" questions do we address ourselves? Is it the etiological question of why particular young men (and, clearly less often, young women) turn to a life of brigandage? Or, is it one of the epidemiological questions: Why are certain categories of people overrepresented in bandit gangs? Why does banditry characterize a particular time period or country but not another? In other words, why are the patterns of banditry in Latin America the way they are? These are standard criminological questions. The challenge to theory from most types of criminal behavior is to address adequately one or the other kind of question, with the hope of accounting, ultimately, for both the etiological and the epidemiological facts of crime.

Latin American banditry, however, presents yet another kind of fact for explanation. That is the fact that a particular image of bandits captured the fancy of entire nations, that the mythology of banditry entered the collective conscience with all the force of hero worship, that criminals by a special other name no longer were criminals, but became revered icons of a martyred peasantry. Why do "bad guys" become, if not outright "good guys," lamented figures of a golden, although tarnished, past? Seldom must criminologists consider such questions, but Hobsbawm's definition of social banditry requires that we do.

Finally, Latin American banditry challenges those who would offer theoretical methods[2] as a means for developing new, testable substantive theory. Largely because of its presumed ubiquity, social banditry begs that we reexamine the bases on which criminological theories are constructed. It points to anomalies, logical inconsistencies, and ethnocentric blind spots that reduce the grandest theories to platitudinous explanations. Social banditry provides a ready point of departure for criminologists to embark earnestly on constructing well-considered theory.

Latin American banditry, then, poses challenges that go to the very heart of criminological theory. Questions regarding its robustness and applicability are raised in the areas of substantive theory—in which etiological, epidemiological, and "mythological" facts must be explained—and theoretical methods.

THE ETIOLOGY OF LATIN AMERICAN BANDITRY

To the question of why young men become bandits, most authors answer in classic anomie theory[3] fashion: there were no, or severely limited, legitimate means of success open to such young men. Their only hope for a reasonable livelihood lay in their willingness and ability to plunder what was held legally by others. Fundamental to anomie theory is the notion that people are pressured to pursue culturally accepted goals of success through culturally approved means for achieving them. Although the pursuit of goals is assumed to be universal within a society, access to legitimate means is not. People may adapt to such a disjunction between cultural institutions in one of five ways, i.e., by becoming (1) a conformist, accepting the goals and pursuing them through legitimate means; (2) an innovator, accepting the goals but pursuing them through illegitimate means; (3) a ritualist, denying the goals but going through the motions of pursuing them legitimately; (4) a rebel, denying both current goals and the means to achieve them, while actively substituting others in their place; or (5) a retreatist, removing oneself from the pursuit of any goals through any means. The innovator typically is most interesting to criminologists because he is the one presumed to be committing the crimes.[4] It is the innovator, too, who is conjured up in these assessments of the motivations for banditry in Latin America.

Like its original application to U.S. crime, anomie theory has a certain intuitive appeal in its explanation of Latin American banditry. The influence of cultural arrangements on ostensibly individual behavior is highlighted. We are encouraged to move the genesis of criminal behavior from the realm of individual pathology to that of social inequality, to recognize that "there but for the grace of God [or the vagaries of birth] go I." We come to see crime, not as wicked or sinful, but as a normal, rational response to having been dealt fewer options than law-abiding folks. The very term "innovator" denotes a certain cleverness, a flexibility by design, even a respectability that is absent from other adaptations.[5] Having internalized the success goals of their culture, the disadvantaged understandably become disaffected and are driven to pursue success outside conventional paths. Latin American bandits, like lower-class criminals in the United States, represent societal rather than individual maladjustment.

As a sensitizing concept, anomie is useful particularly for alerting us to the interplay between the social structures of a Latin American nation and the incidence of banditry found there. As a theory that purports to explain why certain peasants engaged in brigandage, anomie falls short of its promise. For example, all sources indicate that—even at its peak—social banditry was a statistically uncommon adaptation even among the population at highest risk, the peasants. If, by virtue of their class position, peasants are denied access to culturally approved avenues for success, then we should find that the majority of them turn to crime. We do not because they do not. Conversely, the propertied and the gentry should not be represented in bandit gangs, but the Latin American experience indicates that they were. What do we make of this?

The most obvious conclusion is that anomie is no more satisfying as an etiological theory of Latin American banditry than it is of lower-class crime in the United States.[6] Although strain between cultural institutions may set the stage for, even predispose, certain classes of criminal behavior, such strain cannot account for individual lives of banditry or crime. Less obvious, but no less inescapable, is the conclusion that there may not exist in the criminological arsenal any wholly satisfying answer to the question "why did they do it?"

The contributors to this book raise the specters of nearly every major criminological theory in their attempts to understand the motivation of bandits. We take note not just of cultural strain (anomie), but also of social upheaval in which old standards of behavior no longer have currency in the new order (social disorganization), of the transmission of values that promote violence as a means of resolving conflict and as a way of life (cultural transmission/subculture of violence), of political power plays that result in the redefinition of conventional behavior as criminal banditry (conflict theory). Our reaction to each of these explanations is the same: It makes some sense, provides some insight, but it still does not tell us why any of the characters in this book (especially as opposed to their brothers, relatives, or childhood neighbors) became bandits.

Even the theories considered most powerful in explaining etiological facts— the learning or socialization theories—seem to stop with penultimate causes. For example, differential association (the granddaddy of socialization theories of deviance) posits that criminal behavior is learned through the same mechanisms as normative behavior. What differentiates the two is the content of the norms that are learned. Deviance or criminal behavior results when the norms with which one comes into contact are imbalanced in favor of norm violation. Why do certain young men become bandits? Because they have been socialized by a normative system that supports, even expects, such behavior. Why does not everyone raised in that seemingly the same environment become bandits? Because they were differentially associated with norms that favor violation. The non-bandits' associations with such norms were less frequent, less intense, of shorter duration, and of lower priority. This explanation certainly highlights the social and learned aspects of deviance, but it still begs the question of why norms favoring deviance should be differentially experienced and why they should arise in the first place.

Let us examine the efficacy of one last, possibly etiological, theory. Control theory may be considered as a type of learning theory, although the assumptions about human nature, and, consequently, the questions asked about deviance, are opposite those of all other criminological theories. Control theory asks not "why did this person deviate?" but rather "why did that person *not* deviate?" The answer to the latter question is to be found in the development of a bond to normative society, sufficient to control one's inherent tendency to deviate. It is assumed that if one is not appropriately bonded to society, if the stake in conformity is weak or nonexistent, then deviance is the natural response. Again, we are left short of a full understanding of why any particular bandit failed to develop a bond to conventional peasant society.

Latin American banditry is not unique in its recalcitrance to etiological explanation. Criminological theory—singularly or in combination—similarly has failed to specify the origins of any form of social deviance and crime. We would do as well to try to answer the question "where did God come from?" Indeed, without reference to the unique, the bizarre, the individual aberration (phenomena for which the traditionally, sociologically trained criminologist has little use, except insofar as they constitute the bothersome negative cases), criminology may not be capable of providing an ultimate answer to why *anyone* turns to crime. Be that as it may (and it is an empirical question), criminological theory typically fares better in the United States with epidemiological facts. Perhaps the same is true in Latin America.

THE EPIDEMIOLOGY OF LATIN AMERICAN BANDITRY

Latin American banditry appears to be fashioned along the following lines. Although female bandits are not unknown, brigandage is overwhelmingly a male vocation. The incidence and prevalence of banditry are greater in states that are undergoing significant social change and in areas that are removed from the hub, but not the spokes, of such change. Bandits tend (although not overwhelmingly so, especially leaders of bandit gangs) to be from the social classes most likely to be disenfranchised by changes in, particularly, the subsistence or economic basis of the society. Such facts readily fit within the explanatory framework of several criminological theories.

For example, anomie suggests that the highest rates of deviance will be found among those groups that are subject to the greatest cultural strain. It is not difficult to see that a disjunction between pursuit of culturally approved goals and access to legitimate means to achieve them might be especially wide during times of social change. Peasants, whose livelihood is threatened by encroaching modernization and the imposition of other subsistence technologies, might well be the group that experiences the greatest strain, and thereby yields the most bandits. The negative cases, as always, are a problem. But if we invoke the notion of opportunity, we account for more of the facts.

In addition to society's providing differential access to legitimate means for achieving cultural goals, there exists differential opportunity to use *illegitimate* means. Groups (or individuals) may be cut off structurally from both conventional and unconventional avenues for success. This might explain why only those peasants who were unusually mobile could gain a livelihood through brigandage. The same mobility helps to explain why female bandits are an oddity. Especially in agrarian, or pre-industrial, economies, women are bound even more than men to a circumscribed, conventional lifestyle. Although opportunities for legitimate success may be absent or severely limited, there may be no chance for illegitimate success either. It is assumed, then, that people caught in such a bind will take the path of least resistance and remain among the ranks of the non-deviant, but socially disadvantaged, population.[7]

We could apply to the epidemiological facts of Latin American banditry each of the theories discussed in the previous section—social disorganization, cultural transmission/subculture of violence, conflict, differential association, and control—with the same "so what?" result. It is not that the theories are illogical, or even that they are inapplicable to banditry per se;[8] rather, they make so much sense that they are common. We would not feel that we had gained any greater insight into the question of why banditry is distributed as it is than if we had simply left the answer to informed intuition. Part of the discontent with current explanations for social deviance may derive from an overfamiliarity with them. To invoke any one or all of them is an automatic response that requires little contemplation and yields no new knowledge or understanding. The application of the theories is so endemic to the study of crime that even writers (such as those of this book) untrained in criminology summon up the essence, if not the terminology, of such theories.

The other part of our discontent may lie in the fact that our theories are tired. We seldom stretch them or subject them to invigorating exercise, hence they are not intellectually stimulating to us.[9] We take for granted both their strengths in explaining certain kinds of crimes and their weaknesses in failing to account for others. There is hope, however, for a revitalization, which is addressed in the final section of this chapter.

THE MYTHOLOGY OF LATIN AMERICAN BANDITRY

Empirical evidence attesting to the existence of Hobsbawm's social bandit in Latin America is slim. Yet the image of the morally right but legally wrong champion of the "little people" is celebrated throughout Latin America in song, theater, poetry, and prose. For those who would limit criminology to "just the facts, ma'am,'' we would be out of bounds trying to account for such a myth-ological creation. However, some basic assumptions within criminological theory may be useful here.

At the top of the list would be the functionalist assumption that crime is normal. Not only is crime normal in the sense that it is universal across societies and ubiquitous within them, but also in the sense that when a society creates rules it simultaneously creates the likelihood, as well as the form, of their violation. In this way crime no less than ''normalcy'' is a reflection of the society itself, of its values and beliefs, its fears and tolerance limits. By taking this one step further we might come to assume that to glorify this reflection of ourselves is normal too.

First, we triangulate key elements of the criminological theories discussed earlier. Let us assume that a country is undergoing significant social change, such that the conventional way of life for a sizable proportion of the population is threatened, undermined, in a state of flux. Further, although viable alternatives may be developing, structural access to the benefits of the new social order is denied (at least temporarily) to these people. Rather than excitement about new possibilities, the changes engender anxiety mixed with nostalgia for a lost and presumably freer lifestyle.

Might it not make sense in such a situation that those who once were renegades, even predatory criminals, are transformed into heroes? That tales of their exploits are tinged with envy of their having escaped the tethers of conformity? That, rather than chronic ''ne'er-do-wells'' and degenerates, these people become superhuman in their cleverness, their agility, their strength of body and of pur-pose?[10] Such an understanding leads us to recognize that the injustice suffered by the individual, which supposedly provides the motivation for social banditry, need not have been a personal one. Instead, it simply may be symbolic of the perceived social injustice meted out by the forces of change. The bandit becomes a victim, but not a helpless one. He represents the possibility of fighting back, of exerting control over one's life when everything seems patently out of control and uncontrollable.

Obviously, lapses into histrionics are difficult to resist when discussing the mythology of banditry. This *is* the mythology: the exaggerated swagger of de-fiant young men, forced to live outside the law when honoring the ancient code of vengeance for moral wrongs, never forgetting their humble roots or their destiny to die by treachery in their prime. Such larger-than-life images may be easier to understand when the subject is a law-abiding one that serves as a pos-itive role model for subsequent generations. But it may be no less normal or expected when the subject is otherwise and the conditions are right for hero worship of another kind. My task in this section has been accomplished if the reader is led to ponder whether criminological theory (with a strong dose of social psychology) might fare better in trying to explain the myths, rather than the facts, of banditry.

THEORETICAL METHODS AND LATIN AMERICAN
BANDITRY

To engage in theoretical methods is to highlight the ''approaches, assumptions, and techniques of theory construction.''[11] It requires that we cease our knee-jerk application of tried-and-occasionally-true theories and examine critically their foundations. Through theoretical methods Latin American banditry presents the greatest challenge, as well as potential benefit, to criminological theory. One basic notion will suffice as illustration.

The present book attempts to provide examples of and empirical information on Hobsbawm's model of social banditry. Support for the model is uneven, at best. This is not surprising, given that the model suffers from the same maladies as do most typologies. Let us consider those for a moment.

To speak of social bandits, and then to further specify categories of social bandits, presumes a conceptual framework that directs our data-gathering and theory-making efforts along distinct lines. In essence, Hobsbawm has constructed a typology of banditry. The typological approach assumes that ''crimes and criminals are neither all alike nor unique events or persons; instead, a number of distinct 'types' or groups of offenses and/or offenders exist and can be identified and studied.''[12] Bandits are conceived as alike in their manner of livelihood (and their ties to the peasantry) but dissimilar in their motivations and in the uses to which the plunder is put. Thus we have social versus un-, a-, anti-, or non-social bandits (Hobsbawm is not clear on the opposing type). Within the social bandit category we have the noble robber, the primitive resistance fighter or guerrilla units of *haiduks*, and the terror-bringing avenger.[13]

This fits our commonsense understanding that people who rob for a purpose are qualitatively different from those who plunder capriciously. We also appreciate the distinctions among various kinds of purposes, so that those who steal from the rich to give to the poor (no doubt a rudimentary form of income redistribution or welfare) constitute a different type of social bandit from those who rob nobleman and peasant alike in their resistance to any form of authority. The problem here is that the data do not fit these discrete types. Some bandits, indeed, may share the spoils of their plunder with their immediate families or even with entire peasant villages. But they are just as likely to keep what they steal for themselves and to victimize hapless peasants in their path. As has been demonstrated time and again with ''criminal-centered'' typologies, lawbreaking may be patterned and easily typed, but actual offenders do not fit readily ''into homogeneous types of groupings of lawbreakers.''[14] Thus we face the situation of trying to explain the exceptions rather than the rule, of trying to decide which of the behaviors of any particular bandit is more salient—the noble robbing or the terror-bringing vengeance—of trying to fit real-life complexities into simplistic, unidimensional types and wondering why our explanations actually explain so little.

Even if our explanations accounted for all the variation within and between types of social bandits, we still could not claim to have developed a "theory" of social banditry. The typology precludes our doing so. A theory "is a system of interrelated ideas that answers, for *more than one* phenomenon, the question of why/how in a *general, abstract* manner."[15] Social banditry, by definition here, is only one type of phenomenon. The best we can do is to offer an explanation, an "account of some *specific* phenomenon that answers the question why/how for a particular audience."[16] Such an explanation, however, may be a suitable point of departure for constructing a general theory if we recognize that "it is incorrect to assume that all phenomena to be explained by a single theory must be empirically alike. Phenomena have only to be subsumable within a similar causative process."[17]

If we move away from the typological approach imposed by Hobsbawm's model, we open up numerous, potentially more fruitful avenues for explaining the distribution of social banditry. For example, it has been argued that "differences in crime rates in space and time are the result of differences in the patterning of routine activities, those same activities that account for noncriminal behavior."[18] Changes in routine activities produce changes in "three general sets of factors" that determine the crime rate: "the supply of potential offenders, the supply of suitable targets, and the absence of capable guardians."[19] Rates of social banditry in Latin America, then, are viewed as specific, empirical instances of the coalescence of "a likely offender, a suitable target, and the absence of a capable guardian."[20] Much more elaboration would need to be done to make this a satisfactory explanation of social banditry, let alone a general theory of crime, but it promises greater understanding of the phenomenon in the process.

Another example of how we might begin to construct general theory from limited explanations of Latin American banditry is provided in a recent article by Charles R. Tittle.[21] To illustrate the process Tittle begins by describing in detail one of the better-known and respected explanations of gang delinquency, in which gangs are seen as emerging to fulfill status needs otherwise unattainable for lower-class boys. He then indicates that this explanation not only is limited in scope, but also "seems to fail because of minute differences from case to case."[22] From there Tittle suggests that:

this *explanation* of lower-class gang delinquency can be transformed into a *theory of subcultures* by conceptualizing an abstract process that applies to many situations. Thus, instead of referring to lower-class boys, school failure, gangs, and delinquency, the theory refers to subordinates in a status hierarchy, inability to meet the expectations of higher statuses, subcultures, and violations of the norms of a dominant culture. The theory then specifies a process—inability to meet dominant status criteria—that, no matter what the hierarchical system, produces adjustment problems for subordinates. If the subordinates are in close proximity, these adjustment problems will be shared in interaction and a subculture will emerge that helps them overcome those problems. . . . This theory of subcultures accounts for a particular type of delinquency because gang behavior can be regarded as an empirical instance of the abstract categories with which the theory deals. . . . But, more than that, the theory also accounts for prison inmate organization, radical student organizations, underground nationalist movements, and numerous other phenomena that lack obvious similarity with gang delinquency but that logically are embodiments of the abstract categories of the theory.[23]

This theory of subcultures may or may not account satisfactorily for Latin American banditry. If it does, it may explain the existence of bandit gangs but not of the solitary bandit. These are empirical issues beyond the scope of this chapter. The point here is that, although we are likely to be frustrated in our attempts to provide support for Hobsbawm's typology of banditry, our explanations for Latin American banditry could lead us to general theories of such statistically uncommon crimes that would be applicable to other times and other nations. If we have done our work well, not only would our theories explain crime within and among nations, but also we would better understand and appreciate human behavior in all its forms everywhere.

NOTES

1. "Substantive theory is composed of specific ideas that attempt to explain individual offending or patterns of offending." Robert F. Meier, "An Introduction to Theoretical Methods in Criminology," in *Theoretical Methods in Criminology*, ed. Robert F. Meier (Beverly Hills, Calif.: Sage, 1985), p. 12.

2. "The term 'theoretical methods' denotes approaches, assumptions, and techniques of theory construction. . . . They involve a reconsideration of basic assumptions and understandings that underpin our substantive theories." Ibid., pp. 15–17.

3. For overviews of the various criminological theories, see especially, Marshall B. Clinard and Robert R. Meier, *The Sociology of Deviant Behavior*, 6th ed. (New York: Holt, Rinehart & Winston, 1985), and George B. Vold and Thomas J. Bernard, *Theoretical Criminology*, 3rd ed. (New York: Oxford University Press, 1986).

4. The pronoun "he" is used here purposely and descriptively. Given that well over 80 percent of identified criminals are male, it would be misleading to use gender-neutral language.

5. Anomie theory, like the myth of banditry, gives noble motivations to the criminal—he just wants what everyone else does. It may be this phenomenon that helps to explain the elevation of otherwise common criminals—bandits—to hero status through legend; see discussion in later section of this chapter.

6. Please note that anomie theory, as well as the other theories discussed in the remainder of this section, typically are *not* offered to explain etiological facts of deviance in the United States. They are mentioned here because (a) the contributors to this book referred to their tenets and (b) I wanted to explore whether they were more applicable to a non-U.S. setting.

7. The argument could be made that if one *is* successful illegitimately, he or she would *not* come to the attention of authorities, and thereby would not be counted among the deviants and criminals.

8. Indeed, if the measure of a theory is not only its explanation of past cases, but

also its prediction of future ones, then we have an empirical question that is beyond the scope of this chapter.

9. Seldom do criminologists even attempt to apply their theories to crime outside the United States. Although I would not pretend that the present chapter is a systematic application, it is unusual in its reference to Latin American crime.

10. This image is necessary for the pursuer of bandits as well. If the bandit is nothing more than a typical peasant gone bad, the *federales* have no excuse for their failure to capture him.

11. Meier, "Introduction," p. 15.

12. Don C. Gibbons, "The Assumption of the Efficacy of Middle-Range Explanation: Typologies," in *Theoretical Methods*, p. 152.

13. Eric Hobsbawm, *Bandits*, rev. ed. (New York: Pantheon Books, 1981), p. 20.

14. Gibbons, "Assumption," p. 159. "For example, even though residential burglaries often show many similarities and thus can be said to be patterned, it does not follow that these offenses are committed by 'burglars,' that is, individuals who specialize in burglaries to the exclusion of other offenses. And it may be even more difficult to sort real-life offenders into types based on such variables as attitudes, self-concepts, and the like."

15. Charles L. Tittle, "The Assumption That General Theories Are Not Possible," in *Theoretical Methods*, p. 94.

16. Ibid., p. 93.

17. Ibid., p. 109.

18. Albert K. Cohen, "The Assumption That Crime Is a Product of Environments: Sociological Approaches," in *Theoretical Methods*, p. 238.

19. Gibbons, "Assumption," p. 172.

20. Cohen, "Assumption That Crime," p. 238.

21. Tittle, "Assumption That General Theories." pp. 105–106.

22. Ibid., p. 106.

23. Ibid.

12

Conclusion: Banditry in Latin America

RICHARD W. SLATTA

Having examined bandit activity in a number of Latin American nations, we are now ready to review and critique the social bandit model developed by Eric Hobsbawm. On balance we find deficiencies in the model, stemming primarily from Hobsbawm's heavy reliance on folk and literary sources. This does not necessarily negate the value of such materials as historical sources, but it does mandate careful, balanced handling and, most important, cross-checking against other types of sources.

As Richard Slatta's work on the images of gaucho bandits in Argentina shows, literary sources, myths, and legends cannot be dismissed out of hand. Even romanticized and stylized presentations, such as "Martín Fierro" by José Hernández, may resonate with authentic folk values. Hobsbawm merits praise for drawing on the novel types of evidence used in *Bandits*.

But Hobsbawm also invites criticism for not balancing folkloric and literary materials with other documents. As Linda Lewin's work shows, the best course is a blend of official (police and judicial) documents and popular folkloric sources. In Hobsbawm's defense it is well to remember that he creatively used those sources available to him at the time. Much of the painstaking archival research in police and judicial records has been accomplished since the original edition of *Bandits* appeared in 1969.

Despite many reservations we concur with Hobsbawm in his appreciation of the significant social roots of deviant behavior in Latin America, including banditry. It is evident that more types of banditry existed in Latin America than are captured with a simple dichotomy of just social bandits and common criminals.

The bandits of Latin America that emerge from archival sources carry visages different from the ideal type postulated by Hobsbawm. Of prime importance, the close ties of class and camaraderie that theoretically bind social bandits and peasants together do not surface in the Latin American context. One reason is that the locus of some bandit activity in Latin America occurred in thinly populated frontier regions, not in settled peasant areas.

On the South American plains, for example, the seasonal and extensive nature of the ranching industry dictated dispersed, migratory lives for gauchos and llaneros. Although gauchos identified with a local area or *pago*, work demands and legal repression forced them to ride far and wide. "Wanted" posters with detailed physical descriptions circulated among the justices of the peace and military commanders on the pampa. Visits to a village could quickly end a fugitive's freedom.

Gaucho outlaws neither wanted nor needed support from the rural masses. A toss of the lasso and a slice of the knife brought a meal of beef from a wild or stolen cow. Hides from stolen cattle could be exchanged for tobacco, mate tea leaves, and a few draughts of cheap liquor at an out-of-the-way pulpería. Mindful that he needed suppliers and customers, the pulpero asked no questions.

Such plains bandits lived a marginal existence, unintegrated into traditional rural society. Venezuelan llaneros, depicted by Miguel Izard and Richard Slatta as a separate people, provide yet another example of socially outcast frontiersmen, subsisting on the fringes of "civilization," well beyond the reach of central governmental authority.

But even where bandits operated more proximally to peasant communities, their solidarity with the rural masses was weak. In the sertão of the Brazilian Northeast, when the rural poor rendered aid to Lampião they acted more out of fear and duress than out of class or cultural bonding. Mexico's nineteenth-century bandit gangs also seem to have been more feared than admired and supported by peasant villagers.

Perhaps the closest links between settled peasant communities and bandit gangs existed in the coffee regions of Colombia during the Violencia. Gangs, allied along partisan lines with local elites and peasants, took over some areas of Quindío, Tolima, and Valle. They could pose as coffee workers, a form of "social camouflage," to avoid detection by the army. But when Colombian bandits resorted to terrorism to discourage peasant defectors and informants, they turned the rural masses against them.

Bandits everywhere needed some support, such as material assistance (food, arms, clothing), hiding places, and intelligence on the movement of authorities. If the peasantry of Latin America did not provide the necessary assistance, then who did? The local, landed elites, not the peasant masses, had much closer ties to major bandit figures. Far from being class enemies of the elite, major Latin American bandits worked for and with the rural oligarchy and even with governmental officials. This elite-bandit cooperation seriously challenges Hobsbawm's model of class conflict between peasant-based social bandits and the lords of the manor.

Paul J. Vanderwood found that bandits in the states of Hidalgo and Mexico had "accomplices in respected circles" and "had no difficulty finding collaborators among respected citizens." This finding confirms Anton Blok's earlier critique of Hobsbawm. He observed that bandits frequently forged links "with established power-holders" and even worked as paid retainers to the powerful.[1]

Peter Singelmann has shown that in the Brazilian Northeast, the lines distinguishing capangas, thugs hired by the landed elite, from cangaceiros were blurred and easily crossed. Both bandits and hired gunmen came from the same lower-class rural population. Linda Lewin also concludes that bandits of the Northeast acted "on behalf of local agrarian elites." And Billy Jaynes Chandler points out that Lampião enjoyed close relations with some families of the Brazilian coroneis ("colonels" or landed elite).[2]

Merchants and prestigious ranchers on the Argentine pampa engaged in widespread "contraband capitalism," wherein they bought stolen wool, hides, and other goods from gauchos and Indians. These profit-minded middlemen then brokered the fruits of the countryside to export merchants in Buenos Aires.[3]

Outlaws, whether deserters, bandits, or worse, could sometimes count on protection from chronically labor-short ranchers. An estanciero in need of temporary hired hands during the busy roundup and branding season would ask few questions about a gaucho's background.

These ties between rural elites and bandit gangs also lent a degree of legitimacy to the outlaws. A politically powerful family could insulate bandits from police and legal authorities. The elite-bandit relationship also illustrates the fluidity between legal and illicit actions by bandits. In nineteenth-century Mexico yesterday's bandit could become tomorrow's rural policeman with relative ease.

Banditry offered excitement, status, strikingly recognizable dress (like the fancy cowboy or charreada costume of the Plateados gang), and access to power and plunder within the region controlled by a gang. To counter this appeal Díaz outfitted the rural police force smartly and offered them power, prestige, modern arms, good horses, and attractive wages. These incentives were often sufficient to draw brigands away from crime into the ranks of the rural police force.

Hoping to use Lampião against rebellious army personnel (tenentes) marching through the backlands in the 1920s, the Brazilian government commissioned the famous bandit as an army officer. Politicians in need of strongarm men also might lend aid to known criminals. The infamous bandit of the Argentine pampas, Juan Moreira, worked as a bodyguard and "enforcer" for a national political party. The same fluidity between criminal and official ranks could be observed in Bourbon Spain and czarist Russia.[4]

In Argentina, elite governments finally subdued gauchos with vagrancy codes, passport requirements, and forced military service. Long-term repression drove many gauchos away from settled areas to outlaw life on the frontier. As in Mexico, outlaws exchanged places with police and soldiers with an ease that blurred the lines between those who enforced the law and those who broke it.[5]

The social bandit fails to emerge as a distinctive historical type in Latin America. But several other bandit variants did exist. Christon I. Archer identified guerrilla-bandits operating in Mexico during the Independence wars. Interested more in booty and self-aggrandizement than in political ideology or patriotism, they profited from the conflict and disorder of the Independence wars.[6] The same behavior characterized the llaneros of Venezuela and Colombia, for whom looting became a way of life during the Independence and subsequent civil wars. Likewise, Argentine gauchos joined in *montoneras*, populist uprisings, behind federalist caudillo leaders of the interior who promised them booty.

As Louis A. Pérez, Jr., shows for Cuba, elite partisan conflict can stir broader forms of social protest, including banditry. The Colombian Violencia, when partisan loyalties confounded class cohesiveness, gave rise to its own distinctive variation—political banditry. After they had been stripped of their political legitimacy by the national political parties, bandit gangs formed alliances with local elites.

In the 1950s, after the Rojas Pinilla and Lleras Camargo governments had destroyed the political legitimacy of partisan guerrillas, the distinction between guerrillas and bandits blurred. The end result was to force many guerrillas into an outright bandit existence.

The transition from politicized armed struggle to banditry differs sharply from Hobsbawm's conceptualization of social banditry as pre-political. He suggests that the rise of more sophisticated political activity contributes to the demise of banditry. But during the Violencia bandits succeeded organized armed struggle in the countryside.

Hobsbawm recognized "the curious but significant coexistence of banditry with more ambitious or general movements of social insurrection."[7] But Erick Langer shows that Andean peasants adopted banditry or mass mobilization, depending on the strengths of their corporate identity and internal cohesiveness. Where greater internal cohesiveness existed (such as Tarabuco, Bolivia), peasants could mobilize for mass action, even rebellion. Structurally cohesive peasant societies could also use the judicial system and engage (sometimes successfully) in litigation against upper-class encroachment and abuse.

But mestizo areas, like Tomina, Bolivia, lacked the cohesiveness and strong corporate identity necessary for mass mobilization. Here profit-minded gangs of cattle thieves developed. Peasants resorted to the weaker tactic of banditry to confront the socioeconomic crisis engulfing them only when other tactics, such as mass rebellion or litigation, were not available to them.

Latin American banditry diverges from Hobsbawm's model in another significant way. He posits official oppression or injustice as the principal motive or precipitant that forced honest peasants to take up the bandit life. Class oppression by the landed elite was certainly not uncommon in Latin America. But members of the rural masses turned to crime for personal economic gain, not because of unjust acts perpetrated against them. As Lewin observes, in a society of limited opportunity, banditry offered "better work at higher pay." These sharply stratified societies severely limited economic alternatives for the masses during the colonial and national periods.

Rural landed elites jealously guarded and often expanded their holdings at the expense of the rural masses. Monopolistic trade policies diminished somewhat with the Bourbon reforms, but economic opportunity remained limited and the chance for social advancement was virtually non-existent. In the plains regions of the Río de la Plata and the llanos the rural lower classes operated outside the narrow confines of legitimate trade by slaying wild livestock illegally. Contraband trade flourished under Spanish rule, and illicit merchandising of hides remained common after independence.[8]

In some cases, then, the oppressive structure of Latin American rural society, not individual acts of oppression, forced men to criminal acts. Barred from legitimate avenues to wealth, the rural masses found in banditry a means of economic survival. Officials often considered the landless rural masses to be criminal by nature and treated them as such. Venezuelan llaneros exhibited values and behavior of a separate people and ignored or resisted strictures imposed from Caracas. In some ways the poor rural bandit merely accepted a label and a role, based on his race, class, and geographical location, already assigned to him by authorities.

What did Latin American bandits do with their illicit gains? Did they, like Robin Hood, redistribute wealth from the oligarchy to the poor? Not usually. Latin American bandits kept their gains or shared them with elite patrons, but not with the rural masses. Token gestures of largess were sometimes made by a bandit to peasants, but for the most part bandits, not the poor, profited from banditry.

The social composition of bandit leadership also varies from Hobsbawm's model. More often than not, bandit leaders were not themselves of peasant roots. And their actions as often reinforced as challenged existing repressive social structures. It is thus not surprising that the rural poor sometimes betrayed bandits to the police instead of protecting and aiding them as class champions and avengers.

These conclusions about the motives for and beneficiaries of banditry receive additional support from research in the United States. Richard White examined the North American bandit experience—the James-Younger, Dalton, and Doolin-Dalton gangs that operated on the Middle Border. He concluded that "neither class nor traditional values seem to be significant factors in the support of bandits." White remarked also the American bandits' "stubborn refusal to envision the social problems enmeshing them in anything but personal terms. . . . They fought only for self-preservation and revenge, not for a social cause."[9] Like Latin American bandits, gangs of the Middle Border in the United States robbed for their own betterment, not to challenge the sociopolitical structures of the societies in which they operated.

The morality and values of historical Latin American bandits also vary from those of the social bandit. Hobsbawm's noble robber killed only for justifiable reasons, such as self-defense and honorable revenge. Latin American outlaws appeared much less discriminating in their use of force. Argentine matreros, operating in a frontier culture of violence, engaged in knife duels for manly sport, not necessity. Although the supposed goal of such contests was only to mark or scar an opponent's face, many combatants died of knife wounds. During the bloody political conflicts of the early nineteenth century, throat slitting reached the status of a folk art.

Ferocious llanero cavalrymen exhibited similar bloodthirstiness during the Independence wars. In Mexico, brutality and rape served as trademarks for some notorious bands. Desperate Colombian bandits turned to outright terrorism in a failed attempt to force peasant collusion. Violent men in violent cultures observed few of the moral qualms suffered by the archetypal social bandit.

Some Latin American bandits, such as Juan Moreira, Silvino, and Lampião, enjoyed the reputation of invisibility and invincibility of Hobsbawm's noble robber, but most did not. A few famous outlaws achieved intimidating reputations for ferocity, but most faced relentless pursuit by police and military units.

Despite the differences between historical reality and Hobsbawm's model, it is evident that the rural masses did identify with bandit legends. Given the structure of rural society, many understood the unjust persecutions supposedly suffered by famous legends, like Juan Moreira and Martín Fierro in Argentina, Lampião in Brazil, or Pio Romero in Bolivia. As Langer notes, peasant folklore uses a "selective memory" that remembers bandits as class champions, even if historical reality was otherwise.

Some of the bandit groups made a better transition to myth and legend than others. The cangaceiro achieved folk hero status in Brazil, with depictions in a wide range of media, from poetry to the cinema. Thanks to imaginative biographers, Joaquín Murieta achieved similar folk hero status among California Hispanics.

In contrast, the Colombian army's effective psychological warfare tactics gave rise to an anti-myth that depicted bandits of the Violencia as terrorists. After the deaths of some bandit leaders, still-oppressed peasants belatedly recognized them as class champions. But the anti-myth of the murderous bandit, the "son of the Violencia," tarnished the image.

The roots of the social bandit myth and of actual criminality lay in the oppressed status of the rural poor of Latin America. Even if Hobsbawm's model is not borne out by that historical experience, he effectively identified underlying social tensions that traumatized rural society. Or put another way, even if the social bandit did not exist in Latin America, the conditions to make him a believable and significant symbol to the rural masses did.

The social roots of Latin American banditry bear further probing. E. Bradford Burns provides some guidance in his reinterpretation of the nineteenth century in Latin America, *The Poverty of Progress*.[10] He argues that sociocultural conflict between traditional "folk," the unintegrated rural masses, and modernizing urban elites represented a central dynamic of the past century. The folk sought maintenance of traditional values and culture, while elites pushed for integration into world market systems and the adoption of European values.

Bandits did not, for the most part, act as class champions of the folk and "folkish" values. But this does not negate the social conflict described by Burns and others between elites and outlaws, frontiersmen, and other marginal types. Banditry was yet another symptom of the elite-mass conflict, even if criminals did not conform to Hobsbawm's archetype.

Vanderwood elaborates a similar theme in his major study of nineteenth-century Mexico, *Disorder and Progress*. Mexican bandits did not fight for the restoration of a past golden age of traditional rights and freedoms. But they often elected the bandit life because the pressures and strictures imposed by the modernizing regime of Porfirio Díaz provided few legitimate alternatives. The rural poor, socially and economically marginalized by Porfirian policies, could foment disorder and profit by the conflict engendered in the tensions of modernization.

Among the tools of modernity marshaled by elites against the masses was the law. Shifting definitions of law and crime need more critical attention if the complex nature of banditry is to be understood fully. By identifying those behaviors defined as criminal and those social groups most frequently charged, arrested, and labeled as bandits, we can better elucidate the sociopolitical context of crime.

Dretha Phillips indicates the relevance of Latin American banditry to the formation of criminological theory. As with sociology in general, criminological theory has focused ethnocentrically on data from the United States, with some contributions from Western Europe. Although a number of theories bring limited explanatory power to the Latin American context, Phillips finds shortcomings in all extant theories. Theory building still has a long way to go before accounting for the varieties of Latin American banditry.

Despite falling short at the macro level, some theories assist in the analysis of Latin American banditry better than others. As a point of departure, the perspectives of the conflict criminologists offer useful concepts for unraveling what Richard Quinney has termed "the social reality of crime." Works by Quinney, Austin Turk, William Chambliss, Donald Black, and others help to discern how elites use the law to promote their class interests at the expense of the rural masses.[11] Banditry in Latin America must be placed within the broader context of social conflict and change during the nineteenth and twentieth centuries.

Several of these essays present evidence that a culture of violence promoted banditry in the Brazilian sertão, the Venezuelan llanos, and the Argentine pampa. Interpersonal dueling, interfamilial feuding, cattle rustling, fencing stolen goods, and banditry form pieces of a mosaic of violence and conflict that typified such frontier regions.

Silvio Duncan Baretta and John Markoff offer suggestive hypotheses for analyzing such areas in their essay "Civilization and Barbarism: Cattle Frontiers in Latin America."[12] They argue that conflict in such regions stemmed from a culture of violence and the sharp class divisions rending cattle-raising areas. Banditry can thus be placed in a broader context of frontier violence and social deviance and linked to the demands and pressures exerted by "civilized" areas, such as capital cities.

Taken together, these essays examine many facets of banditry in Latin America and revise Hobsbawm's model as applied to the region. The researchers exhibit broad areas of agreement, usually in objections to elements of the social bandit concept. They indicate that many bandit models are needed to accommodate the historical experiences of the region. It also seems that there is far more variability in the types of bandits than a simple dichotomy of social versus anti-social bandit (or common criminal). Most Latin American bandits seem to lie somewhere between the noble robber and the "ignoble" or common criminal. And other clear types, such as the guerrilla-bandit and the political bandit, also existed.

Bandits did not engage in the Robin Hood-style redistribution of wealth from the rich to the poor. If they robbed the rich more often, it was because the rich had more to take. But bandits also despoiled and pillaged the poor, seemingly with few qualms.

Bandits were economically self-interested and forward-looking—more concerned with getting ahead than with looking backward toward the reestablishment of fading peasant values. Singelmann's conclusion for Brazil holds for Latin American bandits in general: "becoming a *cangaceiro* was essentially not a *reaction against*, but an *adaptation to*, the politics and society of the interior Northeast."[13] Banditry provided one of many survival tactics used by the rural masses in their attempts to cope with threatening sociopolitical dislocations.

We have galloped in hot pursuit of bandits across several Latin America countries and through two centuries. We have caught several and unmasked them. They do not precisely fit the description given by Sheriff Hobsbawm, but many of the characteristics that he identified are certainly recognizable. We hope that the wanted posters now more closely match the real bandits of nineteenth- and twentieth-century Latin America. By revising the portraits of these elusive outlaws we assist others in the pursuit and accurate identification of bandits elsewhere. Criminologists can likewise draw on these portraits to refine their theories of criminal behavior.

NOTES

1. Paul J. Vanderwood, *Disorder and Progress: Banditry, Police, and Mexican Development* (Lincoln: University of Nebraska Press, 1981), pp. 67–68; Anton Blok, "The Peasant and the Brigand: Social Banditry Reconsidered," *Comparative Studies in Society and History*, 14, 4 (Sept. 1972): 501–502.

2. Peter Singelmann, "Political Structure and Social Banditry in Northeast Brazil," *Journal of Latin American Studies*, 7, 1 (May 1975): 62; Linda Lewin, "The Oligarchical Limitations of Social Banditry in Brazil: The Case of the 'Good' Thief Antônio Silvino," *Past and Present*, 82 (Feb. 1979): 118–119 (reprinted in this volume); Billy Jaynes Chandler, *The Bandit King: Lampião of Brazil* (College Station: Texas A&M Press, 1978), pp. 64, 70–72.

3. Richard W. Slatta, "Pulperías and Contraband Capitalism in Nineteenth-Century Buenos Aires Province," *The Americas*, 38, 3 (Jan. 1982): 357–361.

4. Vanderwood, *Disorder and Progress*, p. 51.

5. Richard W. Slatta, "Rural Criminality and Social Conflict in Nineteenth-Century Buenos Aires Province," *Hispanic American Historical Review*, 60, 3 (Aug. 1980): 452–455, 461–464.

6. Christon I. Archer, "Banditry and Revolution in New Spain, 1790–1821," *Biblioteca Americana*, 1, 2 (Nov. 1982): 88.

7. Hobsbawm, "Social Banditry," in *Rural Protest: Peasant Movements and Social Change*, ed. Henry Landsberger, (London: MacMillan, 1974), p. 142.

8. Slatta, "Pulperías," pp. 357–360; Jonathan C. Brown, *A Socioeconomic History of Argentina, 1776–1860* (Cambridge: Cambridge University Press, 1979), pp. 9–10, 21–26.

9. Richard White, "Outlaw Gangs of the Middle Border: American Social Bandits," *Western Historical Quarterly*, 12, 4 (Oct. 1981): 395, 402.

10. E. Bradford Burns, *The Poverty of Progress: Latin America in the Nineteenth Century* (Berkeley: University of California Press, 1980)

11. On the conflict perspective, see Austin T. Turk, "Law as a Weapon in Social Conflict," *Social Problems*, 23, 3 (Feb. 1976): 276–291; Richard Quinney, *The Social Reality of Crime* (Boston: Little, Brown, 1970); Donald J. Black, *The Behavior of Law* (New York: Academic Press, 1976); William J. Chambliss and Milton Mankoff, eds., *Whose Law? What Order? A Conflict Approach to Criminology* (New York: John Wiley, 1976).

12. Silvio Duncan Baretta and John Markoff, "Civilization and Barbarism: Cattle Frontiers in Latin America," *Comparative Studies in Society and History*, 20 (Oct. 1978): 587–620; for additional uses of the social bandit concept in Latin America, see Ronald L. Chilcote, ed., *Protest and Resistance in Angola and Brazil: Comparative Studies* (Berkeley: University of California Press, 1972); Robert J. Rosenbaum, *Mexicano Resistance in the Southwest: "The Sacred Right of Self-Preservation"* (Austin: University of Texas Press, 1981); Louis A. Pérez, Jr., "Vagrants, Beggars, and Bandits: The Social Origins of Cuban Separatism, 1878–1895," *American Historical Review*, 90, 5 (Dec. 1985): 1092–1121. For another critique of Hobsbawm, see Ralph A. Austen, "Social Bandits and Other Heroic Criminals: History, Myth, and Early Modernization in Africa and the West," paper presented to the Symposium on Rebellion and Social Protest in Africa, Urbana, Ill., April 22–24, 1982.

13. Singelmann, "Political Structure," p. 60.

Glossary

abigeatista	rustler
acción	monopoly license to kill livestock in the colonial Río de la Plata
agregado	squatter or tenant in Brazil; sharecropper in Colombia
alcalde	local political official
arriero	muleteer
ayllus	clans in the Andean highlands
barrio	neighborhood, district
boleadores	gaucho ostrich (rhea) hunters
cangaceiro	bandit of the Brazilian backlands
cangaço	banditry of the Brazilian backlands
capanga	hired enforcer in Brazil
caudillo	political strongman of Latin America
changador	rustler who stole cattle hides
coiteiro	accomplice who supports and aids a bandit in Brazil
comisario	police chief
coroneis	colonels; local political bosses of Brazil
corrido	Mexican folk ballad that sometimes extols bandits
cuatrero	rustler
curandero	folk healer
defensas sociales	special security units created by Pancho Villa in Mexico
delegado	county police chief in Brazil
desgracia	accidental death in a knife fight between gauchos
estancia	cattle ranch

estanciero	cattle rancher
facinerosos	rustlers
gaitanismo	political movement of Jorge Eliéser Gaitán in Colombia
ganado cimarrón	wild cattle
gauchesco	Argentine, Uruguayan, or Brazilian folk literature about the gaucho
gaucho	horseman or cowboy of the pampas
greaser	unflattering film stereotype of a Latin American bandit
hacendado	rancher
jefe máximo	political chief or leader
jefe político	regional political boss of Mexico
jilakata	local political official in the Andean highlands
ladrón	thief
latifundios	large landed estates—plantations or ranches
literatura de cordel	popular literature of Brazil that often extols bandits
llanero	horseman of the tropical plains of Colombia and Venezuela
llanos	tropical plains of Colombia and Venezuela
mate	caffeine-rich tea favored by gauchos
matrero	Argentine murderer or outlaw
matuanos	ruling creole elite of Caracas
mayordomo	ranch manager
milpa	peasant field for growing corn in Mexico
montoneras	popular uprisings led by caudillos against the government
montonero	irregular cavalryman who followed a caudillo
morador	Brazilian tenant
muchacho	political guerrilla or rebel (literally ''boy'')
município	municipality or county
National Front	Colombian coalition government from 1958–1965
ospinista	follower of Mariano Ospino Pérez in Colombia
pago	home territory, area frequented by a gaucho
pájaro	paid assassin in Colombia (literally ''bird'')
palenque	robber or outlaw in Cuba
pampas	vast grassy plains of Argentina, Uruguay, and southern Brazil
papeleta	internal passport required in Venezuela and Argentina
parentela	extended family in Brazil
payador	gaucho folksinger
Porfirian	relating to Porfirio Díaz, dictator of Mexico, 1884–1910

porteño	resident of the port city of Buenos Aires
propretario	landowner
pulpería	country store and tavern on the pampas
pulpero	tavern owner/storekeeper on the pampas
rodeo	cattle roundup
Rosista	relating to Juan Manuel de Rosas, dictator of Argentina, 1835–1852
Rurales	Mexican rural police force created by Porfirio Díaz
senhor de engenho	sugar estate owner in Brazil
sertão	Brazilian backlands
tenentes	rebel army soldiers who prowled the Brazilian backlands during the 1920s
terrateniente	wealthy rancher, large landowner
trabuco	scatter-gun
vaquero	Mexican cowboy
vaqueiro	cowboy of the Brazilian northeastern backlands
Violencia	violent political conflict in Colombia, 1946–1958

Selected Bibliography

Altamirano, Ignacio Manuel. *El Zarco*. Mexico: Austral, 1901; 1964 (novel about a Mexican bandit).

Archer, Christon I. "Banditry and Revolution in New Spain, 1790–1821." *Biblioteca Americana*, 1, 2 (Nov. 1982): 59–90.

Austen, Ralph A. "Social Bandits and Other Heroic Criminals: History, Myth, and Early Modernization in Africa and the West." Paper presented to Symposium on Rebellion and Social Protest in Africa, Urbana, Ill., April 22–24, 1982.

Baretta, Silvio R. Duncan, and John Markoff. "Civilization and Barbarism: Cattle Frontiers in Latin America." *Comparative Studies in Society and History*, 20 (Oct. 1978): 587–620.

Barroso, Gustavo. *Heróes e bandidos: Os cangaceiros do nordeste*. Rio de Janeiro: Francisco Alves, 1931.

Black, Donald J. *The Behavior of Law*. New York: Academic Press, 1976.

Blanchard, Peter. "Indian Unrest in the Peruvian Sierra in the Late Nineteenth Century." *The Americas*, 38, 4 (Apr. 1982): 449–462.

Blok, Anton. *The Mafia of a Sicilian Village, 1860–1960: A Study of Violent Peasant Entrepreneurs*. Oxford: Blackwell, 1974.

———. "The Peasant and the Brigand: Social Banditry Reconsidered." *Comparative Studies in Society and History*, 14, 4 (Sept. 1972): 494–503.

Boatright, Mody G. "The Western Bad Man as Hero." *Publications of the Texas Folklore Society*, 27 (1975): 96–105.

Buitrago Salazar, Evelio. *Zarapazo the Bandit: Memoirs of an Undercover Agent of the Colombian Army*, trans. M. Murray Lasley, ed. Russell W. Ramsey, (University: University of Alabama Press, 1968 Spanish edition); 1977.

Burns, E. Bradford. *The Poverty of Progress: Latin America in the Nineteenth Century*. Berkeley: University of California Press, 1980.

Campbell, Leon G. "Banditry and the Tupac Amaru Rebellion in Cuzco, Peru, 1780–1784." *Biblioteca Americana*, 1, 2 (Nov. 1982): 131–162.

————. "Recent Research on Andean Peasant Revolts." *Latin American Research Review*, 14, 1 (1979): 3–49.

Carrera Damas, Germán. *Boves: Aspectos socioeconómicos de la guerra de independencia*, 3rd ed. Caracas: Universidad Nacional de Venezuela, 1964; 1972.

Carreras, Julio Angel. "El bandolerismo en las Villas (1831–53)." *Islas*, 52–53 (1975–76): 99–123.

Carrillo Ramírez, Alberto. *Luis Pardo: "El Gran Bandido*,*"* 2nd ed. Lima, 1976.

Castillo, Pedro, and Albert Camarillo, eds. *Furia y muerte: Los bandidos chicanos*. Los Angeles: Aztlán, 1973.

Chambliss, William J., and Milton Mankoff, eds. *Whose Law? What Order? A Conflict Approach to Criminology*. New York: John Wiley, 1976.

Chandler, Billy Jaynes. *The Bandit King: Lampião of Brazil*. College Station: Texas A&M Press, 1978.

————. *The Feitosas and the Sertão do Inhamuns: The History of a Family and a Community in Northeast Brazil, 1730–1930*. Gainesville: University of Florida Press, 1972.

Chilcote, Ronald L., ed. *Protest and Resistance in Angola and Brazil: Comparative Studies*. Berkeley: University of California Press, 1972.

Clinard, Marshall B., and Robert F. Meier. *The Sociology of Deviant Behavior*, 6th ed. New York: Holt, Rinehart & Winston, 1985.

Daniel, James M. *Rural Violence in Colombia Since 1946*. Washington D.C.: American University, 1965.

Della Cava, Ralph. *Miracle at Joaseiro*. New York: Columbia University Press, 1970.

Denisoff, R. Serge, and Charles H. McCaghy, eds. *Deviance, Conflict, and Criminality*. Chicago: Rand McNally, 1973.

Di Tella, Torcuato S. "The Dangerous Classes in Early Nineteenth-Century Mexico." *Journal of Latin American Studies*, 5, 1 (May 1973): 79–105.

Domínguez, Jorge I. *Insurrection or Loyalty: The Breakdown of the Spanish-American Empire*. Cambridge: Cambridge University Press, 1980.

Drago, Harry Sinclair. *Road Agents and Train Robbers: Half a Century of Western Banditry*. New York: Dodd, Mead, 1973.

Einstadter, Weiner J. "Robbery-Outlawry on the U.S. Frontier, 1863–1980: A Reexamination." In *Violent Crime: Historical and Contemporary Issues*, eds. James A. Inciardi and Anne E. Pottieger. Beverly Hills, Calif.: Sage, 1978.

Facó, Rui. *Cangaceiros e fanaticos*, 2nd ed. Rio de Janeiro: Civilização Brasileira, 1965.

Fausto, Boris. *Crime e cotidiano: A criminidade em São Paulo, 1880–1924*. São Paulo: Editora Brasiliense, 1984.

Franco Isaza, Eduardo. *Las guerrillas del Llano*. Bogotá: Mundial, 1959.

Fuentes, Carlos. "Viva Zapata." *New York Review of Books*, 13 March 1959, pp. 5–11.

Gilmore, Robert L. *Caudillismo and Militarism in Venezuela, 1810–1910*. Athens: University of Ohio Press, 1964.

Girón, Nicolé. *Heraclio Bernal: ¿Bandolero, cacique o precursor de la revolución?* Mexico: Instituto Nacional de Antropología e Historia, 1976.

Góngora, Mario. "Vagabundaje y sociedad fronteriza en Chile, siglos XVII a XIX." *Cuadernos del Centro de Etudios Socioeconómicas*, 2 (1961).

Greenwood, Robert. *The California Outlaw: Tiburcio Vasquez, Including the Rare Contemporary Account by George Beers*. Los Gatos, Calif.: Arno Press, 1960.

Guerrero, Julio. *La genesis del crimen en México: Estudio de psiquiatría social*. Mexico: Ch. Bouret, 1901.

Henderson, James D. *When Colombia Bled: A History of the Violencia in Tolima*. University: University of Alabama Press, 1985.

Hennessy, Alistair. *The Frontier in Latin American History*. Albuquerque: University of New Mexico Press, 1978.

Herrera Puga, Pedro. *Sociedad y delincuencias en el siglo de oro*. Madrid: Catolica, 1974.

Hobsbawm, Eric J. *Bandits*, rev. ed. New York: Pantheon, Delacorte, 1969; 1981.

———. *Primitive Rebels: Studies in Archaic Forms of Social Movement in the Nineteenth and Twentieth Centuries*. Manchester: Manchester University Press, 1959.

———. "Social Banditry." In *Rural Protest: Peasant Movements and Social Change*, ed. Henry A. Landsberger. London: MacMillan, 1974, pp. 142– 157.

———. "Social Banditry: A Reply." *Comparative Studies in Society and History*, 14, 4 (Sept. 1972): 503–505.

Huggins, Martha Knisely. *From Slavery to Vagrancy in Brazil: Crime and Social Control in the Third World*. New Brunswick, N.J.: Rutgers University Press, 1985.

Inciardi, James A., Alan A. Block, and Lyle A. Hallowell. *Historical Approaches to Crime: Research Strategies and Issues*. Beverly Hills, Calif.: Sage, 1977.

Inciardi, James A., and Anne E. Pottieger, eds. *Violent Crime: Historical and Contemporary Issues*. Beverly Hills, Calif.: Sage, 1978.

Inclan, Luis G. *Astucia, el jefe de los hermanos de la hoja, or los charros contrabandistas de la rama*, 3 vols. Mexico: Editorial Porrua, 1946 (Mexican bandit novel).

Isla, Carlos. *Chucho el Roto*. Mexico: Ediciones ELA. 1980.

Izard, Miguel. "Ni cuatreros ni montoneros: llaneros." *Boletín Americanista*, 31 (1981): 83–142.

———. "Oligarcas temblad, viva la libertad: Los llaneros de Apure y la Guerra Federal." *Boletín Americanista*, 32 (1982): 227–277.

———. "Sin domicilio fijo, senda segura, ni destino conocido: Los llaneros del Apure a finales del periodo colonial." *Boletín Americanista*, 33 (1983): 13–83.

———. "Tanto pelear para terminar conversando: El caudillismo en Venezuela." *Nova Americana*, 2 (1979): 37–82.

Juliano, Dolores. "Bandolerismo social y milenarismo en la provincia de Buenos Aires." *Ethnica*, 12 (1976): 443–478.

Langer, Erick D. "Rural Society and Land Consolidation in a Declining Economy: Chuquisaca, Bolivia 1880–1930." Ph.D. diss. Stanford University, 1984.

Latta, Frank F. *Joaquin Murieta and His Horse Gangs*. Santa Cruz, Calif.: Bear State Books, 1980.

Lee, Hector H. "The Reverberant Joaquín Murieta in California Legendry."*Pacific Historian*, 25 (Fall 1981): 38–47.

LeGrand, Catherine. "Labor Acquisition and Social Conflict on the Colombian Frontier." *Journal of Latin American Studies*, 16 (May 1984): 27–49.

Lewin, Linda. "The Oligarchical Limitations of Social Banditry in Brazil: The Case of the 'Good' Thief Antônio Silvino." *Past and Present*, 82 (Feb. 1979): 116–146.

———. "Oral Tradition and Elite Myth: The Legend of Antonio Silvino in Brazilian Popular Culture." *Journal of Latin American Lore*, 2 (Winter 1979): 157–204.

———. *Politics and Parentela in Paraíba: A Case Study of Family-Based Oligarchy in Brazil*. Princeton, N.J.: Princeton University Press, 1987.

López Albujar, Enrique. *Los caballeros del delito: Estudio criminológico del bando-lerismo en algunos departamentos del Perú*, 2nd ed. Lima: Juan Mejía Baca, 1936; 1973.

López Leiva, Francisco. *El bandolerismo en Cuba: Contribución al estudio de esta plaga social*. Havana: Imprenta Siglo XX, 1930.

McLachlan, Colin M. *Criminal Justice in Eighteenth-Century Mexico: A Study of the Tribunal of the Acordada*. Berkeley: University of California Press, 1974.

McLoughlin, Guillermo. "Juan Moreira: De la arena a la gloria." *Todo es Historia*, 2, 15 (July 1968): 8–19.

McQuilton, Francis John. *The Kelly Outbreak, 1878–1880: The Geographical Dimension of Social Banditry*. Carlton, Australia: Melbourne University Press, 1979.

Martin, Norman F. *Los vagabundos en la Nueva España, siglo XVI*. Mexico: Jus, 1957.

Matta Machado, Maria Cristina da. "Aspectos de fenomeno do cangaço no nordeste brasileiro," *Revista de Historia*, 93 (1973): 139–175.

———. *As taticas de guerra dos cangaceiros*, 2nd ed. São Paulo: Brasiliense, 1978.

Matthews, Robert P. *Violencia rural en Venezuela, 1840–1858: Antecedentes socioe-conómicas de la Guerra Federal*. Caracas: Monte Avila, 1977.

Maullin, Richard L. "The Fall of Dumar Aljure, Colombian Guerrilla and Bandit." Santa Monica: Rand Corporation, November 1968.

Meier, Robert F. *Theoretical Methods in Criminology*. Beverly Hills, Calif.: Sage, 1985.

Mello, Frederico Pernambucano de. *Aspectos do banditismo rural nordestino*. Recife, 1976.

Meyer, Jean. "El ocaso de Manual Lozada." *Historia Mexicana*, 72 (Apr. 1969): 535–568.

Meyer, Richard E. "The Outlaw: A Distinctive American Folktype." *Journal of the Folklore Institute*, 17 (May 1980): 94–124.

Montenegro, Abelardo F. "José Antonio do Fechado e o banditismo politico." *Revista Brasileira de Estudos Politicos*, 1 (1956): 159–169.

Morrissey, D. "Ned Kelly's Sympathisers." *Historical Studies*, 18 (1978): 228–296 (University of Melbourne).

Morse, Richard M., ed. *The Bandeirantes: The Historical Role of the Brazilian Pathfind-ers*. New York: Alfred A. Knopf, 1965.

Nonato, Raimundo. *Jesuino Brilhante, o cangaceiro romantico, 1844–1879*. Rio de Janeiro: Editora Pongetti, 1970.

Nusbaum, Keith C. "Bandidos!" *Military Review*, 43, 7 (July 1963): 20–25.

Nye, Robert A. "Crime in Modern Societies: Some Research Strategies for Historians." *Journal of Social History*, 11, 4 (Summer 1978): 490–507.

Olmo, Rosa del. *América latina y su criminología*. Mexico: Siglo XXI, 1981.

———. "Limitations for the Prevention of Violence: The Latin American Reality and Its Criminological Theory." *Crime and Justice*, 3 (Summer 1975): 21–29.

O'Malley, Pat. "Class Conflict, Land and Social Banditry: Bushranging in Nineteenth-Century Australia." *Social Problems*, 26 (1979): 271– 283.

———. "Social Bandits, Modern Capitalism and the Traditional Peasantry: A Critique of Hobsbawm." *Journal of Peasant Studies*, 6, 4 (July 1979): 489–499.

———. "The Suppression of Social Banditry: Train Robbers in the U.S. Border States and Bushrangers in Australia, 1865–1905." *Crime and Social Justice*, 16 (Winter 1981): 32–39.

Oquist, Paul. *Violence, Conflict, and Politics in Colombia*. New York: Academic Press, 1980.

Orlove, Benjamin S. "The Position of Rustlers in Regional Society: Social Banditry in the Andes." In *Land and Power in Latin America: Agrarian Economies and Social Processes in the Andes*, eds. Benjamin S. Orlove and Glynn Custred. New York: Holmes & Meier, 1980, pp. 179–194.

Ortiz Vidales, Salvador. *Los bandidos en la literatura Mexicana*. Mexico: Porrua, 1949.

Pages Larraya, Antonio. "Santos Vega, mito de la pampa." *Universidad*, 50 (Oct. 1961): 17–36.

Pang, Eul-Soo. "Banditry and Messianism in Brazil, 1870–1940: An Agrarian Crisis Hypothesis." *PCCLAS Proceedings*, 8 (1981–1982): 1–23.

Paredes, Americo. *"With His Pistol in His Hand": A Border Ballad and Its Hero*. Austin: University of Texas Press, 1958; 1971.

Payne, James L. *Patterns of Conflict in Colombia*. New Haven, Conn.: Yale University Press, 1968.

Payno, Manuel. *Los bandidos del Río Frio*. Mexico: Editorial Porrua, 1979 (Mexican bandit novel).

Pereira de Queiroz, Maria Isaura. *Os cangaceiros*. São Paulo: Duas Cidades, 1968; 1977.

Pérez, Louis A., Jr. " 'La Chambelona': Political Protest, Sugar, and Social Banditry in Cuba, 1914–1917." *Inter-American Economic Affairs*, 31, 4 (Spring 1978): 3–28.

————. "Vagrants, Beggars and Bandits: Social Origins of Cuban Separatism, 1878–1895." *American Historical Review*, 90, 5 (Dec. 1985): 1092–1121.

Popoca y Palacios, Lamberto. *Historia de la bandalismo en el estado de Morelos, ¡Ayer como ahora! 1860 (Plateados), 1911 (Zapatistas)*. Puebla: Guadalupana, 1912.

Quinney, Richard. *The Social Reality of Crime*. Boston: Little, Brown, 1970.

Quirós, Constancio Bernaldo de. *El bandolerismo en España y en México*. Mexico: Juridica Mexicana, 1959.

————, and Luis Ardila. *El bandolerismo andaluz*. Madrid: Turner, 1973.

Ramsey, Russell W. "Critical Bibliography on the *Violencia* in Colombia." *Latin American Research Review*, 8, 1 (Spring 1973): 3–44.

Reyes, J. Ascension. *Heraclio Bernal: El rayo de Sinaloa*. San Antonio, Mexico: Casa Editorial Lozano, 1920.

Rico, José M. *Crimen y justicia en América latina*. Mexico: Siglo XXI, 1977.

Riera, Argenis. "Latin American Radical Criminology." *Crime and Justice*, 11 (Spring 1979): 71–76.

Rodríguez Molas, Ricardo. *Historia social del gaucho*. Buenos Aires: Marú, 1968.

Rosenbaum, Robert J. *Mexicano Resistance in the Southwest: "The Sacred Right of Self-Preservation."* Austin: University of Texas Press, 1981.

Saco, José Antonio. *Memoria sobre la vagancia en la isla de Cuba* (1831). Santiago de Cuba: Instituto Cubano del Libro, 1974.

Sánchez, Florencio. *El caudillaje criminal en Sud América: Ensayo de psicología*. Montevideo: Río de la Plata, 1962.

Sánchez, Gonzalo G. "La Violencia in Colombia: New Research, New Questions." *Hispanic American Historical Review*, 65, 4 (Nov. 1985): 789–807.

————, and Donny Meertens. *Bandoleros, gamonales y campesinos: El caso de la Violencia en Colombia*, 2nd ed. Bogotá: Ancora, 1984.

Schmidt, Steffen W. "*La Violencia* Revisited: The Clientelist Bases of Political Violence in Colombia." *Journal of Latin American Studies*, 6 (May 1974): 97–111.

Schuster, Ernest Otto. *Pancho Villa's Shadow: The True Story of Mexico's Robin Hood as Told by His Interpreter*. New York: Exposition Press, 1947.

Schwartz, Rosalie. "Bandits and Rebels in Cuban Independence: Predators, Patriots, and Pariahs." *Biblioteca Americana*, 1, 2 (Nov. 1982): 91–130.

Sierra Ochoa, Gustavo. *Las guerrillas de los Llanos Orientales*. Manizales, Colombia: Tipografía Departamental, 1954.

Singelmann, Peter. "Political Structure and Social Banditry in Northeast Brazil." *Journal of Latin American Studies*, 7, 1 (May 1975): 59–83.

Slatta, Richard W. *Gauchos and the Vanishing Frontier*. Lincoln: University of Nebraska Press, 1983.

———. "Pulperías and Contraband Capitalism in Nineteenth-Century Buenos Aires Province." *The Americas*, 38, 3 (Jan. 1982): 347–362.

———. "Rural Criminality and Social Conflict in Nineteenth-Century Buenos Aires Province." *Hispanic American Historical Review*, 60, 3 (Aug. 1980): 450–472.

———, and Arturo Alvarez D'Armas. "El llanero y el hato venezolano: Aportes bibliográficos." *South Eastern Latin Americanist*, 29, 2–3 (Sept. 1985): 33–41.

Souza, Amaury de. "The Cangaço and the Politics of Violence in Northeast Brazil." In *Protest and Resistance in Angola and Brazil: Comparative Studies*, ed. Ronald H. Chilcote. Berkeley: University of California Press, 1972, pp. 109–131.

Steckmesser, Kent Ladd. "Robin Hood and the American Outlaw." *Journal of American Folklore*, 79 (1966): 348–355.

———. *Western Outlaws: The "Good Badman" in Fact, Film, and Folklore*. Claremont, Calif.: Regina Books, n.d.

Stein, William H. "Myth and Ideology in a Nineteenth-Century Peruvian Peasant Uprising." *Ethnohistory*, 29, 4 (1982): 237–264.

Tatum, Stephen. *Inventing Billy the Kid: Visions of the Outlaw in America, 1881–1981*. Albuquerque: University of New Mexico Press, 1982.

Taylor, William B. "Bandit Gangs in Late Colonial Times: Rural Jalisco, Mexico, 1794–1821." *Biblioteca Americana*, 1, 2 (Nov. 1982): 59–90.

———. *Drinking, Homicide, and Rebellion in Colonial Mexican Villages*. Stanford, Calif.: Stanford University Press, 1979.

Thompson, I. A. A. "A Map of Crime in Sixteenth-Century Spain." *Economic History Review*, 21, 2 (Aug. 1968): 244–267.

Uninsky, Philip B. "Fleur d'Epine and the Question of Social Banditry in Eighteenth-Century France." Paper presented to the American Historical Association, New York, December 28, 1985.

Vallenilla Lanz, Laureano. *Cesarismo democratico*, 3rd ed. Caracas: Garrido, 1919; 1952.

Vanderwood, Paul J. "Bandits in Nineteenth-Century Latin America: An Introduction to the Theme." *Biblioteca Americana*, 1, 2 (Nov. 1982): 1–28.

———. *Disorder and Progress: Bandits, Police, and Mexican Development*. Lincoln: University of Nebraska Press, 1981.

———, ed. "Social Banditry and Spanish American Independence." *Biblioteca Americana*, 1, 2 (Nov. 1982) (special thematic issue).

Varallanos, José. *Bandoleros en el Perú: Ensayos*. Lima: Altura, 1937.

Varela Zequeira, Eduardo, and Arturo Mora y Varona. *Los bandidos en Cuba*, 2nd ed. Havana: La Lucha, 1891.

Vergara Arias, Gustavo. *Montonera y guerrillas en la etapa de la emancipación del Perú, 1820–1825*. Lima: Editorial Salesiana, 1973.

Vold, George B., and Thomas J. Bernard. *Theoretical Criminology*, 3rd ed. New York: Oxford University Press, 1986.

Weinert, Richard S. "Violence in Pre-Modern Societies: Rural Colombia." *American Political Science Review*, 60, 2 (June 1966): 340–347.

Weller, Robert P., and Scott E. Gugenheim, eds. *Power and Protest in the Countryside*. Durham, N.C.: Duke University Press, 1982.

White, Richard. "Outlaw Gangs of the Middle Border: American Social Bandits." *Western Historical Quarterly*, 12 (Oct. 1981): 387–408.

Williamson, Robert C. "Toward a Theory of Rural Violence; The Case of Rural Colombia." *Western Political Science Quarterly*, 18 (Mar. 1965): 601–616.

Woll, Allen L. "Hollywood's Good Neighbor Policy: The Latin Image in American Film, 1939–1946." *Journal of Popular Film*, 3 (Fall 1974): 278–293.

———. *The Latin Image in American Film*. Los Angeles: Latin American Center, University of California at Los Angeles, 1981.

Zalazar, Ernesto S. *Montonereando*. Buenos Aires: La Rioja, 1967.

Index

Anomie theory, 184, 189 nn.5, 6
Archer, Christon I., 4, 14, 193
Argentina, banditry in, 4–5, 45, 49–53, 63, 126, 193. *See also* Gauchos
Arriaga, Jesús. *See* Chucho el Roto

Bandits: in film, 3, 7, 22, 61, 171–172, 174–76; guerrilla, 2, 4, 14, 40–41, 194, 198; in literature and folklore, 3, 22, 45, 70, 77, 105, 109, 124–25; motives, 11, 26, 73, 86, 101, 106–8, 140, 194; political, 2, 6–7, 169 n.5, 194, 198; social, 1–6, 140; as symbols, 26, 91, 104, 125, 165, 168, 186, 196; women, 17, 98–99, 184. *See also specific country names*
Bernal, Heraclio, 13, 20–22
Berthelin (French captain), 16–17, 99
Blok, Anton, 2, 91, 193
Bolivia, banditry in, 6, 113, 194
Brazil, banditry in, 5, 97
Brilhante, Jesuino, 73, 98, 100, 103, 107
Burns, E. Bradford, 196–97

Cangaceiros, 5, 67, 69, 99–103, 157, 168, 196–98; social organization, 86–87. *See also* Brazil
Cangaço. *See* Cangaceiros

Carranza, Venustiano, 23
Castro, Fidel, 144
Caudillos, 15, 102, 194; in Argentina, ˜52, 55; in Venezuela, 39, 41–42, 44
"Chambelona," "La" (revolt in Cuba), 6, 132, 139, 144
Chandler, Billy Jaynes, 2, 5
Charros, 17
Chávez García, José Ines, 24
Chucho el Roto (Jesús Arriaga), 13, 19–20
Cocada (Manuel Marinho), 87
Colombia, banditry in, 6, 33, 194. *See also Violencia*
Conflict theory, 183, 197
Conservative Party: in Cuba, 131, 134; in Mexico, 16–17
Contraband livestock trade, 38, 42–43, 193, 195
Control theory, 184
Corridos, 19, 26
Criminological theory, 7–8, 181–82, 184–85, 197
Cuba, banditry in, 6, 131, 194

Díaz, Porfirio, 4, 15, 18, 20–23, 44, 108, 193, 197
Differential association, 183

Contents

Contributors

BILLY JAYNES CHANDLER is Professor of History at Texas A&I University (Kingsville) and author of *The Bandit King: Lampião of Brazil* (Texas A&M Press, 1978).

MIGUEL IZARD is Professor of History at the University of Barcelona (Spain). He is author of several books, including an edited collection of essays titled *Marginados, fronterizos, rebeldes y oprimidos* (Ediciones Serbal, 1985).

ERICK D. LANGER is Assistant Professor of History at Carnegie-Mellon University in Pittsburgh.

LINDA LEWIN is Assistant Professor of History at the University of California, Berkeley, and author of *Politics and Parentela in Paraíba: A Case Study of Family-Based Oligarchy in Brazil* (Princeton University Press, 1987).

DONNY MEERTENS, a social anthropologist of the University of Amsterdam, now resides in Colombia. She is co-author of *Bandoleros, gamonales y campesinos: El caso de la Violencia en Colombia* (Ancora Press, 1984).

LOUIS A. PÉREZ, Jr., is Professor of History at the University of South Florida in Tampa and author of *Cuba Between Empires, 1878–1902* (University of Pittsburgh Press, 1983).

DRETHA M. PHILLIPS is Chair of the Department of History, Political Science, and Sociology at Roanoke College in Salem, Virginia.

GONZALO G. SÁNCHEZ is Professor of History at the National University of Colombia in Bogotá and co-author of *Bandoleros, gamonales y campesinos: El caso de la Violencia en Colombia* (Ancora Press, 1984).

RICHARD W. SLATTA is Associate Professor of History at North Carolina State University at Raleigh, Director of ScholarNet (an international telecommunications network for the humanities and social sciences), and author of *Gauchos and the Vanishing Frontier* (University of Nebraska Press, 1983).

PAUL J. VANDERWOOD is Professor of History at San Diego State University and author of *Disorder and Progress: Bandits, Police, and Mexican Development* (University of Nebraska Press, 1981).

ALLEN L. WOLL is Associate Professor of History at Rutgers University, Camden, New Jersey, and author of *A Functional Past: The Uses of History in Nineteenth-Century Chile* (LSU Press, 1982).